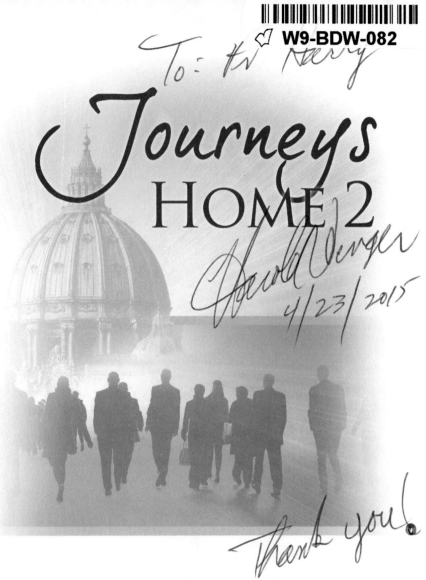

Journeys HOME 2

EDITED BY **MARCUS GRODI**

THE JOURNEYS OF MEN AND WOMEN TO THE CATHOLIC CHURCH

CHResources — Zanesville, Ohio

ALSO BY MARCUS GRODI:

Journeys Home

How Firm a Foundation

Pillar and Bulwark

What Must I Do To Be Saved?

Thoughts for the Journey Home

CHResources
PO Box 8290
Zanesville, OH 43702
740-450-1175
www.chnetwork.org

CHResources is a registered trademark
of the Coming Home Network International, Inc.

Library of Congress Cataloging-in-Publication Data

Journeys home 2 : the journeys of men and women coming home
to the Catholic Church / edited by Marcus Grodi.
    pages cm
 ISBN 978-0-9907921-0-9 (alk. paper)
 1. Catholics--Biography. 2. Coming Home Network International. I. Grodi, Marcus. II. Title: Journeys home two.

BX4651.3.J68 2014
248.2'420922--dc23
[B]

2014036146

Cover design and page layout by Jennifer Bitler www.doxologydesign.com

CONTENTS

INTRODUCTION

MARCUS GRODI

I feel quite sheepish allowing myself to be called editor of this collection of conversion stories, because there are many people who contributed far more than me to this project, especially the writers themselves. But I would particularly like to thank Mary Clare Piecynski and Kevin Lowry who helped compile the material and facilitated the publication process. Jeanette Flood's excellent editing skills deserve a special recognition. Jennifer Bitler did a beautiful job with the cover along with the layout and design of the book.

Together, we wish to dedicate this collection to Father Ray Ryland, whose friendship, witness, and guidance helped all of us.

This second volume of *Journeys Home* gathers together more conversion stories that have appeared in the monthly *CHNewsletter*. Most of these men and women discovered Jesus Christ in some non-Catholic tradition of Christianity, and remain eternally grateful to the many faithful Protestant teachers, friends, and family who helped them know Christ and grow in the Christian faith. Yet in each case and in unique ways, the Holy Spirit opened their hearts to realize that much of what they had been taught about the Catholic Church was never true. They learned to listen to the voice of truth speaking through history, theology, philosophy, Sacred Tradition, Holy Scripture, and personal testimony. In time, their desire to follow Christ faithfully — to remain faithful to the truth He taught and to the Church He established through His Apostles — led them to consider the claims of the Catholic Church.

Having made this journey myself, I realize that many non-Catholic Christian readers may feel skeptical or leery of reading on, convinced that anyone open to the Catholic

Church must have been deceived by the prince of lies himself! However, resisting the temptation to jump into long pages of apologetic arguments, let me at least assure you that this is not the case. These stories are told by humble souls who love Jesus Christ, who desire to obey Him fully, and who have denounced the devil and his horde. They have sought to follow the teachings of Scripture, as well as the teachings of the early Church Fathers and the ecumenical councils.

In doing so, they were startled to discover the truth of the Catholic Church and its teachings. In the process, they also discovered that throughout its history, the Church has included not only thousands of saints but also thousands of sinners, lay and clergy. Too often these real but less-than-perfect followers of Jesus dirtied the fair name of the Catholic Church and provided fodder for the many misunderstandings and exaggerations that have led to so many schisms.

Since 1993, the Coming Home Network International (CHNetwork) has been helping non-Catholic Christians, clergy and laity, discover the beauty and truth of the Catholic faith. Particularly for clergy, this discernment process can require great sacrifice, including sometimes the loss of family, friends, and vocation. We're not here to "push, pull, or prod" anyone toward or into the Church; rather to stand beside them as fellow Christians to share what we have discovered by the grace of God. The CHNetwork provides inquirers and their families with resources, fellowship, and encouragement on the journey and helps them become acclimated to what can often seem the strange, new world of the Catholic Church.

I encourage you to read the following stories with a prayerful and charitable heart. The decision of a Protestant minister to resign from his pastorate and enter the Catholic Church affects more than himself. It affects his family and particularly his spouse and their marriage. In many cases, spouses do not share the same convictions, and marriages are greatly tested.

Though the journeys of laity may not result in the loss of vocation or employment, the emotional, intellectual, and relational impacts can be equally as challenging.

If you are interested in finding out more about the CHNetwork, or in becoming a member, you will find membership information in the back of this book, or on our website, www.chnetwork.org.

Now as you begin, please listen with both your mind and heart, for I believe that you will hear the whisper, and see the work, of the Spirit.

Our Journey Home

Marcus Grodi

former Presbyterian minister

B ecoming Catholic was never my dream or intent. It is still an all too vivid memory to me, sitting alone at age forty in a half-lit basement, having resigned from my Presbyterian pastorate. I ached for having abandoned the weekly privilege of a pulpit from which to proclaim God's truth. *Would I ever have this privilege again? Will I ever again have a pulpit?* Now they estimate that each week, from the "pulpit" of *The Journey Home* television program, I speak to a potential audience of over a billion viewers and listeners. In one night, I speak to more people than I ever could have in my entire career as a Presbyterian minister. This is the humor of our merciful God. When I was contemplating conversion, I had no idea whatsoever how I would support my family, let alone how I would continue in ministry. But this is getting way ahead of myself.

After sharing my conversion story over and boringly over again dozens of times in the past twenty years, I've come to realize shamefully how mechanical it has become in the telling. I've got it all worked out, down to every event, person, place, and thing, with each struggle and motive charted and evaluated, leading with creatively inserted humor to build from despairing confusion to joyful completion upon reception into the Catholic Church. This, though, is only part of the story, for as is the case with the hundreds of converts and reverts I have interviewed on *The Journey Home*, the real journey is usually far too complicated, even embarrassing, to put in a box.

To some extent, I could say that my "journey home" was as equally attributable to personality tendencies as to theological and scriptural apologetics. This is not surprising, since God created each of us uniquely, each with our own set of personality "quirks," all designed as means by which He can draw us closer to Him and by which He can use us uniquely for His purposes.

Most of us don't admit to these personality quirks, but mine admittedly had a great part to play in both of my conversions, as an adult to Jesus Christ and then later to His Church. Each of us is a complicated mixture of our own particular genetics, our environment, our divinely implanted soul or self, and our will. These four, plus possibly other factors, come together to make each of us truly unique — particularly in the eyes of our Creator. One might place the definitive cause behind the quirks of my character on having been an only child, the only one of eight siblings who survived childbirth, but the inability of modern psychologists as well as theologians to unite on any one theory of the human person bespeaks to the futility of seeking that one cause behind our individual uniqueness.

STRANGER IN THE CROWD

One of these quirks is that I have always been incurably insecure. Though over the years I have learned to hide this behind an otherwise confident exterior, inside I always feel like a stranger in every crowd. Some write this off to my being an only child; I see this as the unique thorn or cross to bear that God has given me. This quirk always moves me toward isolation — even when all the doors God continually opens for me require an increased involvement with the public. I speak each week to millions of people when, inwardly, I would prefer to be at home on our farm sharing a coffee with my wife, Marilyn, or brush-hogging our twenty-five-acre farm, or fishing with my sons.

This introverted insecurity also, however, leans me a bit towards the neurotic, always assuming, at least initially, that whenever anything goes wrong, it must be my fault. I've jokingly said that this is why I have a particular affinity for St. Joseph. The story goes that one evening the Holy Family was sitting around the dinner table, and for a brief second there was a bit of a row. Joseph looked at Jesus and Mary, and said, with one of his few words, "Sorry, it must be me."

It was another personality quirk, however, that had a more prominent influence on my journey home: an insatiable, often irritable, desire to know "why." If you want me to do something, I want to know why, or I won't want to do it. I certainly must have been a pain in the neck to my parents, because they'd say "do it," and I'd ask, "Why?" or "Why do it this way; why not another way?" If you didn't give me a good reason, I'd either do it my own way or just give in, but I first had to ask the question.

The reason for sharing these quirks is because describing one's conversion to the faith is not all cut and dried. Each person is unique, and admittedly our motives are never pure or pristine. I only pray that in, through, and regardless of the cacophony of voices that fill our lives, we can truly and clearly hear the voice of Jesus calling and beckoning us each home.

LOOKING FOR ANSWERS

As I mentioned earlier, my entire spiritual pilgrimage can be explained as a result of trying to answer the question "Why?" For example, when I arrived in college, I encountered a culture and lifestyle radically different than what I grew up with. It wasn't that my Lutheran upbringing hadn't prepared me to say no to this lifestyle; it's just that I hadn't been listening. And so, when faced with the challenges, I asked, "Why?" or maybe, more accurately, "Why not?"

Almost immediately, I found myself with both feet in the fraternity drinking and dating scene, to the point where my life became a walking ad for *Bud Light*: "Why ask why?" Eventually I became the beer-chugging champion of my university. I was so caught up in it all that I could no longer see anything wrong with it.

This lifestyle continued until the summer between my junior and senior years. An avalanche of events got my attention, and within only a few weeks I was a "born-again Christian" driven to save the world. It began in a genetics class, studying the evolutionary development of our senses of sight and hearing. I was being taught that these amazing senses had happened by chance over millions of years through mutations and natural selection. The Holy Spirit used this to spark a few "why" questions: "Wait a second, how could this be true? Does anyone really believe this? The majority of all higher-level living things have two eyes at the same location in the front of their heads: is this merely by chance? Did this arrangement happen over time as a result of natural selection? Is there any evidence of fossils showing humanoids or other animals with eyes at less advantageous locations on their bodies?" I realized that for most of the biologists I was studying under, their God was Time; in other words, given enough time and probability, everything could be explained. All order was a chance result of millions of years of natural selection. Facing the absurdity of this is what drew me back to God.

FOLLOWING JESUS, BUT WHAT CHURCH?

Not long after this, at age twenty-one, I experienced a true conversion of faith to Jesus Christ, through the witness of friends, the reading of Scripture, and the preaching and teaching of an Evangelical pastor of a local Congregational church. For the first time in my life, I was actually listening to the Gospel message, and it began changing my life. At this point, my pastor taught me a Proverb that has become my "life verse": "Trust in the Lord with all your heart, / And lean not on your own understanding; / In all your ways acknowledge Him, / And He shall direct your paths" (Prov 3:5–6, New King James Version). Again, though, I began asking, "Why?" Why this local Congregational church, or should I return to my Lutheran upbringing? Why belong to a church at all?

So I visited my childhood Lutheran church, and found two things. The first was positive. As I sat through the familiar Lutheran service, remembering every word of the liturgy, I heard for the first time the Gospel preached there, and I knew that it hadn't been the church's fault that I hadn't grown in my faith; the fault must have been mine. I must not have been listening.

But then I came to another conclusion as I looked down the pew and saw a couple of high school students sitting there, just like I had done, messing around, shooting spit wads, yet at the same time perfectly reciting the liturgy. It struck me that liturgy without an internal change of heart was dead liturgy. Quickly, I turned the blame away from myself to what I concluded was the dead, monotonous liturgy of the Lutheran Church, and left it to become a Congregationalist. I went from one extreme to the other: from a liturgical, creedal church to a nonliturgical, autonomous, democratic church with "No creed but Christ." Here every individual church was free to decide through congregational vote whatever it wanted to believe or how it wanted to worship.

Not long after this, I graduated college and found myself a plastics engineer for a large chemical company, and another "why" question arose: "Why work?" It wasn't so much that I was lazy, but my main project as a plastics engineer was to develop a better butter tub. "Why?!" I pictured myself sitting on the edge of heaven, with Jesus asking me, "Well, Son, what did you do in life?" And my response might be, "Well, I developed a better butter tub!" I asked myself, Is this what I want to do with the rest of my life?

MOVING TOWARDS MINISTRY

At the same time, I was working in my off-hours with young people in a ministry called *Young Life*, a powerful ministry in which more than a hundred teens would gather each week in someone's basement to hear the Gospel. I was a musician who was cutting my teeth on preaching the Gospel message. Over time, I decided that if I were given the choice, I'd rather be in ministry than making better butter tubs, so with the confirmation of my pastor and some of my friends and family (not all!), I sold everything I owned, except my guitar and golf clubs, resigned my engineering job, and went to seminary.

It's important to understand how different this was than a young Catholic man being sent by his diocese to discern priesthood at a Catholic seminary. No church sent me to seminary; rather, I just decided that God was calling me to go. So, I went to a nondenominational, Evangelical Protestant, independent seminary in New England, where the students represented more than forty-six different denominations.

When I got to seminary, all of a sudden I was inundated with more "why" questions. As a Congregationalist, for whom everything was basically up for grabs — except having anyone tell us what we had to believe — I was confronted by every imaginable theological opinion. After dinner nearly everyday, we would sit around, coffee cups in hand, battling over all the big theological issues: Why do we believe in the divinity of Christ or the Trinity? Or what about predestination: what about the people who lived and died without hearing about the Lord Jesus? If they have never heard, then why are they guilty? Are we indeed in the last days, facing the second coming of Christ, or maybe a "rapture," as some of my classmates insisted?

All of us believed in Jesus Christ and the infallibility of Scripture, yet we would argue and argue and argue, and never come to an agreement. It never crossed my mind that there could be anything wrong with Scripture or even Protestantism per se; I assumed, given my neurotic personality quirk, that the problem, of course, must be me. I hadn't prayed enough, or studied enough, or listened enough.

CRISIS OF FAITH

Eventually, I faced a crisis of faith. I read my first "Catholic" book in seminary, by a well-known "Catholic" author (who, unknown to me, was a renegade Catholic theologian), Hans Küng. His book was called *On Being a Christian*, and one of the reasons he is deemed so dangerous is that he is a superb and convincing writer. As I progressed through the book, I found that he was successfully undercutting the very foundation for my faith, which was the Bible *alone*. As a result of reading this book, I found that I, as a Bible Christian who believed only what was found in Scripture, no longer had a solid basis upon which to believe in the Trinity or the divinity of Christ.

For three days, I argued with my professors and fellow students, as they tried unsuccessfully to bring me back. I dropped everything and spent literally an entire night combing the New Testament to find proof for the Trinity, but couldn't because, for one thing, the word "Trinity" is not there.

Then a theology professor pulled me aside and said, "You have to understand: the reason we believe these things is because they are the quasi-unanimous conclusions of the Church throughout the ages. In other words, this is what the majority of Christians, everywhere and in all places, since the beginning of Christianity have believed; so, therefore, we believe it to be true." At this point, it started to become apparent that most of our doctrines in the Protestant churches were based on democratic theology: most of us believe it, so it must be true.

This assumption held me through seminary, until I graduated and was ordained, and pastored my first church. Then came a host of new "why" questions. For example, Why should I wear a clerical collar? As a Congregationalist, I was free to decide for myself. Since none of my fellow clergymen could give me a good reason, I didn't, that is unless it was advantageous for me, like when I wanted respect while visiting the hospital or when I wanted reduced rates at the local golf course. Or I asked, "Why do we worship this way? Why this music? Why this order of the worship? Why do we do the Lord's Supper this way?" In time, I tried everything and changed everything, all with the hope of bringing renewal to everything.

WHAT IS TRUTH?

With all these changes, and as a Congregationalist with everything up for grabs, I began to question, "Why do we believe what we believe?" In essence, could I be certain that what I was teaching was true? This led me to a long study of the creeds and the history of the Church, and, as a result, I became a Presbyterian. I could no longer remain a pastor in a denomination in which every individual church, every individual Christian, could decide for himself what was true; to me, this was institutionalized Narcissism. So I left this to become a Presbyterian because the Presbyterian Church had two things Congregationalists did not: a Book of Confessions, which contained all the major confessions of the history of the Presbyterian Church, and a Book of Order, which is similar to the Catholic Code of Canon Law.

I considered this a good, trustworthy foundation for my pastoral ministry, so in time, I became an assistant pastor in a medium-sized urban church, then the solo pastor of a small rural church, and finally the senior pastor of a large urban church, with a full-time staff of nine, a burgeoning member-ship, and an ample budget. As I took on these responsibilities, however, another "why" question arose: "Why was I single?" In Protestant culture, there really is no place for the "gift of celibacy" — it was a gift that nobody wanted. Generally (at least when I was a pastor), if a minister wasn't married or dat-ing someone, the assumption was that there was something wrong with him. Well, it wasn't that I had to succumb to the pressure; rather, I knew deep in my heart that I needed this special partner, not merely to share life with, but to help me see the blind sides of my character. In the midst of this dis-cerning, the Lord brought Marilyn, the woman whom I would marry, into my life, which immediately doubled all the "why" questions — particularly because it had never been her dream to be a pastor's wife.

Becoming a Presbyterian did not answer all of my theo-logical and pastoral "why" questions, far from it. On Monday mornings, as I had been taught in seminary, I would begin preparation for my upcoming Sunday sermon. I first would make a fresh personal translation of the text from Greek or Hebrew, and then fill pages of exegetical study and reflections. Once I had arrived at a tentative conclusion of the meaning of the passage, and a rough outline of my thoughts, only then would I consult with the row of biblical commentaries on my shelf, to make sure my conclusions were on track.

One day, it struck me that every commentary on my shelf had been hand-picked from scholars I liked, with whose theol-ogies I agreed. I, therefore, was checking my conclusions only against people I already agreed with, so, in essence, I was only checking myself against myself! I had protected myself from any way of knowing whether I — or they — were wrong.

Then one Sunday morning, as I was preaching, it struck me that within a thirty-mile radius of my pulpit, there were prob-ably thirty other pastors in thirty other churches — all of us considering the Bible as the sole authority for our faith — who were all teaching different if not contradictory things, possibly on the same text. Which one of us was correct?

ONCE SAVED, ALWAYS SAVED

As an Evangelically minded Presbyterian Calvinist, I believed and preached "once saved—always saved": that once a person accepts Jesus as Lord and Savior, they have arrived; they are saved by grace through faith *alone*. And because they have done nothing to earn salvation, there is likewise nothing they can do to lose it. As a pastor, I knew many people who needed to break from debilitating sin, and even more of them who needed to live their faith more radically. Because of my preaching of "once saved—always saved" theology, however, I had no theological grounds to challenge anyone — let alone any real authority to do so.

What really hit the fan for Marilyn and me, however, were the pro-life issues. Marilyn was the director of a crisis pregnancy center, and more often than not she found herself working beside Catholics. Our Presbyterian denomination had democratically decided to lean more and more pro-choice. Then, I discovered that the dues my congregation was paying to the head office of our denomination were funding abortions — for the daughters and wives of ministers — and there was nothing we could do to stop this. But if a person is "once saved—always saved," what difference to his salvation does it make whether he is pro-choice or pro-life?

WHERE TO NOW?

With this, I knew I could no longer be a Presbyterian. How could I stand before my congregation when I knew what their donations were funding — when I knew their mixed views on abortion — and yet, at the same time, enable their complacency because of some decision they had made years before that guaranteed their salvation?

So I began admitting to close pastor friends that I could no longer remain in our particular Presbyterian denomination and began exploring more conservative Presbyterian churches. At the time, there were nine Presbyterian denominations in the U.S., each of which believed it was the truer interpreter of Scripture (I think there are more now). Examining each, I determined that none of them were exactly what I wanted, so I found a book of Christian denominations, three hundred pages of all the different Christian traditions in America. I carefully examined each, rejecting them one by one because something in their theology didn't fit with mine, until I stopped myself, wondering who I arrogantly thought I was to stand in judgment of these churches? I was playing God, placing myself over all of them!

I received a phone call from a Presbyterian pastor friend out in Kansas City who, in a panic, exclaimed, "Marcus, you can't leave the church! You must remain loyal, even if all the leaders have become heretics and the church is going down in flames: we need the faithful to remain loyal!" And I answered in words that, at the time, I did not understand — with another "why" question: "If that is true, then why did we leave our last denomination to form this one? And the division before that, and before that, and before that? Why does loyalty to truth require that I stand firm here in this denomination? Why not move on and form a more true church? Because in time, we both know that we would have to move on and form another one and another one, and on into infinity."

You see, our heritage as Presbyterians was "Reformed and always reforming." The way we reformed was always through re-forming, starting one new church after another. Even a Protestant source admits that there are over thirty thousand individual denominations in the world today, growing at the rate of one new denomination every five days!

Essentially, though I had no thought about becoming Roman Catholic, I found myself back at the Reformation asking the big "why" question, and frankly this was a bigger can of worms than I wanted to open.

Realizing that if I could not answer the "why" questions about even the least important issues of our faith, let alone the more crucial ones — like what is necessary for salvation — then I had no business standing in the pulpit before anyone. So, I resigned from the pastorate.

I entered a graduate program in molecular biology with the hope of combining my science and theology backgrounds into a career in medical ethics. Soon, I found myself in a research lab assisting in genetic research as a part of the human genome project. This was exciting work, but after a brief time, I found myself asking God, "Why have You brought me here?" And He answered.

One morning after the long drive to campus, I did something I never did: I bought a copy of the *Cleveland Plain Dealer* newspaper. Sipping coffee, I came across a small ad on the bottom right of the religion page: "Theologian will speak at local Catholic parish: Scott Hahn." Scott and his wife, Kimberly, had been my classmates at seminary. We had known each other for over fifteen years, but had lost contact since graduation. I had heard through the grapevine that they had become Catholics, but I didn't believe a word of it. They had been two of the most outspoken, vehement Calvinists on campus, and I had no mental file-folder for them becoming Catholics — for *any* Protestant minister becoming Catholic! I knew Protestant laity who had become Catholics through marriage, but always presumed they had not known their Protestant faith well enough, or they surely would never have converted.

So when I saw this ad, it piqued my interest: "Was this my old friend Scott Hahn? Did he really become a papist?" and, if so, the big question, "Why?" Or was it possible, and more probable, that he had ostensibly converted so he could clandestinely rescue lost souls from the Catholic Church?

The next Sunday afternoon, I drove alone up to Cleveland to hear him. From my experience with visiting theologians, I envisioned a small clutch of people in a small church basement, eating coffee and donuts, listening glass-eyed to a droning professor speaking far over their heads. Instead, I found an immense church, a full parking lot, a standing-room-only sanctuary, with everyone — cameras and stage lights too — focused on my old friend from seminary. I felt myself a complete, maybe unwanted, stranger in my very first visit to a Catholic church. I was astounded as Scott gave an invigorating talk on the "Fourth Cup", or the Last Supper as the fulfillment of the Jewish Passover meal.

Afterward, Scott was rushed by a crowd of enthusiastic fans. I went over to say hello. He recognized me immediately with, "Hey, what are you doing here? I hope I didn't offend you!" We couldn't talk then, but he encouraged me to listen to the (now famous) tape of his conversion, and then call him.

VERSES I NEVER SAW

So I bought the tape, mainly to discover on the long drive home how he had gotten so messed up. I also bought an interesting-sounding book by Karl Keating entitled *Catholicism and Fundamentalism*. About a half hour into the tape, I had to pull my car over to the side of the road. In just that short period, Scott essentially had provided the answers to the majority of my most disturbing foundational "why" questions. The first of these answers was the first of what I came to call "the verses I never saw." He told the story of being asked by a friend, "What is the pillar and bulwark of the truth?" Scott had answered, as I would have answered, "the Bible." His friend responded, "But the Bible says in 1 Timothy 3:15, that the pillar and bulwark of the truth is the Church." As I listened, I couldn't recall seeing this in my Bible, so that is why I pulled my car over to the side of the road. I had studied and taught a series of sermons on First Timothy and didn't remember seeing this verse; however, when I looked, it was there!

St. Paul wrote that "the household of God, which is the Church of the living God, [is] the pillar and bulwark of the truth." Which church? The Presbyterian Church? Which Presbyterian denomination? My individual congregation? Or Lutheran, Methodist, Baptist, Episcopal, Pentecostal, etc., etc., denominations? Or which branch of these? But surely not the Catholic Church! And besides, as a Calvinist Protestant, I believed that the true Church was invisible, consisting of true believers all over the world, the membership of which was known only to God.

And at that moment, it struck me: how could an invisible church, known only to God, be the pillar and bulwark of anything?

This didn't make me Catholic; it made me more confused and ungrounded.

As I listened, Scott clearly demonstrated how the key foundation of our Protestant faith, *sola scriptura*, was not biblical, nor was it theologically or philosophically sound; in fact, the very Scripture text we used to defend the foundational doctrine, in 2 Timothy 3:14–17, did not actually teach it. St Paul said that all Scripture is profitable for equipping us for good works, but not that it was the sole authority of our faith! In essence, I really had never "seen" these verses either, because I had always read the passages through the lenses of my hidden assumptions.

He pointed out a third verse I had never "seen," 2 Thessalonians 2:15, "Therefore, brethren, stand fast and hold the traditions which you were taught, whether by word or our epistle" (NKJV). *Traditions?* This verse spoke of the importance of passing on faithfully the Apostolic Tradition, which was received primarily through the spoken word, and only secondarily through epistles when an Apostle could not get to his people to speak to them orally.

Even as I sat there in that car, I realized that there was no church in the world that actually lived out *sola scriptura,* because every denomination interpreted Scripture through the lenses of their own passed-on tradition, as they interpreted the tradition of the founder of their movements. It was this nearly limitless assortment of traditions that had spawned the cacophony of opinions coming from pulpits every Sunday, including my own.

After listening to Scott's tape, I found the Protestant foundation of *sola fide* was also beginning to topple. I never questioned, from the time of my Lutheran catechetical formation, that we are saved by faith *alone.* Scott, however, drew my attention to another verse I had never "seen," James 2:24, which states, "You see then that a man is justified by works, and not by faith only" (NKJV). This revelation concurred with what I had always known in my conscience to be true: we are not merely "once saved, always saved" through some one-time surrendering statement of faith in Christ. We must live this out by grace in love for the rest of our lives. Again, as St. James wrote, "But be doers of the word, and not hearers only, deceiving yourselves" (1:22, NKJV). Scott pointed out that Luther had added the word "alone" to Romans 3:28, and when challenged, Luther refused to back down, claiming it was assumed in the text.

When I returned home, I didn't reveal any of this to Marilyn. She already was a bit concerned about my leaving the pastorate to return to school. I didn't think she would be keen about these new revelations. I closed myself away in my study, but instead of reading my biology assignments, I read Karl Keating's book from cover to cover, and he provided even more answers to my many "why" questions. His excellent book particularly pointed out that the many "Fundamentalist" assumptions, to which I had long held, owe their formation not to clear biblical foundations but to the "traditions" or opinions of the founders of Evangelical Fundamentalism.

None of this, however, was making me "Catholic" — just more confused. So I called Scott. I met with him and others, posing every "why" question that rose to the surface and debating all aspects of Catholic doctrine, practice, and devotions that ran cross-grain to my Protestant sensibilities.

Then I read a book by John Henry Newman, entitled *Apologia pro Vita Sua*. I had never heard of this famous nineteenth-century Anglican clergy convert priest until well on into my journey. Once I heard about this universally respected autobiography of his conversion, however, I had to read it. Although his journey was completely different than mine, it was mine. His testimony convinced me that I could no longer be a Protestant. He helped me to realize that, even though the sixteenth-century Catholic Church and culture desperately needed renewal, the schismatic reaction of the Reformation was not the answer, for it had only led to a myriad of more splinters, leading only to confusion.

I could no longer be Protestant, but I couldn't be Catholic! Even though I had to turn from (*metanoia*) my Protestant assumptions and background, I was not yet comfortable turning toward the pervasive strangeness of Catholicism: not just the unfamiliar and uncomfortable doctrines concerning purgatory and Mary; or the unappealing statues and artwork; or the seemingly bizarre devotions to supposed apparitions; or the "superstitious" use of sacramentals, like sticking green scapulars between mattresses to convert family members or the burying of St. Joseph statues to sell homes. No, what concerned me most was trusting my faith to the Church's Magisterium in union with a pope in Rome. All of this ran cross-current to both my Protestant and my "American" sensibilities!

UPON THIS ROCK

I realized that everything came down to one basic doctrine; even the validity of our belief in the Trinity and the divinity of Christ, which cannot be proved through *sola scriptura*, all came down to a belief in the trustworthy authority of Peter, the bishop of Rome. It became obvious to me, the more I studied history, that it was to the authority, and often the courage, of the bishop of Rome as the successor of Peter that we owe all that we now have and believe in Christendom. Certainly, behind him was the protection, guidance, and inspiration of the Holy Spirit, yet at the center of all historic Christianity was the pope. Not the Scriptures, as I previously assumed, for if it wasn't for the historical union of the bishops of the Church in union with the bishop of Rome, there would be no canon of Scriptures that we now call the Bible; there would be no doctrines of the Trinity or divinity of Christ, and there would be no Christendom, for if it wasn't for the Crusades, we would all have long been Muslims.

Realizing this, I read every single book I could find on the authority of the pope. It was through another book by John Henry Newman, however, that I finally became convinced. He himself had been desperately trying to find an alternative to becoming Catholic, to prove from history that Anglicanism was the true "middle way" between Protestantism and Catholicism. His book *An Essay on the Development of Doctrine* was the result. The conclusion of this book in the end convinced Newman to become Catholic. And, likewise, it did me.

There is far too much in the book to summarize here, but basically there were twelve pages in the middle of the book, about the development of the papacy, that brought me "home."

It is not so amazing that the authority of the papacy didn't become clear until the third century, given the constant persecutions of the first three centuries, in which most of the bishops of Rome were martyred. There are lots of things we will never know about the first centuries of the Church because it was mostly underground, in hiding. Once the persecutions ceased under Constantine, however, the structure of the Church, as recorded in the writings of the early Church Fathers, became clearly apparent, under the authority of the bishop of Rome. Most significantly, however, the authority of the pope was clearly recognized across the Church before the canon of the Scriptures and the Trinity were finally defined in the fourth century, and before the divinity of Christ was formally defined in the fifth century. The acceptance of the pope as the authoritative predecessor of the Apostle Peter predated our unified beliefs in the Trinity, the divinity of Christ, and the Bible, and without the unifying presence of the pope overseeing the early councils, Christendom would have had none of these doctrines.

With this, I was ready to become Catholic, and, fortunately by that time, so was Marilyn. At first, she was hesitant to accept all that I was discovering, but her heart had already been so opened to the Catholic Church through her pro-life convictions and work that it didn't take long for her to become as excited as I was about what we were discovering together. Her reading of two particular books — Tom Howard's *Evangelical Is Not Enough* and Thomas Merton's *Seven-Storey Mountain* — had particularly closed the deal for her, as well as the amazingly convincing truth of Juan Diego and Our Lady of Guadalupe.

So, as a result of God's mercy and grace, Marilyn and I entered the Catholic Church together with our two oldest sons in December 1992. It was then that I fully realized the truth of that Proverb I had memorized so many years before. By grace, I had trusted Him, and also by grace, I had been open to challenging the ways I had always "leaned on my own understanding." In the end, God has proven that He will indeed "direct our paths," for through His mercy and love, He has brought us home to the Catholic Church.

Marcus Grodi is the founder and president of the Coming Home Network International, and the host of The Journey Home *program on EWTN. He is the author of several books, including* Thoughts for the Journey, What Must I Do to Be Saved, *and the novels* How Firm a Foundation *and* Pillar and Bulwark.

Towards Unity

Father Jurgen Liias
former Anglican priest

I n a small Lutheran church located in the Black Forest re-
gion of postwar Germany, I received the Sacrament of Baptism as an infant in 1948. My parents, displaced due to the
Second World War, applied for emigration and, in the winter
of 1951–1952, with my younger brother and me, arrived in the
United States and were settled into a displaced-person camp
in Massachusetts. Months later, we were taken into the rectory of St. John's Episcopal Church in Charlestown, Massachusetts. An old bachelor priest, the Rev. Wolcott Cutler, had filled
his large, five-story home with refugees. Though most stayed
briefly, we lived in that rectory for the next ten years. We became caretakers of the building, and my father the sexton at
the church.

Mr. Cutler (as he was called — a deeply committed low
churchman, he would have been offended to be called Father
Cutler) was an extraordinary saintly pastor, who, though from
a rich Boston Brahmin family, had devoted his entire ordained
ministry to inner-city work among the poor. He was seen as
the pastor of all of Charlestown, though ninety percent of the
community was Irish-Catholic. He was a zealous activist for
peace and justice. Mr. Cutler had a profound influence on me
as a child; my mother used to tell me that even as a small boy
I said that I wanted to be like Mr. Cutler when I grew up. The
call to ordained ministry was present as far back as I can consciously remember. Childhood games often included playing
church, with me as the priest distributing communion.

Eventually, Mr. Cutler retired. A new priest with a wife and children arrived, and we were required to leave the rectory. My parents, through intense and diligent work, were able to fulfill the American dream and purchase their own home nearby. The new priest was a high churchman; and in Sunday school he instructed us that we were not Protestants but Catholics — not Roman Catholics, but Anglo-Catholics. This was the best news I had ever heard. After being verbally and physically bullied in our largely Catholic neighborhood for being a "Protestant and Nazi," I was thrilled to learn that I was Catholic, too!

St. John's Episcopal Church was the center of my life. Besides being a refuge where we as immigrants were accepted and loved, it also was the formative spiritual community of my childhood and adolescence. We had a boys' choir and a church Boy Scout Troop. In high school, we had a very active Young People's Fellowship, because of which I had my first preaching opportunity on Youth Sunday. Seminarians from the Episcopal Theological School provided youth leadership, and one in particular solidified my vocation. As a senior in high school, I met with my bishop, and he affirmed my vocation: "Jurgen, you'll make a wonderful priest; now when you go to college, don't major in religion. You'll get plenty of that in seminary." He shook my hand, and I was a postulant!

COLLEGE AND SEMINARY

In 1965, I went off to college. I had been recruited by Harvard College but accepted a full scholarship to Amherst when my mother informed me Harvard meant living at home! My secondary education had been at the Boston Latin School. Six years of Latin and three years of Greek in high school and an interest in archaeology and psychology directed me to choose classics as my major. The greatest providence of college was meeting Gloria Gehshan, a lady from Smith College, on the very first day of freshman year. She would become my wife. We have been together most of our sixty-five years of life.

This was the turbulent '60s and the days of student revolution. I joined the Students for a Democratic Society, the premier New Left organization and was very engaged in organizing teach-ins, demonstrations, and marches against the Vietnam War. This activism for peace and justice was for me an expression of my faith, and Christians like Merton, the Berrigans, Dorothy Day, and Martin Luther King Jr. were my heroes. The underside of this era was also part of my life: sexual promiscuity, drugs, growing cynicism. By the time I arrived at seminary (the Episcopal Theological School in Cambridge) in 1969, I was burned out and found myself in a deep depression.

Spirituality had not been a significant part of my Christian life, but my depression created a quest for inner resources. After dabbling in Eastern religions and New Age philosophies, I embraced Jungian psychology as my new "religion." In my last year of seminary, I interned at an Episcopal church under a priest who himself was an avid disciple of Jung and who had an interest in spiritual healing. Having been well indoctrinated with a biblical hermeneutic of Bultmannian demythologization, in which all the healing miracles of Jesus had been discarded, I was not sure what these folk at the parish thought they were doing, but I dutifully participated. Though a senior in seminary, I had never participated in a Bible study or prayer group before — much less a healing service — but these Wednesday morning gatherings became utterly transformational. For the first time, I began to "experience" the reality of God and the power of prayer.

MY CONVERSION AS A YOUNG PRIEST

As I began my curacy as a deacon in 1972, I continued my explorations in the Holy Spirit. The charismatic movement was emerging in the Episcopal Church. *Nine o'Clock in the Morning* by Bennett, *Gathered for Power* by Pulkingham, and *Miracle in Darien* by Fullam were narrations of priests and parishes totally transformed by the work of the Holy Spirit. "Spiritual Renewal" was the new buzzword in the church; Cursillo, Faith Alive, Marriage Encounter, the charismatic movement — all were efforts to bring new life to the church in the face of what was beginning to become evident: decline and decrease in the Episcopal Church. I was drawn to these movements, not just for the church's sake, but for the sake of my own very thirsty soul.

In this quest, the Lord provided a spiritual mentor, an older woman named Elizabeth. She asked me, "Would you like to receive the baptism in the Holy Spirit?" This was an essential and pervasive theme of the charismatic renewal: that the apostolic experience of the baptism of the Holy Spirit on the day of Pentecost was available today and was the rightful promised inheritance of every believer. My response was rather passive, "Well, why not?" She prayed over me on a number of occasions, but nothing happened. Then in June 1974, in the living room of the home of some Baptist evangelists who were friends of Elizabeth, while being prayed over with the laying on of hands, the heavens opened and the Spirit of God gave me a supernatural vision of the Blood of Christ.

From that point, everything began to change: my spirituality — my prayer became alive, real, and personal; my theology — I began a decided move away from liberalism toward biblical orthodoxy; my preaching — I began to preach Christ crucified; my ministry — the power and experience of the Holy Spirit was central.

My charismatic conversion, however, also produced problems. "Evangelism is a dirty word in the Episcopal Church!" my rector asserted at my proposal to start an evangelism committee. I felt a sense that it was time for a new call. After a few disappointing rector searches, I was called to be the rector of

St. Paul's, in Malden, Massachusetts. It was a small, dying, elderly, urban congregation; my youth was the major qualification of their call.

MY WORK AS AN ANGLICAN PRIEST

St. Paul's was a wonderful adventure for the next fourteen years of my life. The parish had a remarkable transformation. There were all the outward indicators of growth: membership, attendance, staff, income, program; but more importantly, we became the dwelling place of the living God and a mission center of living water (Ezek 47): conversions, healings, deliverances, deep worship, ministry to the poor. We became known as the "Charismatic Episcopal Church." We introduced literally thousands of folks around New England to a deeper experience of the Holy Spirit through weekly healing services, preaching and teaching missions at other churches, and regular "Renewal" conferences hosted at St. Paul's.

During this time, God was planting the seeds of my conversion to Catholicism. I began the discipline of being a penitent. My first confessor was a monk of the Episcopal community of the Society of St. John the Evangelist, Father Carleton Jones. Our monthly meetings introduced me to Anglo-Catholic worship and spirituality. My many years of spiritual direction with Carleton ended abruptly with his sudden announcement that he was becoming a Roman Catholic. I remember vividly the words of the letter he sent to me explaining his decision: "I have come to the conclusion that the unity of the Church is not finally something to be strived for but rather a gift already from the Lord to His Church in the Petrine office."

Radical feminism is a powerful lobby in the Episcopal Diocese of Massachusetts. At one diocesan meeting, a priest and seminary professor declared abortion to be a sacrament. Thus, I felt called to be a voice for the sanctity of life and organized a chapter of the National Organization of Episcopalians for

Life (NOEL). My reputation as a charismatic left me somewhat on the fringes of the clergy as an eccentric, but my pro-life activism drew bitter anger and rejection from many of my colleagues. The abortion crisis, however, posed for me even a larger question: How could the moral compass of the church be so profoundly broken?

Towards the end of the '80s, I sensed that my time at St. Paul's was ending. After being rejected by the few possible prospects in the greater Boston area, I began earnestly to seek the Lord. On the Eve of the Epiphany, 1990, while reading *The New Catholics*, a collection of testimonies of converts to Catholicism, I received a clear word from God that I was to be a Catholic. In obedience to that word, I actually began exploring the Pastoral Provision. I met a number of times with a Franciscan priest to explore the Catholic faith. I also met with Father Andrew Mead, the rector of the Anglo-Catholic Church of the Advent. Strangely, the Holy Spirit seemed to say, "Not yet!" But the conversations with Father Mead produced an invitation to serve with him at the Advent.

Immersion in the deep, rich world of Anglo-Catholic worship and spirituality, far from being alien to my charismatic tendencies, was a profoundly charismatic experience. I was introduced to Keble, Pusey, and Newman, to Benson and Grafton, to the Triduum, the Veneration of the Cross, Benediction, the Angelus, and daily Mass. I remained at the Advent seven years, but again I sensed God was calling me elsewhere. Was it time to go to Rome? Again, God seemed to say, "Not yet!"

In Holy Week of 1997, I received an invitation to become rector of Christ Church Hamilton. Christ Church had been the premier Evangelical Episcopal church of the diocese. It had experienced a wonderful renewal in the late '70s and '80s and began to draw in many faculty and students from Gordon College and Gordon-Conwell Seminary. But the last decade had been a disastrous time of conflict and diminishment and, at the request of the Vestry, the bishop removed the rector. The parish had become a small, financially stressed, demoralized, depressed group, living in the memories of past glory.

Newly equipped with all my Anglo-Catholic experience and paraphernalia (eucharistic vestments, bells, incense), I went to Christ Church. Almost instantly, God renewed the church, liturgically, spiritually, and politically. Attendance doubled the first year and tripled the next, as did the budget. The staff and ministry of the parish were rebuilt; missionary work was revitalized. Seminarians came in droves, and many were ordained (some have even journeyed on to Roman and Orthodox orders). A vision that had animated my ministry, a vision of a church — fully Evangelical, fully charismatic — came to fruition at Christ Church.

But alas, even as we thrived, the din of the political turmoil of the Episcopal Church and the Anglican Communion loomed. I constantly posed the question to the lay and clerical leadership of the church: What is God calling Christ Church to be and do in the midst of this crisis? One answer to that question came in the developments of what would become the Anglican Church of North America (ACNA). A significant group of parishioners thought this was the direction we should go. Another large group, equally faithful and orthodox, was convinced that steadfast witness within the Episcopal Church was God's plan. Each sought my opinion. My theological preferences were with the former; my catholic sensibilities (against schism) were with the latter. I proposed that we accept both directions as authentically led by the Holy Spirit and plan a future of two sister parishes, one a new church plant of the ACNA and the other a continuing Episcopal church at Christ Church. The two sister parishes would continue in mutual affection, prayer, and, where possible, shared ministry — a witness of reconciliation and charity over against the bloodbath of lawsuits and depositions going on in the denomination.

The Vestry adopted this vision for the future. We set a timetable for the next twelve months and invited each member of the parish to discern prayerfully God's specific will for them. We developed the appropriate planning and organizational structures for building of the two new future congregations. I made it clear that I did not believe God was calling me to one congregation or the other. My call was to see through the birth of these two new churches.

This very crisis in the Episcopal Church had been raising questions of ecclesiology, authority, discerning truth, the doctrine of marriage, etc. I became more convinced that as rich and wonderful as the Anglican heritage was, it did not contain the spiritual DNA to resolve this crisis. As good a home as the Episcopal Church had been for me since childhood and as joyful and satisfying a ministry as I had had within her, my intention was to retire from active ministry in the Episcopal Church and then explore admission into the Catholic Church. But again God said, "Not yet!"

I rejoice that through God's grace I have had a very honest, respectful, and mutually affectionate relationship with my Episcopal bishop. Although he approved the parish partition plan, at a private meeting, it was made clear to me that I would not be allowed to remain an Episcopal priest and be involved in the Anglican Church of North America — "You have to choose!"

I finished my work at Christ Church over the next six months. In 2009, I preached and celebrated my last liturgies as rector of Christ Church. The final Eucharist included the Vestries of both congregations mutually affirming and blessing one another. On the following Sunday, October 4, the Feast of St. Francis, I preached and celebrated my first liturgy as rector of Christ the Redeemer Anglican (CTR). I was inspired by the Lord's words to Francis from the San Damiano crucifix: "Go and repair my church, which as you see is in ruins!"

The last three years as rector of CTR were the most joyous and fulfilling of my forty years in ordained ministry. Roughly 250 folks joined me in the exodus from the Episcopal Church; another 150 have since joined. God's provision has been bountiful. But from the beginning, I also knew that this was to be for me a brief assignment; I felt called to be the founding rector and then invite CTR to search for their first new rector. In early January of 2012, the parish had successfully called their new rector. Concurrently, an Anglican ordinariate (Ordinariate of the Chair of St. Peter) was established in North America. At last, I heard the Lord say, "Now is the time!"

I gathered together CTR parishioners to explore, under the brilliant tutelage of Dr. Thomas Howard, the meaning of the invitation of Pope Benedict in *Anglicanorum Coetibus*. For ten weeks, we asked, "What does the Catholic Church really teach?" A convert from Fundamentalism and Anglicanism, Dr. Howard was able to instruct us both biblically and cogently about those subjects most troublesome to Evangelical Protestants: Marian dogma and devotion, the primacy of Peter, the infallibility of the pope, the veneration and intercession of saints, the doctrine of purgatory, prayer for the dead, etc. A second ten-week study program was focused on Anglican-Catholic Ecumenical Conversations and initiatives. I led twelve individuals forward to personally respond to the Pope's invitation to Anglicans and to come into full communion with the See of Rome through the ordinariate.

Though I might have journeyed earlier to Rome in my own personal history, this was a collective historic moment for the beginning of the fulfillment of the vision of the reunion of Rome and Canterbury. That was the dream of our Tractarian fathers, the explicit goal of Pope Paul VI and Archbishop Ramsey at the launching of the Anglican-Roman Catholic International Commission (ARCIC) dialogues, and an implicit hope in the bold ecumenical theology of Pope John Paul II in

Ut Unum Sint and his reenvisioning of a papacy for the whole Church. I am humbled to be invited by God to be a small part of this historic work. At noon on August 15, 2012, the Feast of the Assumption of the Blessed Virgin Mary, after forty years, I officially resigned my Anglican Priestly Orders; at 6 p.m. of that day I was confirmed and received into the Catholic Church. In February 2013, I received word that I had been approved for ordination in the Catholic Church. In fact, I was Pope Benedict's last rescript.

WHY CATHOLICISM?

Since announcing my decision to become a Catholic and to seek ordination through the Anglican ordinariate, I have had many an inquiry from people wondering, "Why?"

My first reason is that this decision is an act of obedience to the guidance of the Holy Spirit. Though a long personal journey of twenty-five years or more, I would add that as personal as it is, it is not just a private or uniquely individual call, not simply a private denominational predilection.

Over the years, I have read innumerable books, have had many searching conversations, watched hours of EWTN, listened to many testimonies and teachings — all of which have contributed to the decision to become a Catholic. But above all it has been a deep, constant, magnetic pull of the Holy Spirit to come to the center of the Church. It is this deep intuitive sense each time I enter a Catholic church or religious community that I am in *the* Church, not *a* church. We speak in Evangelical circles when a person of the Jewish faith becomes a Christian that they have become a "completed Jew." To become a Catholic is for me to become a "completed Christian." As I have already previously articulated, the driving vision of my ministry has been to build a church that was "fully catholic, fully Evangelical, and fully charismatic." I have come to the conviction that one cannot be "fully catholic" apart from communion with the See of Peter. For that matter, one cannot be "fully evangelical" or "fully charismatic" apart from the rich and deep historical meaning of those words in the fullness of the Catholic Church. As has been said to me on a number of occasions by wise and mature Catholic friends, you need leave nothing behind of any Christian tradition that is of true Gospel value. All of it comes only to fullness. To become a Catholic is to receive from my Lord His last providential gift from the cross: "Behold, thy mother."

There is in the Christian life a force of gravity, which draws the believer ever deeper into union with Christ. That union is not only a private mystical union — though it is that — but a deepening union with the Mystical Body of Christ, the Church. It is a dogmatic principle of the Catholic Church that "this Church, constituted and organized as a society in the present world, *subsists* in the Catholic Church" (*Lumen Gentium*, no. 8). If this is true, then this gravitational pull of Christ's Spirit is universally active, drawing all humanity to Christ the Head and to the fullness of His saving grace, which He mediates through His Body the Church. John Henry Newman, an Anglican convert to Rome, insightfully quipped that there was no steady state between atheism and Catholicism! In the human soul, there is always that spiritual battle between the centrifugal forces of the world, the flesh, and the devil drawing us away from the love of God, and the centripetal dynamic of the Holy Spirit pulling us ever deeper into the love of God. There is a *gravitas* to the Catholic Church, to the See of Peter, that is, I believe, a true and objective charism intended by Christ to draw His followers into union with Him in the fellowship of the Catholic Church.

That of course already displays the second reason for my decision: theological. The great divide between the churches of the Reformation and the Catholic Church is in the domain of ecclesiology: What is the Church? In the Protestant world,

Anglicanism has sought to maintain a catholic ecclesiology: organic, universal, and apostolic. Bishops, creeds, sacraments, and conciliarism have been maintained as integral pieces of Anglican ecclesiology, papal primacy alone being set aside. Within that catholic structure, Anglicanism has also asserted a principle of theological freedom and diversity. One *may* believe in spiritual regeneration in Baptism, but one is free *not* to believe it. One *may* believe in the Real Presence in the Eucharist, or one may *dis*believe it. One *may* believe in the authority of Scripture, but one is not *required* to so believe. One *may* believe in the sanctity of marriage, but one may choose *not* to believe it. For much of my life as an Anglican, that freedom was a pleasant gift, but increasingly it had become a source of distress and a profound impediment to my priestly work as a pastor and preacher. How could I proclaim from the pulpit what the Bible teaches or Christianity asserts, when my bishop was saying quite the opposite? How could I advise a person in the confessional when the priest in the neighboring parish would advise the opposite? My authority as a teacher and confessor needed to be based on something other than my own best opinion.

Flannery O'Connor spoke of the glorious freedom she experienced in being delivered from the "tyranny of her intellect." *Credo ut intelligam!* That has become my experience. It is the paradox of true intellectual freedom by submission to "the Church's teaching." It is a glorious freedom, not only in the mind's love for God, but in the vocation of priest in the theological and spiritual formation of disciples of Jesus. Thus, this theological conversion is not first of all a conversion to the peculiar Catholic beliefs about which my inquirers challenge me: "What about Mary?" "What about purgatory?" "What about contraception?" Rather, it is a conversion to the faithfulness of Christ's gift to the Church of an authentic authority to bind and to loose. At its deepest, it is a question of pneumatology even more than ecclesiology. How does the Spirit of Truth actually function in the Church? Whatever complexities and seeming incongruities may be discerned, the Magisterium is at minimum a reasonable and practicable answer to the question of truth that is trustworthy. At best, it is what the Church proclaims, the provision by Christ to His people of the gift of unerring guidance.

Finally and perhaps most urgently, my decision to become a Catholic was driven by our Lord's high priestly prayer, "May they be one, that the world might believe." The unity of the Church has been for me a primary and constant imperative of following Jesus. The unity of the Church is not only an imperative for the internal life of God's people but an essential dimension of her evangelical mission. There is no greater scandal and impediment to the conversion of the world to the love of Christ than her divisions. Pope Benedict established the Anglican ordinariate both as a concrete instrument to begin to organically heal the divisions of the Reformation and as an essential strategy for the sake of "the New Evangelization." As an Anglican, I have received this as a gracious invitation to reconciliation. I can find no valid, faithful reason to decline.

After forty years as an Episcopal priest, Jurgen Liias became a Catholic in August 2012. In April 2013, he was ordained a Catholic priest through the Anglican ordinariate. A community of about twenty-five other former Anglicans have joined him through the Ordinariate of the Chair of St. Peter in forming the parish of St. Gregory the Great in Beverly Farms, Massachusetts.

Hauled Aboard the Ark

Dr. Peter Kreeft

former Dutch Reformed Calvinist

I was born into a loving, believing community, a Protestant "mother church" (the Reformed Church) which, though it had not for me the fullness of the faith, had strong and genuine piety. I believed, mainly because of the good example of my parents and my church. The faith of my parents, Sunday school teachers, ministers, and relatives made a real difference to their lives, a difference big enough to compensate for many shortcomings. "Love covers a multitude of sins."

I was taught what C. S. Lewis calls "mere Christianity," essentially the Bible. But no one reads the Bible as an extraterrestrial or an angel; our church community provides the colored glasses through which we read, and the framework, or horizon, or limits within which we understand. My "glasses" were of Dutch Reformed Calvinist construction, and my limiting framework stopped very far short of anything "Catholic!" The Catholic Church was regarded with utmost suspicion. In the world of the forties and fifties, in which I grew up, that suspicion may have been equally reciprocated by most Catholics. Each group believed that most of the other groups were probably on the road to hell. Christian ecumenism and understanding has made astonishing strides since then.

Dutch Calvinists, like most conservative Protestants, sincerely believed that Catholicism was not only heresy but idolatry; that Catholics worshipped the Church, the pope, Mary, saints, images, and who knows what else; that the Church had added some inane "traditions of men" to the Word of God, traditions and doctrines that obviously contradicted it (how could they not see this? I wondered); and, most important of all, that Catholics believed "another gospel," another religion, that they didn't even know how to get to heaven: they tried to pile up brownie points with God with their good works, trying to work their way in instead of trusting in Jesus as their Savior. They never read the Bible, obviously.

I was never taught to hate Catholics, but to pity them and to fear their errors. I learned a serious concern for truth that to this day I find sadly missing in many Catholic circles. The typical Calvinist anti-Catholic attitude I knew was not so much prejudice, judgment with no concern for evidence, but judgment based on apparent and false evidence: sincere mistakes rather than dishonest rationalizations.

Though I thought it pagan rather than Christian, the richness and mystery of Catholicism fascinated me — the dimensions which avant-garde liturgists have been dismantling since the Silly Sixties. (When God saw that the Church in America lacked persecutions, He sent them liturgists.)

The first independent idea about religion I ever remember thinking was a question I asked my father, an elder in the church, a good and wise and holy man. I was amazed that he couldn't answer it. "Why do we Calvinists have the whole truth and no one else? We're so few. How could God leave the rest of the world in error? Especially the rest of the Christian churches?" Since no good answer seemed forthcoming, I then came to the explosive conclusion that the truth about God was more mysterious — more wonderfully and uncomfortably mysterious — than anything any of us could ever fully comprehend. (Calvinists would not deny that, but they do not usually teach it either. They are strong on God's "sovereignty," but weak on the richness of God's mystery.) That conviction, that the truth is always infinitely more than anyone can have, has not diminished. Not even all the infallible creeds are a container for all that is God.

I also realized at a very young age, obscurely but strongly, that the truth about God had to be far simpler than I had been taught, as well as far more complex and mysterious. I remember surprising my father with this realization (which was certainly because of God's grace rather than my intelligence, for I was only about eight, I think): "Dad, everything we learn in church and everything in the Bible comes down to just one thing, doesn't it? There's only one thing we have to worry about, isn't there?"

"Why, no, I don't see that. There are many things. What do you mean?"

"I mean that all God wants us to do — all the time — is to ask Him what He wants us to do, and then do it. That covers everything, doesn't it? Instead of asking ourselves, ask God!"

Surprised, my father replied, "You know, you're right!"

After I'd had eight years of public elementary school, my parents offered me a choice between two high schools: public or Christian (Calvinist), and I chose the latter, even though it meant leaving old friends. Eastern Christian High School was run by a sister denomination, the Christian Reformed Church. Asking myself now why I made that choice, I cannot say. Providence often works in obscurity. I was not a remarkably religious kid and loved the New York Giants baseball team with considerable more passion and less guilt than I loved God.

I won an essay contest in high school with a meditation on Dostoyevski's story "The Grand Inquisitor," interpreted as an anti-Catholic, anti-authoritarian cautionary tale. The Church, like Communism, seemed a great, dark, totalitarian threat.

I then went to Calvin College, the Christian Reformed college which has such a great influence for its small size and provincial locale (Grand Rapids, Michigan) because it takes both its faith and its scholarship very seriously. I registered as a pre-seminary student because, though I did not think I was personally "called" by God to be a clergyman, I thought I might "give it a try." I was deeply impressed by the caption under a picture of Christ on the cross: "This is what I did for thee. What will you do for Me?"

But in college I quickly fell in love with English, and then Philosophy, and thus twice changed my major. Both subjects were widening my appreciation of the history of Western civilization and therefore of things Catholic. The first serious doubt about my anti-Catholic beliefs was planted in my mind by my roommate, who was becoming an Anglican: "Why don't Protestants pray to saints? There's nothing wrong in you asking me to pray for you, is there? Why not ask the dead, then, if we believe they're alive with God in heaven, part of the 'great cloud of witnesses' [Heb 12] that surrounds us?" It was the first serious question I had absolutely no answer to, and that bothered me. I attended Anglican liturgy with my roommate and was enthralled by the same things that captivated Tom Howard and many others: not just the aesthetic beauty but the fullness, the solidity, the moreness of it all.

I remember a church service I went to while at Calvin, in the Wealthy Street Baptist Temple (Fundamentalist). I had never heard such faith and conviction, such joy in the music, such love of Jesus. I needed to focus my aroused love of God on an object. But God is invisible, and we are not angels. There was no religious object in the church. It was a bare, Protestant church; images were "idols." I suddenly understood why Protestants were so subjectivistic: their love of God had no visible object to focus it. The living water welling up from within had no material riverbed, no shores, to direct its flow to the far divine sea. It rushed back upon itself and became a pool of froth.

Then I caught sight of a Catholic spy in the Protestant camp: a gold cross atop the pole of the church flag. Adoring Christ required using that symbol. The alternative was the froth. My gratitude to the Catholic Church for this one relic, this remnant, of her riches, was immense. For this good Protestant water to flow, there had to be Catholic aqueducts. To change the metaphor, I had been told that reliance on external things was a "crutch!" I now realized that I was a cripple. And I thanked the Catholic "hospital" (that's what the Church is) for responding to my needs.

Perhaps, I thought, these good Protestant people could worship like angels, but I could not. Then I realized that they couldn't either. Their ears were using crutches, not their eyes. They used beautiful hymns, for which I would gladly exchange the new, flat, unmusical, wimpy "liturgical responses" no one sings in our Masses — their audible imagery is their crutch. I think that in heaven, Protestants will teach Catholics to sing and Catholics will teach Protestants to dance and sculpt.

I developed a strong intellectual and aesthetic love for things medieval: Gregorian chant, Gothic architecture, Thomistic philosophy, illuminated manuscripts, etc. I felt vaguely guilty about it, for that was the Catholic era. I thought I could separate these legitimate cultural forms from the "dangerous" Catholic essence, as the modern Church separated the essence from these discarded forms. Yet I saw a natural connection.

Then one summer, on the beach at Ocean Grove, New Jersey, I read St. John of the Cross. I did not understand much of it, but I knew, with undeniable certainty, that here was reality, something as massive and positive as a mountain range. I felt as if I had just come out of a small, comfortable cave, in which I had lived all my life, and found that there was an unsuspected world outside, of incredible dimensions. Above all, the dimensions were those of holiness, goodness, purity of heart, obedience to the First and greatest Commandment, willing God's will, the one absolute I had discovered, at the age of eight. I was very far from saintly, but that did not prevent me from fascinated admiration from afar; the valley dweller appreciates the height of the mountain more than the dweller on the foot-hills. I read other Catholic saints and mystics, and discovered the same reality there, however different the style (even St. Thérèse "The Little Flower"!) I felt sure it was the same reality I had learned to love from my parents and teachers, only a far deeper version of it. It did not seem alien and other. It was not another religion, but the adult version of my own.

Then in a Church history class at Calvin, a professor gave me a way to investigate the claims of the Catholic Church on my own. The essential claim is historical: that Christ founded the Catholic Church, that there is historical continuity. If that were true, I would have to be a Catholic out of obedience to my one absolute, the will of my Lord. The teacher explained the Protestant belief. He said that Catholics accuse us Protestants of going back only to Luther and Calvin; but this is not true; we go back to Christ. Christ had never intended a Catholic-style Church, but a Protestant-style one. The Catholic additions to the simple, Protestant-style New Testament Church had grown up gradually in the Middle Ages like barnacles on the hull of a ship, and the Protestant Reformers had merely scraped off the barnacles, the alien, pagan accretions. The Catholics, on the other hand, believed that Christ established the Church Catholic from the start, and that the doctrines and practices that Protestants saw as barnacles were, in fact, the very living and inseparable parts of the planks and beams of the ship.

I thought this made the Catholic claim empirically test-able, and I wanted to test it because I was worried by this time about my dangerous interest in things Catholic. Half of me wanted to discover it was the true Church (that was the more adventurous half); the other half wanted to prove it false (that was the comfortable half). My adventurous half rejoiced when I discovered in the early Church such Catholic elements as the centrality of the Eucharist, the Real Presence, prayers to saints, devotion to Mary, an insistence on visible unity, and apostolic succession. Furthermore, the Church Fathers just "smelled" more Catholic than Protestant, especially St. Augustine, my personal favorite and a hero to most Protestants too. It seemed very obvious that if Augustine or Jerome or Ignatius of Antioch or Anthony of the Desert, or Justin Martyr, or Clement of Alexandria, or Athanasius were alive today, they would be Catholics, not Protestants.

The issue of the Church's historical roots was crucial to me, for the thing I had found in the Catholic Church and in no Protestant church was simply this: the massive historical fact that there she is, majestic and unsinkable. It was the same old seaworthy ship, the Noah's ark that Jesus had commissioned. It was like discovering not an accurate picture of the ark, or even a real relic of its wood, but the whole ark itself, still sailing unscathed on the seas of history! It was like a fairy tale come true, like a "myth become fact," to use C. S. Lewis' formula for the Incarnation.

The parallel between Christ and Church, Incarnation and Church history, goes still further. I thought, just as Jesus made a claim about His identity that forces us into one of only two camps, His enemies or His worshippers, those who call Him liar and those who call Him Lord; so the Catholic Church's claim to be the one true Church, the Church Christ founded, forces us to say either that this is the most arrogant, blasphemous and wicked claim imaginable, if it is not true, or else that she is just what she claims to be. Just as Jesus stood out as the absolute exception to all other human teachers in claiming to be more than human and more than a teacher, so the Catholic Church stood out above all other denominations in claiming to be not merely a denomination, but the Body of Christ incarnate, infallible, one, and holy, presenting the really present Christ in her Eucharist. I could never rest in a comfortable, respectable ecumenical halfway house of measured admiration from a distance. I had to shout either "Crucify her!" or

"Hosanna!" If I could not love and believe her, honesty forced me to despise and fight her.

But I could not despise her. The beauty and sanctity and wisdom of her, like that of Christ, prevented me from calling her liar or lunatic, just as it prevented me from calling Christ that. But simple logic offered then one and only one other option: this must be the Church my Lord provided for me — my Lord, for me. So she had better become my Church if He is my Lord.

There were many strands in the rope that hauled me aboard the ark, though this one — the Church's claim to be the one Church historically founded by Christ — was the central and deciding one. The book that more than any other decided it for me was Ronald Knox's *The Belief of Catholics*. He and Chesterton "spoke with authority, and not as the scribes!" Even C. S. Lewis, the darling of Protestant Evangelicals, "smelled" Catholic most of the time. A recent book by a Calvinist author I went to high school with, John Beversluis, mercilessly tries to tear all Lewis' arguments to shreds, but Lewis is left without a scratch, and Beversluis comes out looking like an atheist. Lewis is the only author I ever have read whom I thought I could completely trust and completely understand. But he believed in purgatory, the Real Presence in the Eucharist, and not Total Depravity. He was no Calvinist. In fact, he was a medieval.

William Harry Jellema, the greatest teacher I ever knew, though a Calvinist, showed me what I can only call the Catholic vision of the history of philosophy, embracing the Greek and medieval tradition and the view of reason it assumed, a thick rather than a thin one. Technically, this was "realism" (Aquinas) as vs. "nominalism" (Ockham and Luther). Common-sensically, it meant wisdom rather than mere logical consistency, insight rather than mere calculation. I saw Protestant theology as infected with shallow nominalism and Descartes' narrow scientificization of reason.

A second and related difference is that Catholics, like their Greek and medieval teachers, still believed that reason was essentially reliable, not utterly untrustworthy because fallen. We make mistakes in using it, yes. There are "noetic effects of sin," yes. But the instrument is reliable. Only our misuse of it is not.

This is connected with a third difference. For Catholics, reason is not just subjective but objective; reason is not our artificial little man-made rules for our own subjective thought processes or intersubjective communications, but a window on the world. And not just the material world, but also form, order, objective truth. Reason was from God. All truth was God's truth. When Plato or Socrates knew the truth, the logos, they knew Christ, unless John lies in chapter 1 of his Gospel. I gave a chapel speech at Calvin calling Socrates a "common-grace Christian" and unwittingly scandalized the powers that be. They still remember it, thirty years later.

The only person who almost kept me Protestant was Kierkegaard. Not Calvin or Luther. Their denial of free will made human choice a sham game of predestined dice. Kierkegaard offered a brilliant, consistent alternative to Catholicism, but such a quirkily individualistic one, such a pessimistic and antirational one, that he was incompletely human. He could hold a candle to Augustine and Aquinas, I thought — the only Protestant thinker I ever found who could — but he was only the rebel in the ark, while they were the family, Noah's sons.

But if Catholic dogma contradicted Scripture or itself at any point, I could not believe it. I explored all the cases of claimed contradiction and found each to be a Protestant misunderstanding. No matter how morally bad the Church had gotten in the Renaissance, it never taught heresy. I was impressed with its very hypocrisy: even when it didn't raise its practice to its preaching, it never lowered its preaching to its practice. Hypocrisy, someone said, is the tribute vice pays to virtue.

I was impressed by the argument that "the Church wrote the Bible": Christianity was preached by the Church before the New Testament was written — that is simply a historical fact. It is also a fact that the Apostles wrote the New Testament and the Church canonized it, deciding which books were divinely inspired. I knew, from logic and common sense, that a cause can never be less than its effect. You can't give what you don't have. If the Church has no divine inspiration and no infallibility, no divine authority, then neither can the New Testament. Protestantism logically entails modernism. I had to be either a Catholic or a modernist. That decided it; that was like saying I had to be either a patriot or a traitor.

One afternoon I knelt alone in my room and prayed God would decide for me, for I am good at thinking but bad at acting, like Hamlet. Unexpectedly, I seemed to sense my heroes Augustine and Aquinas and thousands of other saints and sages calling out to me from the great ark, "Come aboard! We are really here. We still live. Join us. Here is the Body of Christ." I said Yes. My intellect and feelings had long been conquered; the will is the last to surrender.

One crucial issue remained to be resolved: justification by faith, the central bone of contention of the Reformation. Luther was obviously right here: the doctrine is dearly taught in Romans and Galatians. If the Catholic Church teaches "another gospel" of salvation by works, then it teaches fundamental heresy. I found here, however, another case of misunderstanding. I read Aquinas' *Summa* on grace, and the decrees of the Council of Trent, and found them just as strong on grace as Luther or Calvin. I was overjoyed to find that the Catholic Church had read the Bible too! At heaven's gate our entrance ticket, according to Scripture and Church dogma, is not our good works or our sincerity, but our faith, which glues us to Jesus. He saves us; we do not save ourselves. But I find, incredibly, that nine out of ten Catholics do not know this, the absolutely central, core, essential dogma of Christianity. Protestants are right: most Catholics do in fact believe a whole other religion. Well over ninety percent of students I have polled who have had twelve years of catechism classes, even Catholic high schools, say they expect to go to heaven because they tried, or did their best, or had compassionate feelings to everyone, or were sincere. They hardly ever mention Jesus. Asked why they hope to be saved, they mention almost anything except the Savior. Who taught them? Who wrote their textbooks? These teachers have stolen from our precious children the most valuable thing in the world, the "pearl of great price": their faith. Jesus had some rather terrifying warnings about such things — something about millstones.

Catholicism taught that we are saved by faith, by grace, by Christ, however few Catholics understood this. And Protestants taught that true faith necessarily produces good works. The fundamental issue of the Reformation is an argument between the roots and the blossoms on the same flower.

But though Luther did not neglect good works, he connected them to faith by only a thin and unreliable thread: human gratitude. In response to God's great gift of salvation, which we accept by faith, we do good works out of gratitude, he taught. But gratitude is only a feeling, and dependent on the self. The Catholic connection between faith and works is a far stronger and more reliable one. I found it in C. S. Lewis' *Mere Christianity*, the best introduction to Christianity I have ever read. It is the ontological reality of us, supernatural life, sanctifying grace, God's own life in the soul, which is received by faith and then itself produces good works. God comes in one end and out the other: the very same thing that comes in by faith (the life of God) goes out as works, through our free cooperation.

I was also dissatisfied with Luther's teaching that justification was a legal fiction on God's part rather than a real event in us; that God looks on the Christian in Christ, sees only

Christ's righteousness, and legally counts or imputes Christ's righteousness as ours. I thought it had to be as Catholicism says: that God actually imparts Christ to us, in Baptism and through faith (these two are usually together in the New Testament). Here I found the Fundamentalists, especially the Baptists, more philosophically sound than the Calvinists and Lutherans. For me, their language, however sloganish and satirizable, is more accurate when they speak of "Receiving Christ as your personal Savior."

Though my doubts were all resolved and the choice was made in 1959, my senior year at Calvin, actual membership came a year later, at Yale. My parents were horrified, and only gradually came to realize I had not lost my head or my soul, that Catholics were Christians, not pagans. It was very difficult, for I am a shy and soft-hearted sort, and almost nothing is worse for me than to hurt people I love. I think that I hurt almost as much as they did. But God marvelously binds up wounds.

I have been happy as a Catholic for many years now. The honeymoon faded, of course, but the marriage has deepened. Like all converts I ever have heard of, I was hauled aboard not by those Catholics who try to "sell" the Church by conforming it to the spirit of the times by saying Catholics are just like everyone else, but by those who joyfully held out the ancient and orthodox faith in all its fullness and prophetic challenge to the world. The minimalists, who reduce miracles to myths, dogmas to opinions, laws to values, and the Body of Christ to a psycho-social club, have always elicited wrath, pity, or boredom from me. So has political partisanship masquerading as religion. I am happy as a child to follow Christ's vicar on earth everywhere he leads. What he loves, I love; what he leaves, I leave; where he leads, I follow. For the Lord we both adore said to Peter his predecessor, "Who hears you, hears Me." That is why I am a Catholic: because I am a Christian.

Source: *"Hauled Aboard the Ark – The Spiritual Journey of Peter Kreeft"* excerpt from The Spiritual Journeys, *published by the Daughters of St. Paul (1987). Used with permission of the author.*

Peter Kreeft, Ph.D., is a professor of philosophy at Boston College and at the King's College in New York City. He is a contributor to several Christian publications, is in wide demand as a speaker at conferences, and is the author of over seventy-one books including: Handbook of Christian Apologetics, Christianity for Modern Pagans, *and* Fundamentals of the Faith.

THE TIBER — NEITHER TOO WIDE, NOR TOO DEEP

DR. JAMES PAPANDREA

former Methodist minister

The story of my conversion to Catholicism really goes back to my childhood. My father's family is Chicago Italian and of course that meant Roman Catholic. I was born during Vatican II in 1963 and baptized in the Catholic faith. My paternal grandfather ("Papa Lou") would become a great influence on my faith as I grew up. He made it a priority to get to Mass every week, and, though he didn't talk like an evangelist, no one who knew him would have questioned his faith. My mother, however, was not Catholic, so when my family moved to Wisconsin, we joined a neighborhood Protestant congregation that both my parents were comfortable with, and I was raised Lutheran. I still have fond memories of the Lutheran pastor and the people there.

Having been baptized as a Catholic, I suppose I'm technically more of a "revert" than a convert. In fact, everyone around me always emphasized the similarities between the Lutheran denomination and Catholicism, so I grew up with a healthy respect for the Catholic Church, but also with only a very basic (and often uninformed) knowledge of what Catholicism was. After I was confirmed, I was told that I was now spiritually an adult and able to make my own decisions about my faith. So I left. Like many youth, I suppose, I was bored with my congregation. However, I must say that the Lutherans gave me an appreciation for singing the great hymns (some of which taught me more theology than all the catechism classes put together), but I felt that there should be more to the faith than what I was experiencing in that congregation. I eventually joined another Protestant denomination — the United Methodists — partly because it was where my high school girlfriend belonged. I was also attracted to what they called "pluralism," which, as I understood it, amounted to a license to believe and do anything I wanted without accountability to a higher authority. This sounded pretty good to a young guy in high school and college.

EVANGELICAL ENTHUSIASM

In college, I got involved with Campus Crusade for Christ and became a Fundamentalist. I had a conversion experience in the context of a neighborhood Bible study when I was younger, so this seemed like a continuation of that kind of enthusiasm. Bless their hearts, they meant well, but I could never get on board with their style of evangelism: just walking up to someone you don't know with the "Four Spiritual Laws" booklet in hand, sharing the faith with the hope of extracting the "sinner's prayer" from the poor soul. On the other hand, the deep reverence I have for the Scriptures is a legacy of that time in my life, and so I have to assume that God was at work in me, in and through Campus Crusade.

It was a strange mix in those days, because while I was hanging out and playing guitar with the Campus Crusade crowd during the week, on Sunday mornings I went to the campus Methodist congregation, where I helped out the music leader by playing bass guitar. The Methodists tend to be theologically liberal, especially in Minnesota where I went to college. Thus, I bounced back and forth between the conservative approach of the parachurch organization and the liberalism of a mainline Protestant denomination. The result was that I learned to speak both languages and get along with people in both camps. In the end, the experience planted the seeds of a passion for ecumenical dialogue and the conviction that the truth is not to be found at either extreme, but in the "center of gravity." In other words, the truest expression of the Christian faith is not in Fundamentalism on the right or in extreme liberalism on the left, but in the ancient and historic Church that occupies the center.

I graduated from college in 1985, and, after trying to find my way in the world for a year, I decided to go to seminary. I figured, why not study the most important topic there is — God! I was very naïve, however, and assumed that one seminary was just like another. After all, they all study the same Bible, right? By the grace of God, I ended up at Fuller Theological Seminary in Pasadena, California, which was an interdenominational Evangelical Protestant seminary. I consider my time at Fuller to be my great awakening to the many treasures of the Christian faith, especially the Church Fathers. I learned the tools of biblical exegesis, studied under professors who were both brilliant and spiritual, and grew in my faith by leaps and bounds. It was at Fuller that I went from being a Fundamentalist to an Evangelical — and yes, there is a difference! It was also at Fuller that I discovered the difference between a Reformed ("Calvinist") approach and an "Arminian" approach to salvation. It seemed that many of the people at Fuller were more Calvinist than Calvin was (of course, as a scholar, I now know that they were really just more Augustinian than Augustine was — can I get an "Amen"?). This meant that their understanding of God's providence and even their outlook on life leaned toward a kind of determinism that said, "If you're one of God's elect (and they all assumed they were), then God will take care of everything for you." They assumed that God is going to do what God is going to do, and that left little room for human free will. The problem, as I saw it, is that this approach didn't adequately explain human sin. I would come to find out later that the Methodist (Wesleyan/Arminian) approach is not far from the Catholic (Thomist) approach. It turns out that, theologically speaking, I was a Catholic all along.

Reverend Salmon: Swimming Upstream

When I graduated from seminary with a master of divinity degree, I ended up on the path toward ordination (in part, because I didn't know what else to do with my new diploma). I was still somewhat naïve regarding the extremes of theological liberalism in the Methodist Church, and I was still a bit "holier than thou." Thus, I had no idea that the next decade of my life would be an exercise in swimming upstream.

I was ordained and accepted an appointment as an associate pastor of a congregation of about a thousand members in south central Minnesota. After two years of butting heads with the senior pastor there, I was moved to what they call a "three point charge": two small churches of my own and part-time responsibility as a youth minister at a third (larger) church, all along the beautiful Mississippi Valley at the border of southern Minnesota and Wisconsin. Two years there eventually and inevitably burned me out, and I decided to go back to school to get a Ph.D. I finally felt like I knew what my calling was. As a pastor, while many of my colleagues visited the people of their congregation all week and then wrote a sermon on Saturday, my routine was to work on my sermon from Monday to Thursday, and then on Fridays drag myself outside and force myself to visit a few people. The hospital visits were the hardest, as I felt I had nothing to offer people. I often struggled just to make conversation. I felt I was gifted in the teaching parts of ministry, but not in the pastoral parts; therefore, I decided I was going to teach. I requested and received an appointment to attend Garrett-Evangelical Theological Seminary, the United Methodist Seminary on the campus of Northwestern University in Evanston, Illinois. It was there that I completed a Ph.D. in Patristics, the history and theology of the early Church.

ALL ROADS REALLY DO LEAD TO ROME

It was my study of the Church Fathers that ignited within me the dormant flame of Catholicism. As many others who have gone before me found, one cannot study the history of the early Church without realizing that many Protestant doctrines — *sola scriptura*, for example — were an invention of the Protestant Reformation and do not actually reflect the understanding of the Church Fathers, let alone the Apostles. I also realized that the Catholic understanding of the Eucharist is consistent with the way the sacrament has been understood from the beginning. This was a real revelation for me. In addition, as part of my Ph.D. studies, I got the chance to spend a summer at the American Academy in Rome. My formal studies there were in the history and topography of imperial Rome, but my informal exploration led me to a deeply devotional appreciation for the city of Rome and its churches.

I had been to Rome before. My parents took my brother and me on a trip to Italy when I was fifteen. I fell in love with Rome then, and that love has only grown over time into kind of a passion. But arriving in Rome that summer of 1995, I had a first impression like many people, I suppose. When I saw the grandeur of many of the churches of Rome — grandeur that I viewed as opulence — I had a negative reaction. "Wouldn't it be better to use all this money to feed the poor?" I thought. I would later realize that this is exactly what Judas said when a grateful Mary of Bethany poured out her expensive perfume on Jesus' feet (Jn 12:1–5). I came to understand (and appreciate) that the architecture and decoration of the churches of Rome are part of humanity's gift of gratitude to God. We offer the best of our creations to our Creator, in humble thanksgiving.

Studying in Rome that summer, I began to wrestle with what it would mean to be Roman Catholic. I had no great aversion to the idea, other than the fact that I would be giving up my status as clergy, but I had already discerned that I was not called to parish leadership or liturgical presiding. The more I studied and the more I explored the long history of the Church in Rome, the more I began to think, "I have to be a part of this." At least, that's what was going on deep down in my spirit. It wouldn't come to the surface until later, because at that time there were still too many obstacles. The Tiber seemed just too wide to cross. I had so many connections to Methodism, and I had convinced myself that belonging to a church where you get Communion every week would "cheapen" the sacrament (of course, I now know that the opposite is true, and I love to receive the Eucharist as often as possible).

I continued to study the Church Fathers, and I eventually settled on one who would be the topic of my doctoral dissertation. Novatian was a third-century priest of Rome who wrote an excellent (and orthodox) treatise on the Trinity and who was the acting bishop of Rome for over a year during a time of persecution. However, Novatian's story does not have a happy ending. When the persecution subsided enough to allow the proper election of a new bishop of Rome, Novatian lost the election, because he advocated excommunications for all those whose faith had lapsed under the threat of torture and death. His followers rejected the election of Pope Cornelius, called Novatian their bishop, and began a schism in the Church that lasted hundreds of years. The moral of the story is that the Church would come to the conclusion that the only thing worse than apostasy is schism, meaning the only thing worse than committing idolatry, is splitting the Church. I began to feel more and more the need to return to the original Church.

My conversion to Catholicism, however, was more complicated than simply joining with the Church of the Apostles. It was also about leaving something behind, leaving the denomination in which I was ordained. At this point, I was still determined to continue sticking it out in the United Methodist denomination, as long as I could make it work. This was for two main reasons. First, I was not yet ready to give up my status as an ordained clergyman. Second, I saw the denomination as a mission field and felt obligated to continue to try to save it. Eventually, I got to the point where I knew that my efforts were futile, and I now realize that it was rather arrogant of me to think I could change an entire denomination. It was time to leave. I had to admit that I was in a place that was not right for me and that I had to move on.

CROSSING THE TIBER

In reality, the decision to unite with the Roman Catholic Church was really just a matter of admitting in my head what my heart already knew. The Catholic Church was where I had started out (in baptism), and it was where I belonged. By this time, I had married an amazing woman, Susannah (Susie), who happened to be a cradle Catholic. She was a very good sport about getting married in a Protestant chapel (two, actually: we eloped in a Methodist chapel in Rome and then later had a wedding with friends and family in a Methodist chapel built within a skyscraper in Chicago), but she never felt at home in the United Methodist congregations. Of course, she wanted us both to be Catholic, but I had to come to that decision on my own. When the time came, at my instigation, we did what any self-respecting Protestants would do: we shopped around for a Catholic church. Eventually, we found a Catholic parish with solid preaching and good music, and we started going regularly. I had many meetings with the pastor, and he was very gracious in giving me his valuable time as I asked him all those questions that Protestants ask (interestingly, I now get invited to go into other parishes and talk about the answers to those very same questions).

My biggest stumbling block was probably the concept of praying to the saints. I had reasoned, like many Protestants, that if you pray to the saints, you are ascribing omniscience to them: if you think they can hear your prayers, then you are implying that they are divine, because the only way they could hear prayers is if they are all-knowing — but only God is all-knowing. I also reasoned that if you pray to the saints, you are ascribing omnipotence to them: if you think they can do something for you, then you are implying that they are divine, because the only way they could help you from heaven is if they are all-powerful — but only God is all-powerful. Even though I knew it was an ancient practice, I concluded that prayer to the saints was a form of idolatry. Maybe the Tiber was just too deep to cross. The help I needed came through conversations with a faithful, Catholic friend. She explained to me that praying to the saints is not a form of idolatry. Catholics do not think the saints are omniscient just because they can hear our prayers. Rather, it is a pure gift from God. She also explained that Catholics do not think saints are omnipotent, because Catholics ask for their *intercession*, not their intervention. If we can ask our brothers and sisters in the faith who are here on earth to pray for us (Jas 5:13–18), then why not ask those who are with God to pray for us?

I am still learning to incorporate prayer to the saints into my devotional life, but I am grateful to have a "cloud of witnesses" (Heb 12:1) to intercede for me. My grandparents had a special devotion to Padre Pio (even while he was alive), and to this day my uncle carries on that tradition. I consider St. Pio a patron of our family. I also ask for the intercession of St. Francis of Assisi, St. Hildegard of Bingen, and St. Cecilia (because I'm a musician), St. James (I am a James, after all), and St. John the Apostle (for my vocation as a theologian). Of course, I also pray to our Mother Mary, and, when I'm reading a particular Church Father, I sometimes pray to him as well. Sometimes I even pray to my grandfather, Papa Lou. Because of the intercession of the saints, my devotional life is now deeper and richer than it ever could have been before.

I eventually came to understand that I was really a Catholic at heart all along. When the time came for me to be received into the Church, I sent a letter to the United Methodist bishop explaining why I was leaving the denomination. The envelope included my certificate of ordination (returning it results in the denomination's version of an honorable discharge). Turning in my credentials like that was very liberating. Now, I am happy to be a Roman Catholic layperson, recognizing what my calling is and what it is not.

GLAD TO BE HOME

When I finally came back to the Catholic Church, my first reaction was, "So this is where all the Italians are!"

One of the first things that my wife and I did after I was received into the Church was to have a convalidation ceremony so that our marriage would be a sacrament (so, I've married the same woman three times — and I'd do it again in an instant). Now, as I think about being Catholic and as people ask me about my conversion, there are a few things I will always tell people, the reasons why I'm glad I'm Catholic: Walk into a traditional Protestant worship space and what holds the place of prominence at the front? The pulpit. That's because the preaching of the Word is the center of worship. Preaching is good, but of course preachers are only human. Now, walk into a Catholic church and what is front and center? The altar. That's because we are a sacramental Church. We are a Church that embraces the mystery of the living Word, the Lamb of God. Every time we celebrate Mass we proclaim the Gospel most perfectly (cf. 1 Cor 11:26).

While my personality doesn't normally tolerate mystery very well (I want to answer all the questions), the truth is that the more you try to get to the bottom of the mystery, what you really find is a deeper mystery. The mystery is not explained away, as it is in some other traditions. On the contrary, the mystery is embraced. In a real sense, my conversion (or return) to the Roman Catholic Church had to wait until I was ready to embrace mystery, to let go of having to have concrete answers to all the questions, and to trust in a God who is a mystery. Don't get me wrong, I still write books explaining the Trinity and things like that, but I have learned to be content with submitting to something greater than myself, without having to understand it all. It may seem counterintuitive, but submission is liberating.

I also appreciate the way the Catholic Church is (at least potentially) the "middle way" between the extremes: neither Fundamentalist, nor extreme liberal, but a "center" that embraces the best of both sides; neither all devotional, nor all social justice, but both faith and works; and so on.

Finally, I guess I just came to the point in my life when I longed to be part of the one Church that is connected by an unbroken chain going all the way back to Jesus and the Apostles. I became convinced of the truth of apostolic succession, a principle used in the early Church. It means that what is taught by the Church goes back to the Apostles, because they taught their successors, who taught the next generation of Church leaders, and so on. The institution of the Catholic Church may not be perfect, but I came to believe that it is the closest thing we have to what Jesus and the Apostles intended it to be, in large part because of the sacraments, especially the Eucharist. I just had to be a part of that.

To add blessing on top of blessing, a year after joining our parish, I was offered a full-time job as director of adult faith formation, and I got to live my faith as my day job, a dream I had all but given up on.

Called to the Classroom

Four years later, I left my parish job for a full-time teaching position. Ironically, I now teach early and medieval Church history at the same United Methodist seminary where I studied for my Ph.D. After ten years of waiting (and praying) for a full-time teaching job, I was hired by the seminary, even though they knew that I had become Catholic. I am now the one Catholic on a very ecumenical faculty, all of whom I respect very much and value as colleagues, even though we don't all agree on everything. I have found that I can love and appreciate the Methodists much better from the outside, as a Catholic, and I have plenty of opportunities to engage one of my passions: ecumenical dialogue. I also get to spend my days in the classroom and in the library, teaching and studying the history of Christianity and doctrine. The best part is, I get to take a group of students to Rome every year to see (and touch) the evidence of early and medieval Christianity firsthand and to meet people on both sides of the Tiber.

There is a bridge in Rome over the river Tiber, the *Ponte Sant' Angelo*, the bridge of the Holy Angel. It is lined with sculptures of angels designed by the great master Bernini. Right at the end of the bridge on one side of the river is the Methodist congregation of Rome. On the other side of the bridge is the Vatican. That bridge is symbolic for me, so much so that I used a picture of it as the cover art for my latest musical recording. The bridge is a symbol of both the separation and the connection between the Catholic Church and the Methodists. It is a symbol of the ecumenical dialogue which I value and also a symbol of whatever shared ministry we are able to do as we work together to care for the poor in this world. We all know that people walk that bridge (metaphorically speaking) in both directions. Somewhere, right now, there is a person writing about his conversion *from* Catholicism to a Protestant denomination. This is why the dialogue is so important — to increase communication and mutual understanding, to dispel the myths about Catholicism, and to figure out what we can learn from each other. I still consider myself "bilingual," because I can "speak" Protestant as well as Catholic. It is a gift I use in the service of the universal Church. Nevertheless, I know where my roots are and where my home is, and I thank God for leading me back to the ancient Church of the Apostles and the Fathers.

Dr. James L. Papandrea is associate professor of Church History at Garrett-Evangelical Theological Seminary. He is the author of several books, including Reading the Early Church Fathers, Trinity 101, *and* ROME: A Pilgrim's Guide to the Eternal City. *His latest CD is called* Still Quiet Voice. *Visit his website at: www.JimPapandrea.com.*

LED BY THE GOOD SHEPHERD
TO THE CATHOLIC CHURCH

ED HOPKINS

former Presbyterian and Reformed Episcopal minister

I was raised in a small-town, Southern Baptist church in Virginia, where I, along with my sister and my two brothers, attended Sunday school and, with our parents, church nearly every Sunday that I can remember. In my early teen years, I responded to a preacher's invitation to accept Christ as my Lord and Savior and was baptized. The experience of the waters of Baptism seemed to be one of rebirth. I felt as though my sins were washed away and there was a new beginning and opportunity for me ahead. However, I did not experience much growth in grace during my later high school years, and I went away to college in 1970 very disappointed with my hometown and the Christians that I knew.

COLLEGE MINISTRY

I was a religiously interested skeptic at that time, but a period of soul-searching and contacts with Evangelical friends at college led me back to faith. I began to seriously pray and study Scripture. Within a couple of years, I began to consider theological seminary and preparation for ministry.

During these college years, I was involved with a campus ministry group, the Navigators, that sought to make disciples of the Lord Jesus through a process of discipleship they saw outlined in 2 Timothy 2:2: "What you have heard from me before many witnesses entrust to faithful men who will be able to teach others also." This campus ministry taught me a deep respect for the Scriptures. I have come to see, however, that during that time, I learned some rather dubious interpretations of Scripture. Surely, Paul's words to Timothy were in the context of establishing apostolic leadership for the Church. Timothy was a bishop, ordained by Paul to have oversight over the Christians in Ephesus and perhaps other cities. Timothy was to ordain elders and deacons, root out heresy, and preserve the faith. The context was nothing like what we were attempting to do with young men and women in college.

We tended to miss the corporate dimension of the New Testament faith — discipleship for us was a personal, individual thing. During my last year or two of college, some of us began to see the inadequacy of the model we had been taught, and our campus fellowship began to have more the atmosphere of a house church, including celebration of the Lord's Supper.

I had come to see that the New Testament had much to say about the Body of Christ, the Church: a divinely appointed organization with structure, discipline, and offices. I finally joined a small Presbyterian church, though I was not yet fully "Reformed" or Presbyterian in my theology. The doctrine of the Church, along with the issues of worship and sacraments, would become major areas of interest in my future studies.

Searching for a Church Home

Following graduation, I got married, and a year later, my wife, Debi, and I were blessed with a child. Then in the summer of 1976, we moved to Jackson, Mississippi, where I began studies at Reformed Theological Seminary. Moving several hundred miles away from family was a significant step of faith, but the Lord provided for our needs.

We lived in an apartment a few miles from campus in downtown Jackson, just a few blocks from the State Capitol building. Also downtown was a Catholic church. One Saturday I rode out on my bike for a time of prayer, and passed this church. I stopped, went in, and noticed the inscription over the doorway, taken from John 10:16: "There shall be one flock, one shepherd." I entered the nave — impressed with its beauty — and prayed. Something stirred within me. I went away with a small glimmer of Catholicism traced on my consciousness.

In the first year of seminary, we studied Church history, one of my favorite fields of study. I went beyond the required readings and explored the writings of the early Church Fathers. In their writings, I found a world quite different from that of the Evangelical and Reformed Christianity of my experience.

Around this time, our family began to worship with a house church that was called New Covenant Catholic Church. This was a group of young people, mostly in their twenties and thirties, who were led by a group of men formerly in leadership positions with the Evangelical ministry of Campus Crusade for Christ. Mildly charismatic, much of the teaching of this group was concerned with recovering the teaching of the early Church. There was also a heavy emphasis on "shepherding," which was found in many new house churches in that era. We left this fellowship, mostly because of this "shepherding" approach that we thought to be heavy handed and suspicious. A few years later, this group became part of the Evangelical Orthodox Church, which was later received by the Antiochian Orthodox Church.

I was seeking a more ancient, catholic expression of the faith, which these folks also were seeking, though, at the time we were there, they had not yet quite figured out where they were going. For the rest of our years in Jackson, we worshipped with a nondenominational church that was heavily involved in social outreach and community development. I never felt at home there theologically, but I admired and supported the mission work of this community, which was a place of good fellowship and support. This was a church that transcended racial and cultural lines — something not often seen in the

Deep South in those days. It seemed as though this was the way the Kingdom of God should be. I later found this concern for racial inclusiveness and social justice effectively realized in the Catholic Church.

"Reformed" Way of Thinking

My seminary experience was an enjoyable one. I studied hard and made good grades, and this experience was intellectually fulfilling. I grew more Calvinistic, but was slow to embrace a consistently "Reformed" way of thinking. To my shame, however, it seems I absorbed an anti-Catholic bias during my time there — or perhaps the bias was already there, and the seminary only reinforced it. The reality was that I knew few Catholics and never seriously studied what the Catholic Church taught.

I did come to embrace, however, a deep respect for the ancient creeds, and therefore for the teaching of the early Church. It was my understanding that the Reformers also wanted to go back to the early Church Fathers and thus reform the Church to what it was before the "corruption of the Middle Ages." I have since learned that Reformation-era scholarship knew comparatively little of the writings of the earliest centuries beyond the New Testament. While Lutherans retained much of Catholic Tradition and liturgy, the Reformed movement, and especially the Presbyterians, generally threw out anything they could not find in the Bible.

The principle of *sola scriptura* was the touchstone of orthodoxy at my seminary. It was a given, an axiom, and certainly not debatable. To question this principle was practically to question the faith itself. One might as well object to the deity of Christ as to question whether or not the Bible alone is the final authority for faith and practice. I don't think I ever asked, "But does the Bible itself teach that the Bible is the only authority?" Now I have come to see that the Bible does not teach that the Bible is the only authority. I see that the Bible *does* teach, however, that Christians are to observe the traditions and the teachings, as well as the writings, of the Apostles.

I must credit my seminary professors for clarifying how the New Testament canon was shaped. I learned that it was the Church that determined the canon. I don't think the implications of this reality were drawn out for me then, as I see them now, of course. Nevertheless, the historical reality is that the authority of the Church did form a canon. It was not left up to the interpretation of individuals.

By the time of my seminary graduation, I had come to embrace most of the Reformed faith as taught in the Westminster Standards (the doctrinal standards of historic Presbyterianism), though I could not see the teaching of a "limited atonement" in Scripture. This made me what we called a "four-point," as opposed to a "five-point," Calvinist. I also struggled with the doctrine of infant Baptism until my senior year. Writing a research paper attempting to prove the opposite, I became convinced that infant Baptism was proper.

Ordained Ministry Introduced Me to Catholics

After graduation, I was called to a small Presbyterian church near Chattanooga, Tennessee, where I was ordained and served as a pastor. A few years later, my family, now with two daughters and two sons, moved to Shreveport, Louisiana, where I was pastor of another Presbyterian church for several years. In Shreveport, I first had the opportunity to come to know many Catholics, both clergy and laity. In knowing these dear Christians, many of my prejudices against Catholicism were demolished.

I was active in the Right to Life movement, eventually heading up and helping reestablish the local chapter of the National Right to Life committee. Of course, many of the most dedicated advocates for the life of the unborn were Catholic. As I got to know them, I found them to be devout and sincere men and women who loved Christ. I was able to spend time with several priests and once had a visit with the local Catholic bishop. I was always warmly received, and my position as a Protestant pastor acknowledged with respect. During this time, my wife taught at the local Catholic high school, which gave us both more opportunity to see the world of Catholic life and faith. One of our Catholic friends from Shreveport prayed for me over the years and gently urged me towards considering the Catholic Church with occasional gifts of tapes and books. I now believe her faithfulness in prayer and the gifts she shared were divinely instrumental in our coming into communion with the Catholic Church.

"There Is One Body and One Spirit ..."

I returned to Virginia a few years later, as pastor of another Presbyterian church. I had become increasingly restless in pastoral ministry, however, and resigned from the pastorate to open a bookshop in downtown Lynchburg. At this same time, my wife and I became involved in the work of a classical, Christian school, associated with the Reformed Episcopal Church. The small parish affiliated with the school was without a minister, and I was asked to preach for them on a few occasions. This became a regular, part-time job, and, as I learned the prayer book for liturgy and studied the Episcopal tradition, I found it increasingly appealing. In January of 1997, I was received into that denomination and became rector of that parish.

Over nearly fifteen years of using the prayer book and studying Anglicanism, I moved farther away from my Calvinistic perspective, though for most of my time in that church, I would have thought of myself as an "Evangelical catholic." That is, I had a high regard for the ancient Church, particularly the creeds, and the liturgy (in a fairly low-church expression). Yet, I came to believe in a real presence of Christ in the Eucharist and the sacramental efficacy of Baptism. I once would have seen these as primarily symbolic; now I regarded these as vehicles of grace and among the ordinary appointed means for salvation. I came to believe that "outside the Church there is no salvation," that the Church is the Ark of God, but I still thought of that "one, holy, Catholic, and apostolic Church" as the "invisible" church, as it was obviously broken into too many pieces to think of it as having a visible unity.

Even so, if the Church is one, as Paul declares, "there is one body and one Spirit ... one Lord, one faith, one baptism" (Eph 4:4, 5), how is that unity to be known today? If our Lord prays for the unity of the Church, what is our responsibility to seek and affect that unity?

Protestants seem to love the hymn "Onward Christian Soldiers," but how can we sing this line in good conscience: "We are not divided, all one body we, one in hope and doctrine, one in charity"? I am not aware of anything in current hymnody that seems so profoundly false as this statement. The disunity of the Church is a dreadful scandal, and it seems to me that any serious Christian should do all in his or her power to remedy the disunity of the Church. It now seems to be highly ironic that biblical literalists interpret a concept such as the "Body of Christ" in primarily spiritual terms. Isn't a "body" a material thing? Shouldn't we be able to see a body? Yet over and over, Protestants interpret the *Body* of Christ — the Church — as primarily an invisible, spiritual entity.

When I was still a Presbyterian, the many divisions among the heirs of Calvin often distressed me. In the Anglican world, it is no better, or perhaps, it is worse. Dozens of small "Anglican" groups can be found on the Internet. Apparently, it is fairly easy to find a bishop who is willing to lay hands of "consecration" on another, making yet another bishop and another Anglican jurisdiction.

BY WHAT AUTHORITY?

Throughout the Protestant world, it is the same. For any reason, a person may start a Christian church, and a new denomination — a new schism — is born. This seems to be the inevitable result of the doctrine of *sola scriptura* and the lack of a teaching authority or Magisterium. In the Protestant world, the final arbiter of doctrine is not the Bible, nor Tradition, nor a council, but the sovereign individual. It is one man's interpretation of the Bible against another's. When a man says, "the Bible alone is my authority," what he really means is "only my interpretation of the Bible is my authority," or else he cedes that role to some pastor or teacher that he, for whatever reason, has come to trust. Protestants complain that Catholics have a pope, yet they don't see that Protestants also have popes; indeed, there may be as many popes as there are Protestants.

Of course, my Reformed friends would see the problem and deny that it is this bad. For this reason, we have the confessions, they would say — the Westminster Confession, the Heidelberg Catechism, etc. They seem to think that Calvinism, as articulated by the Westminster standards, is the full-flowering of Christianity. But why should anyone regard the assembly of pastors and theologians at Westminster as more likely to have the right interpretation of Scripture than the councils that produced the Lutheran statements of faith, or, for that matter, the Council of Trent? Even when we have confessions of faith, we must still *interpret* those confessions. Whose interpretation shall be regarded as most accurate and reliable? We go from disputes about the meaning of Scripture, to disputes about the meaning of the confessions. In recent years, we have seen the sad phenomenon of pastors of one Presbyterian denomination pronouncing anathemas upon ministers of other Presbyterian denominations for not holding the same interpretation of the Westminster standards on the doctrine of justification as held by themselves.

THOSE WHO CAME BEFORE US

Another largely unexamined presupposition of the whole Protestant project, as it stands today, is this: using the tools of modern biblical exegesis, we can discern the true meaning of Scripture. I don't know why I never saw this before, but I began to realize the absurdity of believing that a modern exegete can jump back over two thousand years and have a better understanding of the New Testament and the teaching of the Apostles than those men we call the early Church Fathers. If a modern scholar interprets the New Testament in a way not in accord with the *Didache*, Clement, Ignatius, Irenaeus, or Cyprian, who is more likely to be right? Until recently, I tended to read the Fathers and look for affirmation of what I already believed. If they contradicted my confessional stance (first Westminster, then the Thirty-Nine articles) I would set the early Church teaching aside, intending to "come back to it later." However, some of the questions raised by the Fathers concern the very core of the Christian faith. One may put off deciding for a time, but one can't do that forever. One must eventually take a stand. If I must decide, who, then, is more likely to have the correct interpretation? I think the safer bet, or the more logical, reasonable decision, would be to side with the early Church Fathers.

Another significant change in my perception of spiritual reality has to do with the doctrine of the communion of saints. In the Creed, I confessed to believe in the communion of saints, but what does that really mean? A few years ago I discovered a Charles Wesley hymn, with the lines, "Let saints on earth in concert sing, with those whose work is done; for all the servants of our king in heaven and earth are one ... E'en now we join our hands with those who went before, and greet the ever-living bands, on the eternal shore." Hearing this for the first time moved me deeply, and the vision it unfolds is a wonderful one. Those who have crossed the stream of death are still living; they sing with us. If they may sing with us, why may they not pray for us? If we are in communion with them, why may we not seek their intercession for us?

As I was drawn to the doctrine of the communion of saints, I happened to watch a video on the life of Edith Stein. She was a remarkable woman. A Jewish, university teacher of philosophy in Germany between the wars, as a young adult, she became an atheist, then later was converted to Christ and became a Carmelite nun. She died in the gas chambers of Auschwitz. She was later canonized as St. Teresa Benedicta of the Cross. I was moved by her story and found myself invoking her prayers for my son.

I no longer found it a strange thing to think of asking for the prayers of the Blessed Virgin or other saints. There is a Christian inscription from around 250 AD that says, "Pray for your parents, Matronata Matrona. She lived one year, fifty-two days." What a beautiful vision this brings to mind: an infant alive in the presence of God and the holy angels, interceding for her parents.

AUTHORITY IN THE KINGDOM

I have always been intrigued by the parables of the Kingdom. The theme of the Kingdom of God is so crucial to understanding the teaching of our Lord. How closely related are the Church and the Kingdom? Are they the same? Is the Church the gate of the Kingdom, or something like the visible expression in time of the timeless, transcendent Kingdom? That they are closely related seems clear in such passages as Matthew 16:18–20. Jesus speaks of the building of the Church on the Rock (*Petros*), and the keys of the Kingdom are given to Peter.

Surely, the Kingdom of God is not a democracy. A flock of sheep is not a democracy. Families are not democracies. Kingdoms have a top-down government. Several of the Kingdom parables speak of a ruler or landowner going away and leaving a trusted servant in charge. Peter and the Apostles are the trusted servants. The New Testament clearly puts Peter in a position of some prestige or respect above the rest of the Twelve. It would seem reasonable, even necessary, that upon Peter's death, another would take his place. A precedent for filling the place of a departed Apostle is set in Acts 1, with the appointment of Matthias to take the place of Judas.

Therefore, it is surely not unreasonable to expect that the rule of the Church, or Kingdom of God on earth, should be under a visible head or regent in place of the Lord and King, Jesus. If anyone filled that role in the Church between 30 and 60 AD, then it was surely Peter. It would then seem most reasonable that upon his demise, someone would have been recognized to take his place. Of course, the records from the second century on indicate that this was indeed what happened — the Fathers are careful to trace the succession of the bishops of Rome back to Peter (see Irenaeus, *Against Heresies*, book 3, chapters 2–4).

Irenaeus' *Against Heresies* seems especially appropriate for modern times, in which heresy and schism abound. Irenaeus counsels: "What if there should be a dispute about some matter of moderate importance? Should we not run to the oldest churches, where the apostles themselves were known, and find from them the clear and certain answer to the problem now being raised?" (book 3, chapter 4.1). Ireaneus counsels that to settle disputes we need both Scripture and Tradition. For this Tradition, we look *ad fontes*, to the source in the oldest churches.

John Henry Newman famously observed: "To be deep in history is to cease to be Protestant." I found this to be true in my case. As I read more Church history, especially the early

Church Fathers, and Reformation history from Catholic writers, my Protestant viewpoint was slowly eroded. It became clear to me that if there is one Church, which Jesus established, the Catholic Church under the bishop of Rome has the most clear and convincing claim to be that Church.

A MATTER OF CONSCIENCE

After this realization, it then became to me a matter of conscience. I was convinced that the denominations to which I had belonged were in schism from the one Church that our Lord established, and I came to believe that to continue in separation from that Church would be to sin against my conscience and my Lord. My wife and I enrolled in our local parish's RCIA (Rite of Christian Initiation for Adults) program and after several months of study, we were received into the Catholic Church on June 24, 2012.

Though I am deeply sorry for the schism of Protestantism and my part in perpetuating that schism, I rejoice in the ministry I have received from the churches and teachers of my former denominations. In my childhood church, I became aware of the reality of God, was first awakened to faith, and was baptized. In the college ministry of the Navigators, I was taught to be zealous for Scripture and learned a concern for evangelism and mission. In seminary, I was instructed by good and godly men who taught me to think and write. In my sojourn among Presbyterians, I saw a zeal for social concern, and, among the Anglicans, I learned to love beautiful liturgy. Along the way, many Catholic ministries, such as Catholic Answers, as well as local parishes and friends have been very helpful. Finally, through the Coming Home Network International's ministry, especially through the *Deep in History* conference, we were able to see the intellectual integrity, spiritual depth, and amazing beauty of the Catholic faith. Along the way, our gracious good Shepherd has patiently led us, and we now rejoice to be at home in His flock. Thanks be to God.

Ed Hopkins was formerly a minister in the Presbyterian and Anglican churches. He and his wife, Debi, have four children and two grandchildren and live in Lynchburg, Virginia.

Following God:
Jesus Loves Me This I Know

By Marian Prentice

former Baptist and Free Methodist

From my earliest memories Jesus was my best friend. I loved church, worship, and my Bible, which I unfailingly carried everywhere. My dad used to joke, "Don't you trust my driving? Is that why you always take your Bible?"

The Lord's grace throughout my life has always been abundant. In reality, I can't recall a time when I have not loved, desired, and pursued God. I always wanted to hear more about Jesus and to share Him with others. Both of my parents were "church going people" and had been raised in Protestant denominations (my father was a member of the Church of Christ and my mother was raised Baptist). We were a family of faith. I was raised to have high moral standards and know that the Bible was the manual for making daily decisions. We were in church every Sunday and I am thankful for that foundation. However, we were perpetual visitors/strangers since we never joined a church. I did not grow up with the experience of a church family.

Regardless, my love for Christ was strong. At the age of ten, I recall walking down the aisle at a Baptist Church in Dayton, Ohio, to ask Jesus into my heart as my personal Savior. It was a long walk to the altar that day because, again, I was a visitor in that church, not to mention just a child. I remember shaking inside from the fear of it, yet my love for God and the desire to move towards Him was infinitely stronger than my fear. I left my parents in the pew and walked down that aisle in front of three hundred strangers! But I didn't care what others thought. I wanted Him. It was this way of thinking that I believe eventually led me home to the Catholic Church: I wanted more of Him, no matter what.

At age twelve, it was my decision to be baptized in the Baptist church we were attending. I remember realizing that Sunday night that something wonderful had happened, but no one else seemed to think so or even talk to me about it afterwards. After all, we were taught that Baptism was just "an outward sign of an inward change," so nothing really was supposed to happen anyway. But to me, it was a momentous event.

In high school, once I had my driver's license, I drove myself in my dad's seafoam green Volkswagen to a Baptist church across town to be able to worship each Sunday night (we went as a family Sunday mornings). I didn't care that it was a long drive or that I didn't know anyone there. I just wanted to be in the House of the Lord.

FOLLOWING GOD: TO THE JOY OF SERVICE

I began frequenting a United Methodist church, during my time at The Ohio State University. But, between school and falling in love with the man who would become my husband, church attendance and my daily relationship with God began to take a back seat. I wouldn't say that I walked away from the Lord, but He was not the center of my life during those four years as He had always been. After Phil and I married, we started our life in a Baptist church just off campus and, when we moved away from that area, we attended a mainline United Methodist church for a while. Soon, we bought our first house across town and we changed churches yet again and began attending a Free Methodist Church, which eventually became our church home for twenty years. It was a great joy to become active in that church.

For the first time in my life I had a church family and I loved it beyond words. My husband and I were blessed with good teaching, as we both got back on track with God. We formed deep friendships, many of which we still have and treasure today. We were there Sunday mornings, Sunday nights, Wednesday nights, and always for any kind of special service or Bible study. I was privileged to be involved in ministry in that church and learned a great deal as I grew deeper in the Lord.

The joy of service was, and always has been, abundant in my life as a Christian. I took 2 Corinthians 5:15 seriously: "and He (Christ) died for all that those who live might live no longer for themselves, but for Him who for their sake died and was raised." I taught Sunday School and Kid's Club classes, adult Bible studies, served as Children's Ministry Director, directed Vacation Bible School, and served on the Church Board. I also participated in Bible Study Fellowship, an International, inter-denominational Bible study. I am very thankful for this solid foundation and experience.

While raising our two children, working part-time, my days were filled with training them in the faith. Both of our children attended Christian schools (as well as public) and both graduated from evangelical, Christian colleges. After leaving the Free Methodist Church, we were in the Nazarene denomination for seven years. When I became involved in charismatic worship, the Lord expanded my church family to include a parachurch organization, Women's Aglow.

FOLLOWING GOD: TO MISSION FIELDS

When I turned fifty, God opened my heart to a different direction in service to Him and drew me to missionary work. I have been privileged to serve on Short Term Mission teams to Venezuela, Ecuador, Mexico, Cuba, and, most recently, China. The China venture was birthed through Vineyard Columbus, a nondenominational church where my husband and I were members for the past ten years. God also opened my heart to prison ministry where I teach several classes and have the privilege of mentoring at Ohio Reformatory for Women.

Over these fifty years, God has been — and is still — teaching, stretching, and surprising me with many new things. However, this last path was in a direction that I never, ever, thought I would travel. Five years ago, I thought my life was set and settled as I began my sixth decade. But it began with a stirring; I sensed a deep yearning for beauty and reverence in worship. I realized that I wanted more — somehow I knew there was more. And I was right!

FOLLOWING GOD: TO THE CATHOLIC CHURCH?

I believe it was the Holy Spirit who nudged me as I was surfing TV channels one day and came across EWTN, just as they were airing Mass. I was mesmerized. I had never seen a Catholic Mass before and couldn't stop watching. Something was unmistakably awakened in me and I knew I had to investigate this faith.

However, from an early age, my parents had taught me that Catholicism was very wrong. Still, I have early memories of a budding Catholic interest that began as intrigue more than anything substantive. Maybe it was the attraction of the "forbidden fruit." I remember watching Pope Paul VI on TV and hearing my parents ridicule him, but not understanding why. I would sit, mesmerized, watching movies about priests and nuns (mostly Bing Crosby movies). I was so impressed with the reverence of it all that once I recall putting a pillowcase on my head as if I were a nun, making the sign of the cross and genuflecting!

As a young woman I remember saying, "I love God so much that if I were Catholic, I'd be a nun!" I even recall as a teen — never known to my parents — finding a Catholic bookstore and buying a crucifix, which I kept hidden. I remember the actual purchase being rather scary, feeling as if I were betraying someone. I kept the crucifix for a long time and would take it out to hold it and just gaze at it in wonder.

At sixteen, I had a boyfriend who was Catholic and I just knew that I could make him see "the truth" and abandon his religion. However, even in talking with him about our religious differences, I was learning the faith — I just didn't know it then. Ultimately, my parents ended our relationship because they were against all things Catholic.

Now as I look back, it is clear that God was planting the seeds of His holy Church in my young mind and heart. Never having studied the Catholic faith, I believed the typical Protestant misconceptions about Catholics: they worship Mary and the pope; believe salvation is attained by works alone; are idolaters, because they pray to statues; engage in necromancy (communicating with the dead), because they pray to dead saints; and don't believe in hell, because they have purgatory, whereby you can pray someone into heaven regardless of the life they have led. None of these Catholic beliefs were in the Bible, I was told. But after seeing that beautiful Catholic liturgy on TV, I began the quest to see for myself what Catholics believe, not what I was told they believe.

I watched EWTN, in particular *The Journey Home* program, listened to *Deep in Scripture* and *Catholic Answers Live*, viewed Catholic websites, and devoured at least 30 books on Catholicism and countless conversion stories. With every source I investigated, the draw to Catholicism was more and more intense. As a Protestant, I already went deep in Scripture and exegesis (the explanation or interpretation of Scripture), since I prepared many teachings for church or prison. Therefore, the more I studied the Catholic interpretation of Scripture, the more I knew that what I was learning was true. It all made sense as each of my "issues" melted away and I became more and more convinced of Catholic teaching.

At the very start of my research, I asked the Lord to keep me from error as I began this journey. I put my trust in Him and knew that He would answer my earnest prayer. Periodically, I would "check in" with Him: "Father, is this okay?" As time went on, the prayer became: "What are you doing in me?" because I was slowly — but surely — becoming Catholic!

With my husband's support, I decided I would begin to attend a local Catholic church on Saturday evenings. Nervous, I sat in the back and just took it all in. What I remember most about that first time at Mass was the reverence of worship, the quiet, and the beauty. What I had been hungering for was satisfied in that Mass. I began attending Saturday night Masses regularly while going on Sunday mornings with my husband to our Protestant church. As time when on, I couldn't wait to go to the Catholic church each week. I learned how to participate in the Mass (except for receiving Communion) and I worshipped in such a deep way. I absolutely loved it.

By September 2010, I had the courage to register for RCIA. I had done so much reading and studying in the three years prior to those classes that hearing it all "from the horse's mouth," so to speak, served to cement it in my mind. The Holy Spirit was confirming in me that what I was learning was true. I indeed discovered that my Protestant idea of what Catholics believed was false. I learned that what Catholics *do* believe is firmly rooted in Scripture and the Tradition that had been lived out by the early Church long before there even was a written Bible at all! I realized that *sola scriptura* (living by the Bible alone) is not taught anywhere in the Bible. *Sola fide* (salvation by faith alone, apart from whether or not we live out our faith) had long been a belief that I couldn't square with Scripture, so that was not a hurdle for me. On the night in RCIA that we were taught about the Mass and what all the ritual actually means, I left in tears. I was totally overwhelmed at all the symbolism and the love I felt for Jesus who died for me. How could I *not* become Catholic?

As a Protestant there were many Scripture verses that had either never made sense to me or for which I had never heard an adequate explanation. Now as a Catholic, those same verses make sense and it is a joy to finally understand them. One of the Scripture verses I finally came to understand was when Jesus called Peter "the Rock" on which He would build His Church (Matthew 16). I was taught as a Protestant that by "rock" Jesus meant the truth of the Gospel message and also that, in the original Greek, the two words "rock" were different, one being "big rock" and the other being "smaller rock." Therefore, I was taught, Jesus couldn't have meant that He would build His Church on Peter. However, I had always read it over and over and I could not seem to accept any interpretation except what the Catholic Church teaches (even though I really *tried* to accept the Protestant view). Now in RCIA, the question was solved. Jesus spoke Aramaic, not Greek. In Aramaic, there is only one word for "rock," *kepha* (which, in fact, means a substantially-sized rock), but in Greek, the language into which Jesus' words were translated, the words have linguistic genders and must be altered to match the context. Also, I had previously reasoned that there were only a few times in Scripture that God changed a person's name (Abram to Abraham, Jacob to Israel, Saul to Paul, for example) and each time that new name signified new, God-given roles in His plan of salvation. Jesus changing Simon's name to Peter ("Rock") was not, therefore, inconsequential.

Another Scripture that had never been fully explained to me was John 3:5, when Jesus said: "Truly, truly I say to you unless one is born of water and the Spirit, he cannot enter the Kingdom of God." The Protestant teaching that "water" in this Scripture actually refers to "natural birth" just never made sense to me. I came to understand in RCIA that this is a clear reference to Baptism. Previously, I was taught Baptism was just an outward sign, to which no grace or divine action was attached. However, once I read a number of Scripture passages that refer to Baptism as a Sacrament, which accomplishes the forgiveness of both original and actual sin, that verse in John made perfect sense (see 1 Pet 3:20-21, Acts 2:38-39).

I am sad to say that prior to my research it had not dawned on me that there was anything "Christian" before the Reformation. When my eyes were opened to Christian history predating the Reformation, I began to read the early Church Fathers (most of whom I didn't even know existed). After I read about men such as Eusebius, Athanasius, Polycarp, to name a few, "the Catholicism of the early Church became so obvious.... that I knew that if [I] were to follow the truth then [I] had no option but to become Catholic" (Jimmy Akin, *The Fathers Know Best*, Catholic Answers, p. 9).

That realization made me feel safe — yes, that's the word, s-a-f-e. The burden was no longer placed on me to decipher and choose between the varying beliefs and private interpretations of the Scriptures from the current 32,000 different Protestant denominations (all of whom believe the Holy Spirit has told them that their interpretation is true). I think because I trusted the Church on the things I *did* understand, it helped me to choose to trust the Church on some of the other issues that were harder for me to understand, such as purgatory. However, because I know that the Catholic Church is the true Church guided by the Holy Spirit, I can rest in that and let God move me along as I mature in this new faith. I love the *Catechism of the Catholic Church*, because I no longer have to guess or depend on my private interpretation. I can refer to the *Catechism* and know what is true. And I feel safe!

FOLLOWING GOD:
TO LOSING MY REPUTATION?

To be honest, the days leading up to the Easter Vigil in 2011 when I would enter the Catholic Church were full of anxiety. I was so certain in the truth of the Church, and yet my mind swelled with questions: What am I doing? What will my friends say? Will my children still respect me? What about the "reputation" I have as a solid and respected teacher of the Word of God? Will I even have any ministry left if I do this? And, yet, I wanted this so much. The Lord heard all my angst and provided for me. I read Leona Choy's book *My Journey to the Land of More* and it was just what I needed. At age eighty, Leona, a well-established, Protestant author and fellow missionary to China, had also embarked on this journey to the Catholic Church later in life. Her life and journey paralleled my own in many areas that I felt such camaraderie with her about my journey. Her words summed up perfectly what I was thinking and feeling throughout much of my journey. Just like Leona, I felt like I was entering a foreign country and leaving behind all I had ever known. I now know, however, that I didn't have to turn my back on my faith as a Protestant Christian. Rather, I was coming home to the *fullness* of the Christian faith.

I also had other sources of support and encouragement in my journey. When I signed up for RCIA, the parish provided me with a wonderful sponsor who loves Jesus. She and I "clicked" from the start. I was also given a mentor by the Coming Home Network who was so good at putting my anxiety and angst into perspective. This mentor understood the difficultly in "changing countries" and faithfully prayed for me.

In the end, I came to the conclusion that I believed the Catholic Church is the one, holy, Catholic, and apostolic Church founded by Jesus Christ. Because of all of the support and prayers from those special people God put in my life and the familiar, comforting nudge from the Holy Spirit, I willingly surrendered to what God had been asking of me: to become Catholic.

FOLLOWING GOD:
TO THE FULLNESS OF FAITH!

The moment that Father Jerry announced at Easter Vigil that I was now Catholic, I got weak in the knees and nearly fell over out of sheer happiness! As I received Communion for the first time that night, the experience was electrifying. The tears fell at the realization that in my whole life of loving Jesus, *He* had seen to it that I could take Him completely — Body, Blood, Soul, and Divinity — into my being. As I returned to the pew afterwards and knelt in total gratitude, joy, and awe, the shape of a heart appeared in my mind's eye. I was overcome. God had always loved me, but now I was home.

Since my reception into the Catholic Church, my joy has neither left, nor waned; it has only increased. Jesus is still my best friend. I still love to learn and study. I still love the holy Scriptures. And, now, I love being Catholic!

My husband goes with me to Mass a couple times a month and is very supportive, but he is not yet ready to join me. Some of my family members are supportive and some are not. The Lord has provided me with a few Protestant friends who support this journey and I am making new friends in my Catholic parish.

So, the journey continues! Thomas Merton once said: "a life befriended by God is a life where growth always means a step beyond what is familiar." And to that I say, "Thanks be to God!"

Marian Prentice and her husband, Phil, live in Pataskala, Ohio, and have been married for forty-three years. They have two grown children and two grandsons. Marian and Phil are both retired and attend The Church of the Resurrection in New Albany, Ohio. Phil entered the

Catholic Church at the Easter Vigil 2014. Marian is active in prison ministry, RCIA, and parish Bible studies. She and Phil both love the fall season and give hayrides for many groups on their twenty-four acres during the month of October.

Upon This Rock — That Doesn't Roll

Dale Ahlquist

former Baptist

He was called the "Father of Jesus Rock." Everyone who was an Evangelical or Pentecostal Christian in the 1970s knew who he was. He wrote such songs as "I Wish We'd All Been Ready," "U.F.O.," "One Way," "I Am a Servant," and "Righteous Rocker, Holy Roller." He was the one who lamented playfully, "Why Should the Devil Have All the Good Music?" He had brilliant lyrical and musical gifts. He could hold audiences in the palm of his hand, easily making them roll with laughter, rock with praise, or be quiet and thoughtful.

His name was Larry Norman — and he was married to my sister.

My brother-in-law was certainly one of the most influential people in my life. As a teenager in the 1970s, I, too, wore my hair long, played the guitar, and wrote songs. I was also an outspoken Christian, and everyone who knew me knew I was a Christian. I was unafraid to share my faith, unafraid to defend it.

Larry not only helped pay for my college education, he provided some fascinating summer employment in his office and recording studio in Los Angeles, which was a long way from my home in St. Paul, Minnesota. With him, I always felt right in the thick of things. During those interesting summers, I had long talks with Larry about everything: music and movies and art and love and the world and God.

BETTER THAN C. S. LEWIS

His primary influence on me did not come from those talks, his dynamic personality, his creative intellect, the fact that he was married to my sister, or that he was too religious for the rock-and-roll people, yet too rock-and-roll for the religious people. It came from a simple passing remark when he saw me reading *Mere Christianity*.

"You like C. S. Lewis?" he asked.

"Yeah," I replied.

"Have you ever read any G. K. Chesterton?"

"I've never heard of G. K. Chesterton."

"Chesterton is a lot better than C. S. Lewis. In fact, if you read Chesterton, you wouldn't even need to read C. S. Lewis, because all of Lewis is inside Chesterton."

To me this bordered on blasphemy, but the comment stuck in my head. I soon began to notice Lewis' references to Chesterton here and there. I went on to read how C. S. Lewis had been a confirmed atheist — until he read *The Everlasting Man* by G. K. Chesterton. Lewis said that a young man who is serious about his atheism cannot be too careful about what he reads. He called *The Everlasting Man* the best book of apologetics in the twentieth century. But it would be four more years before I actually read a Chesterton book, and a lot of things changed in those interim years. Larry divorced my sister, and his career as a Jesus rock singer began a steady decline. I graduated from college and got married in 1981.

My wife, Laura, and I went to Italy on our honeymoon. She had been born there and spoke the language. We were in Rome on a rather momentous day: May 13, 1981, the day Pope John Paul II was shot. We were in the Church of St. Peter-in-Chains, looking at Michelangelo's statue of Moses, when we heard the news. As we walked back to our hotel room, we watched the city transform from utter chaos to an eerie calm. After the sirens died down, the streets became strangely empty. A silence descended on Rome. It was as if everyone went home to pray. A few days later, street vendors were selling postcards of the Pope waving from his hospital bed.

Little did I know that my path to Rome *began* in Rome; the city amazed me in every way, with the weight of its history and beauty, and with the urgency and significance of what was happening during our visit. Regardless, the farthest thing from my mind at the time was that I would ever become a Catholic. I was only there as a tourist, an outsider. Born and raised a Baptist, I knew my Bible sideways and diagonally, and I knew all the things that were wrong with the Catholic Church. Yet, a seed was planted while I was in Rome; an unlikely seed in an unlikely soil. It had nothing to do with the churches, shrines, or holy sites I saw. It had to do with the reading material I brought with me on my honeymoon: a book by G. K. Chesterton.

People get a good laugh out of the fact that I read *The Everlasting Man* on my honeymoon. What makes it even funnier is that my bride was reading *Les Misérables* and crying her eyes out. In contrast to her experience, my sensation upon reading my book was the same as that described by Dorothy L. Sayers the first time she read Chesterton: she said it was like a strong wind rushing into the building and blowing out all the windows. It was utterly fresh, and it knocked me over! I knew I had encountered a writer like no other. His words resounded with a splendor of confidence and truth from the opening sentence: "There are two ways of getting home; and one of them is to stay there." In the book, which is a condensed history of the world, Chesterton demonstrates that Christ is the center of history, the center of the human story. He brings together history, literature, mythology, science, and religion, and swats the skeptics who scoff at the Christian claims. "The most ignorant of humanity know by the very look of earth that they have forgotten heaven."

Chesterton gave me a completely new perspective of the coming of Christ: a baby, outcast and homeless. "The hands that had made the sun and the stars were too small to reach the huge heads of the cattle." He awed me with his description of the crucifixion, when the darkness descended, and "God had been forsaken of God." Then the resurrection: which was the first morning of a new world, when "God walked again in the garden."

I did not know at the time that Chesterton was a Catholic convert. It was a fact that I avoided as I continued to collect and read books by Chesterton: *Heretics, Orthodoxy, All Things Considered, Tremendous Trifles,* even books with giveaway titles like *St. Francis of Assisi, St. Thomas Aquinas,* and the Father Brown mysteries. I simply could not get enough of this unique writer. I found that there was no subject that he did not address, that he said something about everything and said it better than anybody else.

I could not understand why hardly anyone had heard of G. K. Chesterton, why he was not required reading in the schools, why his sweeping ideas, his energizing wit, and his profound insight were not discussed and debated and searched out and savored by everyone.

In 1990, I completed a master's thesis on Chesterton and that same year was delighted to learn of a Chesterton conference being held in Milwaukee. I drove six hours from the Twin Cities, and when I walked into the room there were about twenty people sitting in a few rows of folding chairs, listening intently to an Englishman named Aidan Mackey giving a talk on Chesterton's poetry.

I immediately knew I was among friends, among people who had discovered the same treasure that I had discovered. As I had the pleasure of getting to know these Chestertonians, I was not surprised to find that they were incredibly articulate, morally grounded, and fun-loving. I suppose I was a bit surprised to find that almost all of them were Catholic. It was the first time I had ever met Catholics who could actually explain and defend their faith.

A year later, I was back and presenting a synopsis of my thesis at this same conference. It was warmly received, and I was soon contributing a regular column to a modest Chesterton newsletter. I invited friends to attend subsequent conferences with me, and as the Midwest Chestertonians continued to tap me to do work for their small group, I had an urge to do even more, to get more people to discover Chesterton. Here was a complete thinker. No holes. No loose ends. His Christian faith, his philosophy, his art, his politics, his economics, his literature, and his laughter were all of a piece, truly a seamless garment, and I regarded this neglected literary master as a prophet holding the cure for what ails the modern world. People who had not heard of him and had not read his works were simply being cheated! So, with the help of some co-conspirators, I started the American Chesterton Society, and, soon after that, helped launched *Gilbert! The Magazine of G. K. Chesterton* — and this all happened *before* I became a Catholic!

But let's back up a minute.

I BEGAN TO FEEL A BURDEN

My father was a Baptist missionary's son. He was born and raised in the jungles of northeast India, in Assam, among the headhunting tribes of the Garo Hills. His father was a doctor and a pastor, who not only brought the Good News of Christ to the natives, but the medical miracles that healed thousands of people. Dr. Ahlquist was a beloved man, who was tragically killed in an automobile accident on a mountain road when my father was only eighteen years old. My father came back to America, and a few years later met my mother at a Baptist church in St. Paul. She was a farm girl who had come to the big city to study nursing. My father became a high school biology teacher, and he and my mother had six children. We went to church four times a week. I was a counselor at a Billy Graham Crusade when I was fourteen years old. I led youth groups, Bible studies, and "singspirations." By the time I was in college, I could recite whole books of the Bible from memory. I was active in InterVarsity Christian Fellowship in college and challenged my professors about, well, everything. I even taught a weekly class to other students on Christian apologetics.

It was while I was in college, however, that I began to feel a burden that would not go away. I was very troubled by the deep divisions within Christianity. I took the opportunity to visit every single church in Northfield, Minnesota, a classic college town. I wanted to see what they were like, and, this way, I got a taste of over twenty different denominations (but since this was Minnesota, an undue portion of them were Lutheran.) For the most part, there wasn't much difference, but there was always *some* difference. The most telling event came one Sunday when I attended a "New Testament" church. It was new indeed and was meeting in a temporary facility. There were only thirty people there, a group of maybe seven or eight families. I soon learned that it was the final Sunday that they would be meeting together because the following Sunday they were going to be splitting up into two different churches, not for evangelistic reasons, but because they had had a disagreement. This tiny nascent group could not even hold itself together, and so one faction was breaking away to form a new church.

To me, it epitomized everything that was wrong with Christianity. Instead of working out their differences and mending their divisions, instead of *uniting* in Christ, they splintered off into a still smaller group, with a new name, a new denomination, thus rendering themselves more insignificant and ineffectual in a world that needed Jesus. It was clear to me that though they were utterly sincere and devout in their faith, there was no way that such a show of sincerity or devotion honored the Body of Christ. It was division. It was brokenness.

WHERE TO PRAY?

I got married a year after college, and, after our Italian honeymoon, Laura and I began to look for a church that we could attend regularly. We soon gave up. Nothing seemed quite right. I eventually became a "lone ranger" Christian. When we had kids, we had "home church," and why not? There was nothing that was done in a Protestant church that we couldn't do at home. We read the Bible, we sang, we prayed, and I sermonized. Once in a while, we did attend a church and had the exact same experience: some Scripture readings, songs, and prayers wrapped around a sermon.

Even though my theology was still Baptist, I no longer wished to be known as a Baptist, but simply as a Christian. I noticed, too, that the mega-churches in the Twin Cities that had previously called themselves Baptist had also dropped the word "Baptist" from their names. I also saw that they were looking less and less like churches. Their "sanctuaries" had become mere auditoriums. Regardless of whether they were latent Baptists or blatant Baptists, the fact was, there were still over fifty different Baptist denominations.

All the while, I was reading Chesterton and yearning for a place to pray.

During the week, I would "sneak" into Catholic churches and kneel and pray, reciting one of the many Psalms that I had memorized, such as Psalm 130: "Out of the depths, I cry to you, O Lord. Lord, hear my voice.... My soul waits for the Lord more than watchmen for the morning, more than watchmen for the morning" (vv. 1–2, 6).

Why did I go into *Catholic* churches? Well, they were usually the only ones open, and, importantly, I sensed a presence

there that I did not sense in any Protestant church: a sanctuary
— a *holy* place.

WHAT HAPPENED BEFORE THE REFORMATION?

Soon, I had a brand-new problem. I found myself longing
for the ancient, historical faith. I had to admit, reluctantly, that
Baptists were a relatively recent phenomenon in the history of
Christianity. What, I had to ask, was going on during the huge
period of time before the Reformation? None of that portion
of history had ever been explained to me. It had only been
explained away. I started to dig into that history, reading the
early Church Fathers and books on the history of the Church.
I also read the *Catechism of the Catholic Church*, and Chesterton's most Catholic books: *The Thing, The Catholic Church and
Conversion*, and *The Well and the Shallows*.

Chesterton describes the three stages a convert goes
through. The first is deciding to be *fair* to the Catholic Church.
However, there is no being fair to it. You are either for it or
against it. When you stop being against it, you find yourself
being drawn towards it. Then comes the second step, the fun
one. It is learning about the Catholic Church, which is like
exploring an exotic country full of strange new animals and
flowers that you had never imagined existed. It is fun because
there is no commitment and you can run away anytime you
want. Which leads to Chesterton's third step: running away.
You do everything you can to avoid becoming Catholic. You
know it is the right Church, and you will not admit it, because
admitting it means changing your life forever. Your head is
convinced, but your heart is still trying to talk you out of it.

One by one, I had dealt with each of my Baptist objections to Catholicism. Any good Baptist is raised with a subtle
(and sometimes not-so-subtle) anti-Catholicism. The Baptist
way could almost be described as a point-by-point reaction

against and rejection of Catholicism. We rejected the papacy, the priesthood, the Eucharist, celibacy, saints, Confession, crucifixes, and so on. We identified ourselves by the name of a sacrament we also rejected. Though we insisted on a "believer's baptism" and full immersion, we also insisted that it had absolutely no effect on a person whatsoever. It was merely a symbol. The Bible was our final authority in all matters, and we were quite convinced that the Catholic Church deliberately kept its members from reading the Bible in order to keep them ignorant and malleable — which is quite a trick, especially if you can do it for two thousand years.

There is a major hole in the logic of those Christians who protest against the Catholic Church: you cannot use the authority of Scripture to attack the authority of the Church when it was the authority of the Church that recognized the Scripture's authority. The hierarchy, the sacraments, the major doctrines of the Catholic Church were all well in place — centuries in place — before the biblical canon was in place, and, of course, it was the Catholic Church that authorized the biblical canon. Chesterton says he can understand someone looking at a Catholic procession, at the candles and the incense and the priests and the robes and the cross and the scrolls, and saying, "It's all bosh." But what he cannot understand is anyone saying, "It's all bosh — except for the scrolls. We're going to keep the scrolls. In fact, we're even going to use the scrolls against the rest."

THERE'S SOMETHING ABOUT MARY ...

I also learned that the Catholic Church, in spite of its reputation among Baptists, is intensely scriptural. Ironically, at any Catholic Mass you will hear far more Scripture than at any Baptist service. And it was also my observation that every Protestant sect at some point simply disregards certain Scriptures that are not convenient to its own teachings.

There is not enough space here to deal with all of my objections to Catholic doctrine and how each was resolved, but I must mention one. The first hurdle and the final hurdle for me was Mary. I'm sure it is the same for most Baptist converts to the Catholic Church. Mary represents all the things we object to in one package. She is the pagan remnant in the Catholic faith, the goddess-worship, idolatry, bigger-than-Christ in all the prayers, art, and music devoted to her, appealing to the ignorant who do not read their Bibles, and so on.

My objections to the Catholic view of Mary were deeply ingrained. The first thing that helped me overcome them was reading something that Cardinal Leo Suenens once said when speaking to a group of Protestants. He said, "I'm going to say to you what the angel said to Joseph in a dream: 'Don't be afraid of Mary.'"

I was indeed afraid of Mary.

Do not be afraid of Mary. This is the first step. And it was like Chesterton's three steps of conversion. I had to start by deciding not to fear Mary, but to be *fair* to her. Then, it was a matter of discovering her. Then, running away from her.

The next thing that helped me with Mary was something I read when I went on a retreat to a Trappist monastery in Iowa. (Imagine! Here's a guy who thinks he's running away from the Catholic Church, and he goes on a retreat to a monastery! Though I have never been too bright, I have still always managed to outsmart myself.) In that place of silence and solitude, I read how the monks there model themselves on Mary because Mary is the model Christian. She obeyed God's call, she carried Christ within her, and she then revealed Him to the whole world. She stayed close to Him, and, so, she experienced the suffering of His death, the glory of His resurrection, and the coming of the Holy Spirit. We are to imitate her. What she did, literally, we must do in every other way. Who can argue with that beautiful image? It is an image worth meditating on every day, which is exactly what devotion is, and why so many have meditated on and been devoted to Mary. In doing so, they have also fulfilled her prophecy in Scripture by rising up and calling her "blessed."

After a few more intermediate steps, I went to another monastery on a retreat (again, I was retreating in the *direction* of the Church). The priest there looked me in the eye and asked, "Why haven't you converted yet?" I mumbled something about Mary. He did not loosen his gaze, but asked, "Do you believe that her soul magnifies the Lord?"

The literal Baptist in me had never considered that verse literally before: "My soul makes God bigger." I had run out of excuses.

THE FINAL STEP IN MY JOURNEY HOME

It became clear that every other Christian sect was exactly that — a sect, a section, something less than the whole. I discovered, as Chesterton had discovered, that "the Catholic Church is not only right, but right where everything else is wrong."

The hardest thing I have ever done — and what I don't doubt delayed my decision — was to tell my parents that I was going to become a Catholic. They were good, Christian people who had raised me to be a man of God. I did not want to make them feel that I was rejecting them, but that it was because they had imbued in me a love of the truth that I pursued that truth to its fullest expression. After that first awkward evening when I broke the news to them, we had many deep discussions about the Catholic faith. They asked a ton of questions. They did not like all my answers, but I was at least able to answer their questions, since I had asked all those questions myself during my pilgrimage. Many of the answers did make a great deal of sense to them. My father said to me, "You're telling us things we never knew."

I was received into the Catholic Church on the Feast of the Holy Family in 1997, along with my two oldest children, Julian and Ashley. At the same time, my wife, who had not been a practicing Catholic when we met, returned home to the Church.

Not long after my conversion, I was invited by Marcus Grodi to be on *The Journey Home* to talk not only about Chesterton's conversion, but my own. As I walked off the set at the end of the program, the producer came up to me and said, "We should do a whole series on Chesterton." About a year later, I was taping the first season of *The Apostle of Common Sense.* My conversion led to a new vocation. I became, as some have said, "The Apostle of the Apostle of Common Sense," and I have had the privilege of traveling the country giving talks on the life-changing writer, G. K. Chesterton. The literary society became a full-time Catholic apostolate with a unique form of evangelism.

Chesterton said, "Becoming a Catholic does not mean leaving off thinking. It means learning how to think." I can scarcely convey how astounding that comment is from someone like Chesterton, who was not exactly a dunce before his conversion. However, I discovered firsthand that the Catholic faith was not only central to Chesterton's profound thought, it is central to *everything*.

One of Larry Norman's songs described Jesus as the Rock that doesn't roll. Though the image of Jesus as a rock is a valid one, one of the many metaphors that describe Him — the Lamb, the Lion, the Vine, the Shepherd, the Door — the image of the rock is far more important for the man, Peter, whom Jesus Himself named the Rock: the Rock upon whom He would build His Church. Peter is truly the Rock that doesn't roll because of Jesus' promise that the gates of hell would not prevail against the Church that He built on Peter. There is only one, true Church, and everything else that calls itself a church is something that has separated from it. Everything else is a splinter. You cannot call thirty thousand different denominations "the Church." You cannot even call fifty different Baptist denominations "*the* Church." You can only look to the Church that they all left behind. We have nearly lived through five hundred years of the Reformation. It is time for the reunion. Lord, hear our prayer.

I did have one reunion of sorts with Larry Norman. After a twenty-year silence, we reconnected over the phone and through email. I interviewed him for *Gilbert Magazine*, and when I was on a speaking tour in California, we got together for just a few minutes. He was very ill. He expressed his awe at my accomplishment in helping lead the Chesterton revival. I told him he created a monster that day he told me to read G. K. Chesterton, and I thanked him. We said, "I love you" to each other and "good-bye." Less than five months later he was dead. Grant him eternal rest, O Lord.

Dale Ahlquist is the president of the American Chesterton Society, co-founder of the Chesterton Academy, creator and host of EWTN's G. K. Chesterton — The Apostle of Common Sense, publisher of Gilbert Magazine, *and author or editor of several books on Chesterton, including* The Complete Thinker: The Marvelous Mind of G. K. Chesterton. *For more information, visit www.chesterton.org.*

SURPRISED BY TRUTH –
AND BEYOND

KEVIN LOWRY

former Presbyterian

> *Sometimes I think the greatest thing that ever happened to me spiritually was getting kicked out of Franciscan University of Steubenville.*

That was the opening line of my conversion story, "Son of a Preacher Man," in Patrick Madrid's classic book, *Surprised by Truth 2*. The story was written several years ago, so what follows will reiterate the early years and bring the story up to date. More great things have happened to me spiritually since then — although none of them appeared to be blessings at the time!

A PREACHER'S KID FROM CANADA

I grew up in a small town near Toronto, Canada, the son of a Presbyterian minister. My parents are wonderful people — and in my opinion, they're living saints. While studying theology at a Baptist seminary in the 1960s, my dad heard so much anti-Catholic rhetoric that he decided to take a Knights of Columbus correspondence course to hear the other side of the story. Partly as a result of that course, he ended up leaving the Baptists to enroll in a Presbyterian seminary. This was one of his first steps toward an appreciation of Catholicism.

After my dad graduated from seminary, my parents became missionaries in Nigeria. Malaria forced them to return to Canada prematurely, but their experience in Nigeria changed their lives forever. The Catholic missionaries they were exposed to had a powerful, yet practical faith. When civil war broke out, the Catholic religious stayed, while others fled the country. Their fearlessness in doing Christ's work had a profound impact on my parents.

The experience in Nigeria had another formative effect on my dad in particular. After witnessing a disorganized approach to trade in Nigeria (just buying a stamp could take forty-five minutes), he wondered whether the Lord was calling him to further education in business. After hitting the 99.9th percentile on the GMAT (Graduate Management Admission Test) and then topping his MBA class at the University of Western Ontario, he was the recipient of a full scholarship to the Ph.D. program at M.I.T. Despite humble beginnings, he earned his doctorate there in international business. From that point forward, the unusual fusion of faith and business would characterize his career — and eventually be passed along to me!

DENOMINATIONAL DAZE

After a stint in academia, my dad accepted a position as the full-time minister of a Presbyterian church. In addition to attending this church, I was exposed to countless Protestant denominations: United Church, Pentecostal, Baptist, Methodist, Evangelical, Quaker — you name it. As I grew in my faith, I discovered that the one common belief within Protestantism was that Christ died on the cross to wash away our sins. Pretty much everything else was negotiable.

Occasionally, I would encounter the Catholic Church. Of course, I didn't understand much about Catholicism, and it seemed very complicated and foreign. Like many of my Protestant friends, I thought that no single denomination had a monopoly on truth, and that Catholicism was simply another denomination. I sincerely believed it was okay that no church had the whole truth, and that we would all be enlightened and unified when the general resurrection occurred.

I knew a lot of people who also held this point of view. They would shop for the denomination that was right for them, the one that best suited them theologically and in the way it worshipped.

You can see the problem. Rather than seeking Christian truth — especially if it meant they had to abandon their personal beliefs — many were content simply to find the group of people who taught doctrines with which they were comfortable. They wanted to worship with others whose perception of God and His demands on them were similar to their own.

I say this not out of any antagonism toward Protestants. These people were my friends, and they were sincere. But they had fallen into subjectivism: they were searching for a church that held their beliefs instead of seeking a Church whose beliefs they ought to hold. That's backward. Our call is not to conform the Christian faith to *ourselves*, but to conform ourselves to the faith. After all, who needs to change: we or God?

I Enter Franciscan University — Twice!

In spite of my denominational confusion, I had an idyllic childhood, watching my parents live out their vocations to love and serve the Lord in full-time ministry. Since I had started school early as a child and later skipped a grade, I graduated from high school when I was sixteen. Full of exuberance and self-confidence, I believed I was ready for college.

At that time, my dad read a now-defunct Catholic magazine called *New Covenant* (published, significantly, by Our Sunday Visitor). The magazine ran an article about Franciscan University in Steubenville, Ohio. After reading about this unique school, my dad thought the dynamic Christian environment might help me through my rebellious years.

At sixteen, I enrolled in the university. Although I was there to study psychology, I double-majored in beer and billiards. Three semesters later, my enthusiastic dedication to these pursuits got me academically dismissed — kicked out of the university. I returned to Canada humiliated.

The Lord soon provided me with a job at Sony of Canada, where I matured, improved my work ethic, and discovered that I enjoyed the world of business. After four years with Sony, I wanted to be on track to the top of the company. That required a degree, so I returned to school — this time to study business.

By the grace of God, Franciscan University allowed me to reenter.

A CLOSET CATHOLIC!?!

The second time around at Franciscan, I worked hard. However, I finally had to take the Catholic theology courses I had avoided during my first three semesters. So I would call up my father, and say, "Hey, you wouldn't believe what I heard in class today. What do you think about this?" My dad, with characteristic patience and wisdom, would explain the Catholic and Protestant perspectives, and then explain why the Catholic viewpoint makes a lot of sense. Over time, this approach led me to accept as reasonable many Catholic teachings; they weren't as bizarre or unfounded as I had once believed.

One topic had a significant impact on me. In my ethics course, we studied the Catholic teaching on birth control. As a Presbyterian, of course, I saw nothing wrong with artificial contraception. However, as I considered the Catholic teaching on it, I came to see that anti-contraception arguments were simple and compelling, and I began to understand why the "modern miracle" of contraception has such sinister effects on society.

Artificial birth control breaks the natural connection between marital love and the conception of children. Contraception makes it easier for extramarital relationships to happen and even thrive. Contraceptive sex is self-indulgent — hardly an authentic expression of love and total self-donation to another person. This realization led me to see that artificial contraception enables women to be demeaned, even unwittingly, by being treated by men as mere objects, used selfishly for gratification, and so I eventually rejected the conventional Protestant acceptance of contraception.

The issue of contraception raised a bigger doctrinal question for me. Until recently (the 1930s), all the older Protestant churches taught that birth control was wrong. Nineteen hundred years after Christ's life on earth, did Protestants wake up to the truth that contraception was fine, or had they caved in to societal pressure? The Catholic Church had consistency in the development of doctrine over its two-thousand-year history. I wondered why, if God doesn't change, Presbyterian teaching could — and how could it change by a simple majority vote?

During my final semester, as my mind reeled from my steadily forming doubts about my Christian identity, my father changed hats and came to Franciscan to teach as a visiting professor of business. I had thought my dad would reaffirm me in my crumbling Presbyterian faith and help me sort out the theological questions that beset me. He didn't.

I soon realized that my dad was a closet Catholic.

THE TOUGHEST WAY TO BE CHRISTIAN

His own appreciation and understanding of the Catholic faith was growing as I struggled with theology in the classroom. During this time, I also fell in love with a beautiful American girl named Kathi. She too had a Protestant background, and we were similarly bewildered at the Catholic teaching in our classes. It was like learning a new language or culture. Nonetheless, we married in her small hometown's Wesleyan church and subsequently moved to Cleveland, where I took a position in an accounting firm. My parents moved back to Canada for the sake of my sisters.

In Cleveland, Kathi and I struggled to find the right denomination for us. We were spiritual nomads, shopping for a place to call home. We tried a Full Gospel church, wildly open to the Spirit but without sufficient doctrinal grounding. We visited a Catholic church, but the people seemed cold and distant, and it was so large that it was rather frightening. We then tried a Christian and Missionary Alliance church, which I liked, since it had Presbyterian roots and was relatively mainstream. The people were friendly, too, so we stayed there for our first year in Cleveland.

Yet I continued to struggle internally with many theological questions, looking as I was for a "biblically based" church. Why were there so many different denominations, all claiming to be grounded in Scripture and with teachings opposed to one another?

In college, I had majored in accounting because a friend had told me that it's the toughest of the business majors, and I wanted to take up that challenge. But then it occurred to me that Catholicism is the toughest of the Christian denominations. As a Protestant, I could shop around until I found a church with people whose beliefs mirrored my own. As a Catholic, even if I didn't live up to that ideal, the ideal was still held out as the goal. But it seemed easier for me to change churches than to change myself.

ROME BECKONS

Around this time, my dad had an opportunity to visit the Vatican for a week. He had created a computerized Bible study program called the *Findit Bible*. The software had been selling well in Europe, and my father's distributor had arranged for him to have an audience with Pope John Paul II to present him with an Olivetti computer loaded with several of my father's Bibles. His meeting with the Pope and his new friendship with Archbishop (later Cardinal) John Foley led him to write an article on Christian unity for the *Presbyterian Record*, the magazine of The Presbyterian Church in Canada. On the cover of that issue was a full-page photo of my dad shaking hands with the Pope.

When the issue came out, all hell broke loose. For almost twenty years, my father had been the clerk of the General Assembly of The Presbyterian Church in Canada (PCC) — an extremely visible role. Responses to the article poured in, many praising his efforts towards church unity. Others bordered on being hate mail. One letter was simple, yet beautifully compelling: "Why doesn't Dr. Lowry just become Catholic?"

After the ruckus had died down, my dad and I made a trip back to Steubenville together. As we drove there, we listened to a tape by Scott Hahn, who was coming to teach at the university the following year. We were enthralled by the moving and dramatic story told by this articulate, former Presbyterian minister who became Catholic after struggling with so many of the same issues that troubled us. I was surprised to learn that the birth control issue was also his starting point for serious investigation into the Catholic faith. It was an inspiring testimony, and the Holy Spirit used it to give me a clear sense of direction for the first time in years.

"I WANT TO BECOME CATHOLIC"
At the end of the tape, my father turned to me and said, "You know, I can't argue with anything this guy is saying." I went home after the trip and announced to Kathi, "I want to become Catholic." Just like that. She was shocked.

As we spoke, all my reasons and feelings came pouring out. I wanted to love and serve the Lord in all that I did, and I finally felt I had found my way home. The Catholic Church offered a depth and beauty unparalleled in the Protestant world. So many of the questions I had grappled with were deftly resolved by Catholic teaching. How could so many denominations be based on the Bible, yet have such vastly different interpretations? How could the prerequisites for salvation be viewed so differently by so many people? How could matters of faith and morals be decided simply by majority vote? The teachings of the Catholic Church were intellectually compelling, her doctrine was scripturally sound, and I was finally convinced that one Church actually did have the whole truth: the Catholic Church.

Although Kathi was hesitant at first, she agreed to go through RCIA (Rite of Christian Initiation of Adults) with me. She knew she was under no obligation to convert, and I think she attended in an effort to save me from what she perceived as a dead Church.

PRAYING THE ROSARY BRINGS SPIRITUAL CONVERSION

Still searching for answers, I boldly called Scott Hahn. We agreed to meet at Mass at Franciscan University the following weekend. After Mass, as we talked about searching for the "right denomination," Scott's face lit up. He reached into his suit pocket, fished out a beautiful Irish rosary, and handed it to me. "I wondered why I put this in my pocket this morning," he chortled.

Sheepishly, I stammered something about not having the slightest idea what to do with his gift. Before I knew it, Scott was writing out a list of books I should read! It struck me at the time that it was rather like a physician writing a prescription. Well, the medicine worked! I read those books and prayed the Rosary regularly as Kathi and I went through RCIA.

Back at the Catholic parish we had originally found so huge and uncaring, we began to meet deeply spiritual people who loved the Lord. We continued to study and grow in our faith, even as we had our second son and, only a few months later, discovered we were expecting another child. We stayed in touch with the Hahns, and Scott's wife, Kimberly, gave tremendous encouragement to Kathi in both spiritual and practical matters. Kathi's apprehensions were evaporating rapidly, and she began to share my enthusiasm for the faith.

I continued praying the Rosary. I prayed for things that seemed nearly impossible, but to my shock and amazement, I often received them. My interior life changed rapidly, too. Although my intellectual conversion had taken many years, the Rosary brought about my spiritual conversion in a matter of weeks.

I desired the sacraments, having a particular hunger for the Eucharist. I remember going to Mass during the RCIA process and having to leave before Communion, dragging along Kathi and our infant children. I longed to have a place at the eucharistic table.

KATHI AND I RECEIVE THE SACRAMENTS

At Easter in 1992, Kathi and I were received into the Catholic Church. My parents attended and looked on with what I can only now describe as envy. The night was vivifying: I was baptized (since I hadn't been baptized as an infant), and we both received the Sacraments of Confirmation and First Communion. Kathi and I were thrilled to discover our marriage was now a sacrament.

This first step in a lifelong journey of faith was a true celebration of God's love. In becoming Christian when I was young, I felt that I had chosen God. In becoming Catholic, I felt that God had chosen me.

I still tell my Protestant friends that my becoming Catholic isn't an abandonment of my Christian faith; it's the fulfillment of it. As Catholics, we're given the spiritual tools to live a sacramental life.

As a Presbyterian, I didn't even understand what the word "sacrament" meant (outward sign of inward grace, instituted by Christ for our sanctification) nor what the sacraments were (the seven sacraments are Baptism, Confirmation, Eucharist, Penance or Reconciliation, Anointing of the Sick, Holy Orders, and Marriage). Yet as a Catholic, I recognize the sacraments as the primary, practical means by which we seek to draw closer to God.

In particular, frequent reception of the Eucharist has been of enormous value. It provides spiritual strength for the journey, a way of tapping into the divine life and opening my soul wide for transformation. Reconciliation is not only a means for obtaining forgiveness of sin, it's also truly a sacrament of healing — both spiritual and emotional. Marriage, that great preparation for the mission of building up the Church, is often an underestimated sacrament. Despite the challenges that are part of every marriage, it is a means of tremendous grace.

MY PARENTS ALSO BECOME CATHOLICS

My parents continued to move in the direction of the Church. My dad in particular wanted to convert, but believed that since his commitment to my mom preceded this desire, that he should wait for her. They decided to go through an RCIA program together.

Since Dad's role in the PCC was so highly visible, he also wanted to avoid scandal and hurt among people he cared for. He continued to preach in a Presbyterian church on Sundays, although on one of my visits to Canada, I discovered a little secret: he was also attending daily Mass (without receiving the Eucharist) Monday through Saturday!

In the fall of 1992, my parents returned to Steubenville. The following February, they came into full communion with the Catholic Church. I was deeply moved when I was able to serve as my dad's sponsor in a beautiful ceremony led by Father Michael Scanlan, president of the university. My dad later accepted a permanent teaching position in the business department at Franciscan.

My parents were utterly thrilled to enter the Church, and several months later, my dad was also able to bring his departure from the PCC to an unexpectedly positive conclusion. The General Assembly invited him back to provide a farewell address, and to thank him for his many years of dedicated service. Although he got a couple smiling comments about "being in a Catholic way," the event was suffused with a spirit of mutual respect and gratitude. He counts it as a blessed ending to that chapter of his journey.

PRACTICAL CONSEQUENCES

In the time since we became Catholic in 1992, Kathi and I have been blessed beyond description, and have experienced abundant joys — and challenges. For example, one of the practical consequences of our desire to submit our fertility to God was His blessing, in the form of more children. We now have eight. The birth of our seventh child in particular provided us with some hard-won lessons.

When Kathi was about five months pregnant, she began to experience problems and went to visit her obstetrician. As a physician who had made the courageous decision to become "NFP (natural family planning) only" in his practice, he was someone we trusted implicitly. Yet when he called me at the office, I knew something was up.

It turned out that Kathi had excess amniotic fluid building up around the baby, and what followed was a mind-numbing, rapid succession of complicated medical tests and procedures. The diagnosis turned out to be a frightening congenital condition — polysplenia syndrome. The survival rate past adolescence, we learned, was only ten percent.

We spent the next couple months in mourning for our baby boy who hadn't even been born yet. We didn't know if he would survive his birth, but assuming he did, a surgery was needed right away to correct some internal, structural anomalies. During the time leading up to his birth, we prayed fervently, and Kathi regularly sent out email updates to family and friends. Her emails frequently found their way to prayer chains; in particular, our close family friend Father Ray Ryland (former Episcopalian minister and chaplain of the Coming Home Network International) led the prayer efforts.

Through what we believe was the prayer of hundreds, if not thousands, of people, our son David survived his birth, and I had the profound honor of baptizing him prior to his surgery. Subsequent testing determined that he did *not* have congenital heart disease, the cause for such a high mortality rate, so despite some ongoing challenges, his prognosis is good.

David's birth had some unexpected graces attached. Through the process, Kathi determined that we would not stop at child number seven. "I'm not going out like this!" she would say. Our beautiful youngest daughter Hannah is evidence of Kathi's courageous openness to life, despite the hardship of her pregnancy with David.

Surprisingly, our family was also brought closer together through David. As we all came to recognize the fragility of his life, it had the effect of helping us to grow in appreciation for one another.

FAITH AT WORK

The experience also caused us to reevaluate our priorities from a family perspective. My work in a CPA firm had demanded long hours for many years. After much prayer and emotional discussions, we decided it was time to make a change. The day I informed my good friend and mentor at the firm, he handed me the number of a recruiter. "Give this guy a call," he said.

Within twenty-four hours, I had an interview that turned into a role with a dynamic company as vice president of finance. Five minutes into the interview, I was convinced that I wanted to work for them — as soon as I heard that the local executive team had recently been discussing how to tithe their bonuses. What an amazing gift! However, there were hardships there too, as we were buying companies and growing rapidly. Within my first year at the company, some disputes among the shareholders arose, and the company was put up for sale.

I had hoped my work life was stabilizing, but instead it went into overdrive. The process of selling the company took much longer than anyone had anticipated, and it once again demanded tremendous sacrifice. Then finally, we were sold — to a good company that unfortunately already had a fully staffed finance department. I was put on the list to be terminated.

Through what again I can only describe as the grace of God, after several months helping out with the transition to new ownership, I was given another opportunity. One of the founders of the original company asked if I would consider a new challenge. In the end, I was promoted to senior vice president in an operations role, and eventually had responsibility over the Ohio operations of the company. What a tremendous blessing.

Since that time, I have been given many more opportunities, including becoming a member of Legatus' Columbus chapter, and a director on the board of Our Sunday Visitor, the Catholic publisher whose magazine had initially brought me to Franciscan University!

In addition, Our Sunday Visitor published my first book, a labor of love entitled *Faith at Work: Finding Purpose Beyond the Paycheck*. The book encourages everyone with a job to continue down the path of conversion by fully integrating faith and work. I'm convinced this helps people to become happier, better team players, and better able to handle workplace relationships and challenges.

On top of all this, the Lord provided another opportunity — to take a hiatus from the corporate world and serve full time as chief operating officer of the Coming Home Network International. It was a privilege serving the organization, Marcus, and the staff.

Although life continues to provide many difficulties, I have been blessed beyond description. I am deeply thankful for the many challenges God has provided — as with getting kicked out of Franciscan University many years ago, they have all turned into spiritual blessings!

More than anything, I am grateful for the many people who have enriched my life, especially my family, my relationship with Jesus Christ and His Church, and the rich and mysterious faith to which He brought me home.

Kevin Lowry is an enthusiastic Catholic, husband, and father. He served as the chief operating officer of the Coming Home Network International from 2010-2014. His first book, Faith at Work: Finding Purpose Beyond the Paycheck *was published by Our Sunday Visitor. Kevin's website and blog can be found at http://gratefulconvert.com.*

GOD CLOSED A WINDOW
AND OPENED A DOOR

KATHRYN STUART

former Evangelical and Reformed Calvinist

Reflecting on my life, I recognize God's hand leading me through the times of joy and sorrow. I can now trace the turns in the road that led me to the best thing that happened to me in my life: coming home to the one, holy, Catholic, and apostolic Church.

DEEP ROOTS

In December 1939, when I was six months old, I was baptized in St. John's Evangelical and Reformed Church in Coshocton, Ohio. On the documents that hung in one of the Sunday school rooms were the names of some of my relatives who had been instrumental in bringing the congregation to our town. Before that, other ancestors were listed as charter members of the denomination in the rural areas where they settled after immigrating to this country in the mid-1800s. In 1942, my parents divorced, and my mother and I moved in with my grandmother. It was Sunday school and church every Sunday except in the case of illness or very bad weather, since we did not have a car. Learning the Bible stories, singing, and spending time with other children, many of whom were our extended family members, formed a bright spot in my week. Afterward, a covered-dish dinner was a bit like a family reunion with grandparents, aunts and uncles, great-aunts and great-uncles, and cousins — first, second, and third! It was a comfortable place to be.

Drawn by His Presence

However, my parents' divorce left a deep wound in my heart, because I idolized my father; he had been my best buddy, and, after the divorce, I rarely saw him. My tenacious little heart wouldn't give up, and almost every Saturday, I would sit on the front steps and look down East Elm Street watching for him to come to take us home. It was a hurt that never went away and one that I cried over when I was alone. I thought I had done something wrong that made Daddy leave me.

The children in the neighborhood would go to the Kiddy Show downtown on most Saturdays. We always took a shortcut through the churchyard of Sacred Heart Catholic parish. I felt drawn to this unfamiliar church on the hill more than to my own. One day, I made an excuse on our way home, left the other children, went back to Sacred Heart, and entered the church.

The huge, seemingly ancient, double wooden doors closed behind me and shut out the sun; I was standing in a dimly lit vestibule. A bit frightened at first, I slowly made my way into the sanctuary and knelt down in the back pew. I had Catholic friends, but knew nothing of their beliefs and practices. Moved by the quiet beauty, I cried and told God how hurt I was; He was the only one I trusted my pain to. At home, I would kneel down, at the window in my bedroom, and say to God, "You'll have to be my Father."

But that day, in that Catholic church, I found something that never occurred at my window: kneeling in that dim sanctuary, I recall being vividly aware of a Presence. The Presence had a kind and compassionate personality, and somehow I knew that the personality was a strong, but gentle, male. I felt that this personality was emanating from the area where the mysterious red light was hanging in the dark church. That Presence was so real and so reassuring that it drew me back through that big door Saturday after Saturday.

After having suffered from rheumatic fever that summer, I came back to the huge, thick, wooden door, but I was too weak to push it open. Tears began to fall, and I panicked, thinking I couldn't get in. I can still recall how fast my anxious heart was beating that afternoon. Finally, I pushed the door with all my might, and it opened. After that day, I was afraid to go back.

However, I sought that Presence all throughout my life. As a teenager, I went to the youth group at our church and would steal away upstairs and sit in the sanctuary trying to find that Presence. He wasn't there. Once when Mother and I went to a wedding at the big Methodist church, I wandered away from the reception and went back upstairs and sat in the pew, hoping to find what I had found at Sacred Heart. He wasn't there, either.

The Need for Truth

Our Calvinist Evangelical and Reformed denomination merged with others and became the United Church of Christ. For a couple of years, I taught an adult Sunday school class; I wanted to simply use the Bible as my curriculum, but I was told I needed to follow the church teaching somewhat. I didn't know what that meant — we were Protestants — didn't everyone believe the same thing? I sincerely tried but found that I couldn't teach the Bible through the Calvinist and Zwinglian lenses of our denomination. They just didn't fit together. I found that one had to twist the Scriptures, take verses from here and attach them to others in order to make the Bible say what I was supposed to teach. I wasn't comfortable with that.

A turning point in my life came on a Sunday in October of 1979 when I found myself on the patio crying and praying. If God is God, I thought, then there is *His truth*, and men need to conform to it, not the other way around! Something was dreadfully wrong. I remember asking the Lord if I was supposed to believe that the Holy Spirit was not doing His job; I couldn't begin to believe that. I told the Lord that Sunday afternoon that, from that moment on, I wanted *His* truth and nothing but His truth. But, to take up the question of Pontius Pilate, what *was* the truth? The ongoing question in my mind was "Where is the church — *the* Church?" The only answer I got from Protestantism was "The church is invisible." I didn't argue, but it wasn't an answer I could reconcile with Scripture. Was Jesus' prayer for unity unheeded and unanswered? What of the biblical witness that the unity of the faithful would be the thing that draws others to the Church?

That very week, I went to the library and picked up my first two books on the Reformation — an old book simply called *John Calvin* and another general book on the Reformation. This began a personal study of the Reformation that lasted from October 1979 to January of 2011 and evolved into a long study of the works of Luther. For thirty-two years I persisted in my study, which included fifty-five of the sixty-three volumes of the Erlangen Editions of *Luther's Works*, some of Jaroslav Pelikan, and most of the romanticized versions on the Reformation.

In 1981, I turned my Sunday school class over to another because, through my studies, I had found a series of self-willed opinions thrust up in the face of the Catholic Church. I found that Luther's novel inventions were decisively the "traditions of men" into which the Bible must be made to fit. I began to get a glimpse of why I couldn't make the Bible fit the doctrines of my denomination.

I could no longer in good conscience call myself a Protestant, and my mother and I walked out the door of St. John's United Church of Christ.

SOLA FIDE

Justification by "faith alone" was one of those doctrines on which Protestantism either stands or falls. I learned that Luther literally *added* the German word *allein* ("alone," or *sola* in Latin) to Romans 3:28 in his translation of the New Testa-

ment. Paul states, "Therefore we conclude that a man is justified by faith without the works of the Law." Luther's translation
read, "Therefore we conclude that a man is justified by faith
alone without the works of the Law." The Catholic Church sent
Luther a message saying it was not acceptable to add the word
"alone" to Holy Scripture. In Luther's answer, which you can
read in its entirety in Luther's "Open Letter on Translating," he
states, "You can go back and tell your papist that a papist and
an ass are the same thing." He then wrote that, no, the word
"alone" was not in the original; and, yes, he *did* add it where it
was not. He went on to say, "I, Dr. Luther, will it and my will is
as good as the Thomists," including a diatribe about having to
add "alone" to make it say what *he* wanted it to say and that "I,
Dr. Luther, am a doctor above all the papal doctors."

That was a huge eye-opener. When I related it to other
Protestants, they often laughed and thought it was funny
that Luther was so feisty. I quit talking and kept studying. I
searched for the biblical basis of *sola fide*, and I found nothing.
The only place the Bible states the words "by faith alone" is in
James 2:24, in which James says, "You see that a man is justified by works and *not* by faith alone" (emphasis added).

Luther went on to radically pit faith against works and to
even say that works are sinful because through them one would
be attempting to earn salvation. Because Luther's teaching contradicted what was clearly stated in the Letter of St. James, Luther said that it was an "Epistle of Straw with nothing of the
Gospel in it." He was opposed by other Reformers and finally
said that he cared not what others did about the Book of James,
but "I will not have it in my Bible." He threw out seven books
of the Old Testament on the same grounds. So much for *sola
scriptura*! Luther never actually put *sola scriptura* into distinct
words, but intimated it in a hundred ways. It bothered me that
we, as Protestants, were holding others and ourselves to "the
Bible alone" when the Bible doesn't even teach "the Bible *alone*."

For a time I was angry; I'd believed those who had taught me "by faith alone," "by Scripture alone," a "symbolic Lord's Supper," etc. (our denomination followed Zwingli, who held the lowest doctrine on Holy Communion — pure symbolism). I could find no one to talk to who had delved into anything beyond a biography of Luther. Even minister friends of mine had never dug into the origins of their doctrines. When I tried to encourage it, I was branded as a troublemaker and ignored.

An Episcopal priest friend of mine brushed me off saying, "There had to be *something* good come out of the Reformation." He was a new priest at St. Paul's Continuing Episcopal Church in Coshocton, and he and his family became our best friends. They helped me through some very hard times in my life, and I finally had someone to talk to about the deeper and richer things of God. The priest was a Scripture scholar par excellence (my mother insisted there was no better preacher).

My years in the Episcopal Church were years of growth spiritually, but there was still that longing for what I had experienced as a child — the presence of the Lord. It was a quiet need that I concluded finally would be satisfied only in heaven. But in this world it manifested itself in a continual frustration to study more — and more and more. I really wanted to know the truth.

The Truth I Had Known without Knowing

Decades passed, and I was having some kind of spells for which the doctors didn't have an answer; it was taking less and less to wear me out. In October 1991, I caught my foot on a piece of carpet and catapulted across the hall. I fell headlong into a wall, pulling ligaments and muscles in my neck, injuring my right shoulder, and popping out my back in three places. A couple of months later, one doctor finally listened to me when I said that there was no feeling in my left leg. It was a worker's comp case, and it was a big struggle to get anyone to take me seriously. I ended up with lots of pain, stiffness, and muscle spasms.

I was housebound for a while, and right around that time my cable television company added the Eternal Word Television Network (EWTN) to its lineup. I began to watch EWTN and listen to Mother Angelica as she talked about "offering up" pain and suffering to the Lord. It was an immense help that seemed providential. I watched all day, every day, while I was recuperating. After I went back to work, I videotaped six hours a day of the programming and watched it in the evening. The more I heard of the teachings of the Catholic Church, the more I knew I was hearing the truth I had sought for so many years. Scripture was falling into place.

One day, Mother Angelica and a guest were talking about the Eucharist. As they explicated the Catholic teaching regarding the Real Presence of our Lord in the Blessed Sacrament, my ears perked up. I became engrossed in what they were saying — it seemed as though they were talking to me. Part of the way through the discussion, a realization dawned on me that hit me with the impact of a velvet sledgehammer. My mind ran back to Sacred Heart Church that summer I was nine, and suddenly I knew that the experience had been real — it had been Jesus in the Blessed Sacrament that I had "known." Stunned and in awe, I exclaimed, "Oh, my God" — a prayer and exclamation rolled into one.

I began to put together in my mind the reasons why I had never found the Presence in any Protestant church, although I looked for it always and everywhere.

Watching TV that day, I heard with my ears the truth that Jesus was present in the Catholic Eucharist — Body, Blood, Soul, and Divinity — but I realized that it was a truth I had known without knowing, for all those forty-four years.

Finally, John 6 made sense in a way it had never made sense before. It was ironic to me that the "Bible believers" I had studied with took this chapter figuratively, and the Catholic Church (which I had been taught did not follow the Bible) took it literally. I found it refreshing. Although, through my studies I had already become so disgusted with what I learned about the Reformation, it had never occurred to me to *convert* to Catholicism. I had never known anyone who had converted! Yet, somewhere in the very depths of me, I seemed to know that the Catholic Church was not just another denomination into which I could "church hop." Converting would be a big deal.

FIRST CORINTHIANS 11

The discovery of the truth about the Holy Eucharist was the push that launched me into yet another study. I went to Luther. I read a letter that Luther had written to a friend in which he said that he had heard a very learned man say that perhaps it would be better if Jesus just came into and was present along with the bread and wine. He stated, "I liked that better." And so he invented the concept of consubstantiation (literally, "with"-substantiation). That was too much for Calvin, and he came up with receptionism — what you believe is what you get — "the divine gift" is manifested through the believer's faith alone. Zwingli, whom many denominations seem to follow today, said that the Lord's Supper was purely symbolic. I saw in the changing doctrine of the Protestant communion the warning St. Paul had given regarding those who would be "holding the form of religion but denying the power of it" (2 Tim 3:5).

I was interested to see how Luther formed his beliefs about Holy Communion, as taught from his *Small Catechism*:

> ### What is the Sacrament of the Altar?
> It is the true body and blood of our Lord Jesus Christ, under the bread and wine, for us Christians to eat and to drink, instituted by Christ Himself.

Where is this written?
The holy Evangelists, Matthew, Mark, Luke, and St. Paul.

Notice that Luther leaves out John 6, and in his writings he states that John 6 has nothing to do with Holy Communion but is about believing the Word (by faith alone). In order to substantiate his claim, Luther uses the Scripture of St. Paul, 1 Corinthians 11:23–26:

> For I received from the Lord what I also delivered to you, that the Lord Jesus on the night when he was betrayed took bread, and when he had given thanks, he broke it, and said, "This is my body which is for you. Do this in remembrance of me." In the same way also the chalice, after supper, saying, "This chalice is the new covenant in my blood. Do this, as often as you drink it, in remembrance of me." For as often as you eat this bread and drink the chalice, you proclaim the Lord's death until he comes.

However, Luther truncated this Scripture passage. What Luther did not include in his catechism on the Eucharist were the verses *immediately following* the above quotation from 1 Corinthians 11:

> Whoever, therefore, eats the bread or drinks the cup of the Lord in an unworthy manner will be guilty of profaning the body and blood of the Lord. Let a man examine himself, and so eat of the bread and drink of the cup. For any one who eats and drinks without discerning the body eats and drinks judgment upon himself. That is why many of you are weak and ill, and some have died. (vv. 27–30)

The portion he excluded is fundamentally important, and the Catholic Church rightly includes its teaching. Luther used Scripture in a dishonest way to form Protestant beliefs and practices on the Eucharist (what a strange way to uphold *sola scriptura*).

TOWARDS HIS REAL PRESENCE

Upon learning about the truth of the Eucharist, I was intrigued: just what else does the Catholic Church believe and teach? By the summer of 1992, I was deep into the study of Catholicism. I wasn't alone in my study; my eighty-nine-year-old mother and our Episcopal priest and his wife were studying with me. We spent our Sunday evenings tearing apart every Catholic teaching and holding it up to a scriptural analysis. We were surprised that the Bible "fit" as written into the doctrines of the Catholic Church. It passed every test!

After what had been thirteen years of personal study of the Catholic Church, I had come to the conclusion that I could never go back into any form of Protestantism.

In September of 1992, I began RCIA classes. By that time, RCIA was just a formality, because our Sunday study group had examined and reexamined every Catholic doctrine, and we were all in agreement: the Catholic Church had the fullness of Christian truth! At Easter Vigil 1993, I came into the Church — I came home! I had the feeling that I had finally made an honest woman of myself.

My mother would have converted, but she was ill and frail; she was Catholic at heart and prayed the Rosary faithfully twice a day until the end of her life in December 1993. I had the privilege of traveling to Florida to attend the ordination of my former Episcopal priest into the Catholic priesthood in September of 1994.

I have never had a doubt that the Lord orchestrated my conversion; I believe it began when my father left, and I committed myself to seeking out my heavenly Father. I believe that it was the Lord who led me to enter Sacred Heart Church to pray. Finally, I know it was Jesus, present in the Blessed Sacrament, who met me there when I was nine years old and brokenhearted. I believe God knew that His presence, which I had tasted, would turn into a lifelong pursuit until I finally found what my soul truly longed for all those years.

No one can ever tell me that Jesus is not truly present in the Blessed Sacrament, because He let me experience it decades before I even knew the doctrine existed! Although I knew and loved the Lord for many years, I have come to know and love Him in deeper and richer ways in His Church — in the sacraments; in His Word; in a deeper spirituality; but particularly in receiving Him, Body, Blood, Soul, and Divinity. I love Scripture in new and deeper ways.

On my seventieth birthday in June 2010, I became an Oblate Novice of St. Benedict in association with St. Vincent Archabbey in Latrobe, Pennsylvania. On September 1, 2011, my sisters took me to Latrobe where we stayed for three days and where I made my final profession and was confirmed as a full Oblate of St. Benedict. I took the name Grace Marie, since it has all been, from start to finish, God's grace, grace, grace!

I think of what Blessed Elizabeth of the Trinity said when she was asked, "Are you sometimes homesick for heaven?" She answered, "I am sometimes homesick for heaven, but apart from the Beatific Vision, I have everything here that I will have in heaven."

Kathryn E. Stuart lives in Coshocton, Ohio, and is a parishioner of Sacred Heart parish. She is an Oblate of St. Benedict associated with St. Vincent Archabbey, Latrobe, Pennsylvania. She has four children, seven grandchildren, and five great-grandchildren.

CRADLE MENNONITE TO ROMAN CATHOLIC

HAROLD WENGER

former Mennonite pastor

On May 1, 2011, with great joy, I confessed my faith, was confirmed as a Roman Catholic, and received my first Holy Communion at Holy Cross Catholic Church in Mesa, Arizona. The church was packed with over a thousand reverent people for the 10 a.m. Mass, which made it so joyful and welcoming. For a sixty-eight-year-old Mennonite, career pastor, and missionary, this was a dramatic move!

MENNONITE ROOTS

As a "cradle Mennonite," I grew up in Chesapeake, Virginia, the oldest of nine children. My ancestors were Mennonites from the Anabaptist movement, which started in Switzerland in 1525. They migrated from Europe to Pennsylvania in 1727. My Mennonite parents struggled to provide for us materially, and my father worked very hard. Unfortunately, my father grew lukewarm and critical of hypocrisy in our denomination. During my growing years, he hardly ever went to church (he returned to the Lord when I was eighteen, and at age ninety, he is still a faithful Mennonite), but my late mother always took us to church. I remember her singing and praying with us at bedtime every evening when I was a child.

I enjoyed going to church, attending summer Bible school, and memorizing Scripture. I accepted Christ as my Savior at a revival meeting (meaning I was convicted of sin and sought forgiveness) when I was nine or ten and then was baptized with a group of my peers — in the name of the Father, the Son, and the Holy Spirit. My upbringing as a Mennonite taught me serious discipleship as obedience to the Word, following Jesus, nonconformity to the world, pacifism or conscientious objection to war (we called it non-resistance), and the importance of foreign missions. I have great appreciation for my Mennonite spiritual heritage and for those who nurtured me along the way.

When a cousin of my father, who was a missionary in Ethiopia and Tanzania, spoke at our church, I felt the call of God to mission in Africa.

A CALL TO MISSION ABROAD

At Eastern Mennonite College, I met a black-haired girl with a beautiful smile named Christine Headings (a Mennonite from Ohio), whom I later persuaded to marry me. We became husband and wife on August 28, 1965. She agreed to go to Africa with me, and we served as English teachers in Zambia from 1966 to 1969, where I did alternative service as a conscientious objector under the Mennonite Central Committee instead of doing military service in Vietnam. We served a second term in Sierra Leone. Upon returning to the States, we studied at Associated Mennonite Biblical Seminaries in Elkhart, Indiana, where I received good biblical teaching and Anabaptist theology and earned my master of divinity degree in 1975.

Near the end of my seminary training, we wrestled over our call to mission. I believe that God sent a senior missionary couple to challenge us to return to Africa where there was such great need. So Christine and I went to Swaziland in 1975 with our three young children, and we served six years, initially teaching with African Independent Churches. In 1976, African students revolted in Soweto, near Johannesburg, South Africa, and a good number came to Swaziland. At that point, some of the churches organized the Council of Swaziland

Churches, and a Catholic bishop was chosen as the chairman. At the organizational meeting, he looked at me, a young missionary, and nominated me as secretary. I thanked him and said I had come to serve the churches, but I thought that they should choose a Swazi leader for secretary. With a twinkle in his eye, he said that since I had come to serve the churches, I should do what I was told! So I was secretary under a gifted and eloquent Catholic bishop. Several years later, he died in a tragic accident, and his funeral service was a great celebration of life. I was impressed with the Catholic funeral Mass!

In 1981, after six years in Swaziland, there were mounting personal and professional reasons to return home, so I applied for pastoral ministry back in the States. After seven years as pastor of Mennonite churches back in Pennsylvania (Pittsburgh and Altoona), I had the longing to return to Africa. Christine struggled over that call, but then agreed with me. We served in Tanzania as Bible teachers for six years, followed by six more years in Mozambique as country representatives for Mennonite Central Committee. It is now hard to believe that we spent a total of twenty-four years in Africa!

PRIMED TO COME HOME

Throughout our years of service in Africa, we were exposed to many positive aspects of the Catholic Church. A list of reasons for my "Big Move" to Catholicism began to mount:

Liturgical Worship and Communion. In Mozambique, we had worshipped primarily with the Anglican Church, and I was ordained a subdeacon to assist the priests with the sacraments and to preach. While I remained officially a Mennonite pastor in the Allegheny Mennonite Conference, we were practically Anglicans for six years. We came to love the liturgical worship and regular communion.

After we returned to the United States, I served as pastor at a Mennonite church in Virginia for two and a half years. I encouraged communion once a month to which the congregation reluctantly agreed, but I missed the liturgy with weekly communion.

Discontent and Spiritual Hunger. As pastor of that small church in Virginia, I began to experience a lack of fulfillment and affirmation. After months of struggle and prayer, we felt that God gave me the freedom to resign. We decided to move to Arizona in 2005 to be near our daughter and grandchildren, even without a job or position lined up! I made contact with Mennonite churches in Arizona and had serious discussions with the chair of a search committee, but when I learned how wide open they were to same-sex relationships (an issue that had already made me uneasy about the larger Mennonite Church), I told the chairman that we would not make a good fit. There were very few Mennonite churches in Arizona and no other opportunity for me. At the same time, following the difficult experience in Virginia, I was struggling over my sense of call to pastoral ministry. With encouragement from my father and realtor friends, I decided to pursue training as a realtor. I saw it as a source of income and the kind of business that would give me flexibility in schedule. I was able to get my license right away and began a new challenge in business.

After stepping back from ministry, we soon joined Koinonia Mennonite Church in nearby Chandler, where our daughter and family were attending. It is an expanded house church with an attendance of around sixty. We came to appreciate the fellowship and joyful worship, and I did occasional preaching. As in Virginia, I again encouraged more frequent communion, which was increased to six times a year. In 2010, for various reasons, I became discontented enough with the church to go visiting elsewhere. I felt a spiritual hunger for something more. The next nearest Mennonite church was about forty-five minutes away in Phoenix, and I was not interested in the other Protestant churches around.

But I was curious about the Catholic Church. This interest was sparked by many positive encounters with Catholics in Africa, such as the Catholic bishop in Swaziland and wonderful Catholic nuns and sisters, especially in Tanzania and Mozambique. While in Virginia, my spiritual director was a wonderful Catholic priest. I had drawn much inspiration over the years from the writings of Catholics such as Henry Nouwen and Mother Teresa. My call to mission left me with a great curiosity about Christianity throughout the world and a longing for richer, liturgical worship. The fact that the Catholic Church has a similar focus on Jesus and the Gospels, rather than starting with Paul and justification by faith — as did many other Protestant denominations — also sparked my interest.

Spiritual Retreat. As part of my search, in November 2010, I went to Holy Trinity Monastery in southeast Arizona for a spiritual retreat. There I met a former Episcopal priest, who shared his Catholic conversion story with me. He listened patiently to my questions about the Real Presence, Mary, the pope, and the Church's attitude to war. He counseled me and gave me a book about the conversion of a Protestant minister and his wife to the Catholic Church. I was deeply moved by their journey from a conservative, anti-Catholic, Presbyterian church to the Catholic Church. It had a powerful impact on me as I realized my own anti-Catholic bias from childhood, though not as strong as theirs!

That First Mass. I first went to Mass at Holy Cross Catholic Church on October 10, 2010, and found it packed with about a thousand people for the 10 a.m. Mass. The beauty of the Mass — the reverence, the music, the singing of the Gloria, the Scriptures, the confession of sins, the Profession of Faith, the sacrament of Holy Communion, the whole Christ-centered worship experience — moved me to tears. In my heart, I felt greatly blessed to have been there and had a strong desire to return. I dared to continue going to Mass (to the dismay of Mennonite friends), and with great excitement, I invited friends and family to go with me, of whom several did. With growing desire, in December, I went to see the director of Christian education and signed up for the RCIA class beginning in January 2011.

In the RCIA class, I had to review the basics of the faith again. I remember being touched by the Nicene Creed (which is not used in Mennonite worship) and commented to the teacher: "As a Mennonite that is exactly what I believe." As we continued, I realized the Creed's importance for the unity of the Church's faith. During the course, I had many questions, and I kept borrowing books from the parish library. The teachers were so clear on Church doctrine and practice and explained it with passion. I struggled with new terminology, new practices, and with the Church's great respect for Mary. At some point along the way, I realized that in my heart I was ready, that I really wanted to be Catholic, that I respected and trusted the teaching authority and Magisterium of the Church, and that I did not have to understand everything. I could hardly wait to be received and to receive Holy Communion.

The Real Presence. The Real Presence of Jesus in the Eucharist is such a joyful, faith-building sacrament, the heart of our faith. Using a phrase from Scott Hahn, it is "heaven on earth." From my reading, I am convinced that Protestants have had to ignore or reinterpret the teachings and practice of the early Church in order to circumvent the clear message of the Scriptures, as in John 6 ("unless you eat my flesh and drink my blood"). I had taught the symbolic view for so many years, criticizing the Catholic view as absurd. However, with further study, I rediscovered early Church history, and realized that the Catholic Church has faithfully maintained the clear teaching of Jesus and the Apostles. From the Coming Home Network International, I received the book *Ignatius of Antioch & Polycarp of Smyrna*, by Dr. Kenneth Howell, confirming the Catholic faith of these early leaders. In fact, I chose St. Polycarp, a second-century bishop and martyr, as my Confirmation name! Now I find it such a joy to receive the Body and the Blood of Jesus in the Eucharist, and I sometimes go to Mass twice on Sunday. Already I am privileged to serve as an extraordinary minister of Holy Communion.

Clarity of Faith and Doctrine. I had tired of endless dialogue over issues of theology, biblical interpretation, leadership, worship style, homosexuality, etc. In the Catholic Church, I found a fixed structure and leadership, with clear lines of authority, and I respect that. I appreciate the Nicene Creed, the clear teaching, the *Catechism*, and the Magisterium of the Church. I trust that the Spirit of God will continue leading the Church to work through difficult issues, and to continue proclaiming the faith of the Apostles. Plus, I have come to greatly admire Pope St. John XXIII, Pope St. John Paul II (whose life story has amazed and inspired me), and Pope Emeritus Benedict XVI, whom I consider one of the greatest theologians of our time.

Coming Home. It is a surprise to everyone — even myself — that I am now a Roman Catholic, but it truly feels like coming home to the "Mother Church." My father thinks it is a temporary phase, one of my sisters is shocked, and our three children are respectful. My wife, Christine, has done considerable reading as well and has gone with me to Mass a number of times, but she is not ready and is still serving as an elder at Koinonia Mennonite Church (but we are still deeply in love!). I remain grateful for my heritage in the Mennonite Church: for the emphasis on Jesus as Lord and Savior, for the strong sense of community (now enlarged with the community of saints!), for the teaching on peace and nonviolence (which is still very important to me), and for the emphasis on nonconformity to the world. However, I now realize the tragedy of the broken and divided Christian world, which continues to splinter into thousands of groups. There are scores of Mennonite groups alone, and more every year. Yet we all confess one Lord, one faith, and one Baptism.

At age sixty-eight, I have begun a new spiritual journey, with so much to learn, so many new resources, and such awareness of my human weaknesses. I have become part of the Church established by the Lord Jesus, part of the worldwide community of faith, and an heir to the treasures of Christian history and the witness of the saints. I am excited with my continuing journey and ready to tell my story to anyone who will listen! Glory be to the Father, to the Son, and to the Holy Spirit.

Harold Wenger currently resides in Mesa, Arizona, with his wife, Christine. They have three children and three grandchildren. He is employed as a realtor.

CROSSING THE TIBER

STEVE RAY

former Baptist and Evangelical

I can still smell the green vinyl of the used couch in our living room as I knelt with my mom, with my face buried in my hands and my nose pressed into the vinyl. She had decided I was old enough — after all, I was four years old. She didn't want to wait any longer. She was eager.

When I was born, I was taken to the front of Joy Road Baptist Church in Detroit, Michigan, held aloft and dedicated to Christ. The thought of baptizing an infant was repugnant. Where do you find *that* in the Bible?

My parents had "found Christ" less than a year earlier. After twelve years of painful miscarriages, my parents had discovered Jesus through the preaching of Billy Graham. The radio was on one morning as my mother was getting ready to go shopping. With keys in one hand and purse in the other, she stopped in the kitchen before heading out the door. She heard something she'd never heard before.

She heard the compelling voice of Billy Graham passionately explaining the precious blood of Jesus that was shed on the cross. It was shed for my mom to pay for her sins. It could save her from hell and insure her a place in heaven. My mom, raised without any religion, heard John 3:16 for the first time: "For God so loved the world that he gave his only-begotten Son, that whoever believes in him should not perish but have eternal life."

When I was older, she told me that she had fallen on her knees on the kitchen floor. With tears rolling down her cheeks, she "accepted Christ as her personal Lord and Savior and asked Him to come into her heart."

At the same time, my dad thought he had cancer and was having a nervous breakdown. He went out on the front porch one night, and after looking up to the stars he pleaded, "If there is a God up there, please reveal yourself to me. I don't know if you even exist, but if you do, I need your help!" He then went to bed.

The next morning he went through his normal routine and ended up at his office at Ford Motor Company in Dearborn, Michigan. A friend walked up and said, "Charlie, can I tell you something?" My dad said, "Yes, of course, what is it?" The friend boldly proclaimed, "Charlie, you need Jesus Christ in your life." It had been less than twenty-four hours since the prayer of desperation.

Do you think it was a Catholic who approached my father? Unhappily, it was not. Catholics too often think their faith in Christ is a "personal thing; not something you talk about." But this Baptist friend had a different opinion: the Gospel of Christ *was* something you talked about, and you talked about it to as many people as you possibly could. My father prayed the "Sinner's Prayer" with his friend. Within a matter of days, my parents were members of Joy Road Baptist Church.

On my desk sits one of my most valuable possessions; a black, leather, King James Version, Scofield Reference Bible. The gilded pages of this Bible are filled with notations, underlined verses, scribbled notes, and comments. This was my father's first Bible and became one of the loves of his life. He wrote the date, May 1954, inside the cover.

After their dramatic conversions and much prayer, I was born nine months later, after twelve years of miscarriages. Two brothers followed.

ACCEPTING JESUS

Now we are back to the green vinyl couch in our small house on Marlowe Street. Mom thought I was old enough to accept Christ as my own personal Lord and Savior. So after some coaching and explanations in words a four-year-old could understand, she led me in the Sinner's Prayer. I can still remember that moment, and the smell of old vinyl always brings that memory to the forefront of my mind.

Now came the task of raising this young boy to love Jesus and the Bible. It began with memorizing Bible verses. I was a rich little kid because my parents were smart. They paid me 50¢ for each Bible verse I memorized (I now do this for my grandchildren, but the price has gone up to $1.00). Mom knew a young mind was fertile and supple and could memorize easily. After all, Proverbs reminds us that if you "train up a child in the way he should go, ... when he is old he will not depart from it" (22:6).

Of course, John 3:16 was the first verse we memorized. It was the heart of the Bible and the perfect summary of the mind and heart of God in His relationship to His people. My brothers and I also learned to say the books of the Bible, the faster the better: "Genesis, Exodus, Leviticus, Numbers ..." We raced to see who could say them the fastest, keeping it under fifteen seconds!

We never missed any of our church's events, especially not the ever-anticipated Summer Vacation Bible School, where prizes, ice cream, racing around, sticking flannel graph elephants onto Noah's ark, and all kinds of other fun stuff abounded.

My parents, though, moved between churches. My dad would question the pastor and disagree about biblical passages and theology. Through the years, our family attended Baptist churches, Reformed, Methodist, nondenominational, charismatic, and ultimately I ended up bouncing between an Evangelical Presbyterian and a Baptist church. It was great being a boy in a Baptist family in the '50s and early '60s.

But time marches on, and interests march on as well. At fifteen years old, my mind shifted to girls and motorcycles and the Beatles and other things upon which my parents frowned. The kids in our church youth group were not "cool," and I left them behind.

Just before the beginning of twelfth grade, I heard Billy Graham on the television. I always had a soft spot in my heart for God that was never calloused over by my cultural rebellion. Mr. Graham's compelling arguments sank deep into my heart followed by the mellow baritone voice of George Beverly Shea singing, "Just as I am without one plea, but that thy blood was shed for me." That did it. I was out the door with tears running down my face. I walked down our long country driveway, and I said to the Lord, "I am only seventeen years old, but tonight I give my whole life to you!"

THE PERFECT LIFE

On the first day of twelfth grade, a friend introduced me to a cute girl with long blond hair. Janet had just moved to Michigan from Costa Mesa, California. She had been baptized as an infant and raised as a nominal Presbyterian. But that summer she had gone to a Bible study at school and had been led to a "new life in Christ." She was baptized by Pastor Chuck Smith in Pirates Cove in the Pacific Ocean. (For those who don't know Pastor Chuck Smith, he is the founder of Calvary Chapel. One of their boasts is that eighty percent of their members are ex-Catholics.) Janet was quickly caught up in the excitement of her new Christian life.

She told me that God spoke to her for the first time in her life that morning at her new school in Michigan. She heard, "That is the man you're going to marry." But I had other goals, and they no longer involved girls. I was now dedicated to Bible study, prayer, and preaching the Gospel of Jesus Christ to everyone. Four years later, in 1976, we did marry, and it was the best thing I ever did. (We now have four children and ten grandchildren and counting.)

Janet and I loved being Evangelical Protestant Christians. We homeschooled our children, taught Bible studies, evangelized, and started our own very successful family business. With a great family, wonderful Evangelical friends, a flourishing business, a love for the Bible and evangelism, and a life full of joy, we felt we had it made. All our family and friends were not only Protestant, but also anti-Catholic. To even have a member of the family "go Catholic" would have been unthinkable, an egregious betrayal of the Christian faith and the family traditions.

We taught studies on how to evangelize and always had people in our home, though not all our visitors were Evangelicals. Mormon and Jehovah's Witness missionaries, atheists, New Agers, and Catholics were always targets for evangelism. We knew the best arguments and Bible verses to unleash on any one of them. Catholics were usually pretty easy to pick off the tree. They generally didn't know the Bible and, from our perspective, had no idea how to get saved. We believed Catholics prayed to Mary instead of Jesus, thought they got to heaven by works instead of faith, and followed tradition instead of the Bible — in everything, they were upside down.

Then it happened — we converted to the Catholic Church!

PROBLEMS ARISE IN PROTESTANT LOGIC

People often ask, "What was it that made you willing to lose everything to become Catholic?" Protestants asked us, "Why would you leave biblical Christianity to follow the traditions of men in the Catholic Church?" Others asked (and still do), "What did you see in the Catholic Church that made you want to leave everything you knew to begin such a radical new path in life?"

My answer is, "I saw *nothing* in the Catholic Church to make me want to be Catholic!" And the Catholics I knew were the biggest argument *against* the Catholic Church. Out of principle, neither my wife nor I had ever set foot in a Catholic church. We had never met a Catholic priest or religious, and, most unfortunately, we had never encountered a Catholic who could explain or defend their faith.

Our journey to the ancient Church began by seeing the problems within Protestantism — problems that were incurable (if these problems had been corrected, Protestantism would have had to become Catholic). Sometimes one has to realize they are very sick before they visit a doctor. Janet and I came to realize over time that something was dreadfully wrong with Protestantism. I will briefly explain the three "biggies" that hit us.

PROBLEM NUMBER ONE: WORSHIP

Janet interrupted me one Sunday on our way home from the Baptist church, saying, "I can't listen to preaching anymore and call it worship. Something is missing, but I don't know what it is." In the nineteenth century, Charles Haddock Spurgeon, one of our favorite preachers, had once said that no form of worship was higher than a good sermon. But Janet knew this was not correct. It was the first crack in a locked and bolted door. What was worship? Was it preaching? Was it loud music — "pump up the volume"? It seemed that Evangelicals did not know either since they were constantly trying all kinds of new worship services to entertain and inspire.

The act of worship has always involved offerings and sacrifice. Not just the offering basket passed back and forth through the pews but real sacrifice. Pagans, Jews, Hindus, early Christians — they all knew this. From the beginning of time, people have brought a sacrifice or offering to the gods. The Jews offered sacrifices, and we inherited their God. The Protestants had preaching, but what did the early Church have?

Janet and I have since had the privilege of visiting the oldest churches in the world. We have visited and explored the first churches ever built in Israel, Egypt, Italy, Turkey, and Greece. Every one of them had something in common with all the others. As the focal point in the front and center of every ancient church is an altar! An altar was always a place of sacrifice, and sacrifice was offered by a priest. In 1 Corinthians 10, St. Paul speaks of the sacrifice of Jews, pagans, and Christians. All offer a sacrifice. Where was this in my Baptist church? We had exchanged the ancient model for a new religion. No longer a priest and an altar, instead we had a preacher in front of a podium. The Catholics had the Holy Sacrifice of the Mass.

And to my great amazement, I learned that the very first Christians believed the same thing about the Sunday sacrifice as Catholics today! The disciples of the Apostles referred to what we called "communion" as the very Body and Blood of Jesus, the same flesh that was nailed to the cross (see St. Ignatius of Antioch, *Letter to the Smyrnaeans*, 6, 7, ca. AD 110). The *Didache*, written during the New Testament period, calls the Eucharist a sacrifice and reminds the first-century Christians to confess their sins (Confession) before offering their Sunday morning sacrifice (section 14).

PROBLEM NUMBER TWO: THE BIBLE ALONE?

The second major difficulty Janet and I came across was "who speaks for God?" It is the Bible, correct? That is what I thought. But in my house I have thousands of books on the Bible. Each was bought to teach me what the Bible meant and how to properly interpret each page, especially difficult passages. I realized over time, however, that even among my close-knit circle of Evangelical Protestants we could not agree on significant issues. Should you baptize infants? My Baptist tradition said, "Absolutely NOT!" Yet my wife who was raised Presbyterian had a certificate of infant baptism in her files. Can you lose your salvation once you are born again? "In no circumstances," said my particular tradition. Yet citing alternate Scripture verses to defend their position, other Evangelicals said, "Of course you can lose your salvation, if you deny Christ and chose a life of sin."

So, who interprets the Bible? Who is the arbiter when conflicts arise? How can I be certain? Ultimately, I realized that within Protestantism it is up to me to decide these deep matters of theology and salvation. Did I have to become my own pope? This became a huge discussion.

I realized early on that the New Testament was not codified and closed as a collection of twenty-seven inspired books until the end of the fourth century. How did the early Christians know how to get saved, what to do on Sunday morning, or how to please God? And it was these early Christians *without a New Testament* who were eaten by lions, burned at the stake, and beheaded in front of cheering crowds. How could they follow Christ so faithfully without the "Bible alone"?

The Bible itself never promotes "Bible alone." We realized that *sola scriptura* was unscriptural. The early Church had the Apostolic Tradition, bishops in the apostolic succession and, only later, a gradually recognized and collected New Testament. And where did the authority to chose and close the canon of Scripture come from? As St. Augustine said, "I would not believe the holy Gospels if it were not for the authority of the Holy Catholic Church" (*Against the Epistle of Manichaeus Called Fundamental*, 5, 6, ca. AD 397).

St. Paul himself said that it was the church of the living God that was the pillar and bulwark of the truth, not the Bible (see 1 Tim 3:15).

PROBLEM NUMBER THREE: MORALS

The third issue was no less monumental. What about morals? We had just returned from studying with Dr. Francis Schaeffer in Switzerland. *Time* magazine referred to him as the missionary to the intellectual, and he spoke uniquely to those searching for the truth. He was a Presbyterian minister, very Evangelical, in the tradition of the John-Calvin-Bible-alone-and-faith-alone persuasion. He encouraged us to return to America and speak out against abortion. This we did.

However, our first attempt met with dismal failure and disillusionment. The pastor told me to my face, "You will NOT talk about abortion in my church. We are here to get people saved and make disciples for Christ. We have no business being involved in politics and medicine. Plus, many women in this congregation are getting abortions, and I am not going to allow you to rock the boat."

Something was seriously wrong with American Evangelicalism! I knew enough from my reading of history that ALL Christian traditions from the beginning of Christianity until the beginning of the twentieth century condemned as sinful not only abortion but also contraceptives. Had God changed His mind? Who spoke for God in this matter?

It did not take a rocket scientist to realize that among the thousands of Protestant traditions, sects, churches, and denominations that one could find a group to fit any idea of morals desired. Maybe someone had had an abortion and didn't want to feel guilty. They could find a church to tickle their ears. What if someone were more concerned about a good music ministry than morals? No problem, the mega-church down the road might fit that customized request with no problem.

I realized that many Americans decide on their church the same way they choose their restaurant at lunch time. We drive down Main Street, and on one side of the street are Burger

King, McDonalds, KFC, and Pizza Hut. What I feel like today determines what restaurant I choose.

Now it is Sunday morning, and I drive down Main Street again. On the other side of the street, I find Methodist, Baptist, Pentecostal, Presbyterian, Mormon options, and so on. How do I choose where to go? Again it is very simple. What do I feel like this morning? Do I want good preaching or a good children's ministry? Do I want a pastor who meddles in my choices or someone who makes me feel good? Americans sadly too often pick their church the same way they pick their restaurant!

A New Catholic Friend Rattles My Cage

These three were not the only issues. But worship, Scripture, and morals were right up there on top of the heap. We did not see any solution. I began to question the foundations for the faith altogether. Had I gone much further, a form of agnosticism might have set in.

At that very moment in our lives, a long-time Evangelical friend and pastor announced to us, "Steve, my wife and I have decided to join the Catholic Church." Janet and I were stunned. I immediately blurted out, "Al, that is the stupidest thing I've ever heard; you are way too smart to be a Catholic!"

This friend, Al Kresta, is now a well-known commentator on Catholic radio, a speaker, and an author. We are still best friends, and I never cease thanking him for being there at the right time to rattle my cage and force me to look in a new direction.

Our first response, though, was to study and prove him wrong. Janet and I decided we would mount a defense. Al knew the Bible as well as I did so to collect an array of Bible verses would prove ineffective. A better strategy had to be found. Ah, that's it! We'll go back in history to the first Christians and prove to Al that primitive and apostolic Christianity was Protestant! There were no pope-mobiles or processing cardinals, no Vatican or ecumenical councils.

Surprise, surprise! We were not prepared for what we discovered. But first, why were we never encouraged to read the Fathers of the Church? We had always stated, "The Fathers are not inspired; the Bible is inspired, and that's all we need." But this new finding was a real eye-opener. These first Christians lived, preached, worshipped, and died before the New Testament was even in existence. They were authentic witnesses to the life, Tradition, and practice of the Apostles themselves. They still had the apostolic voices ringing in their ears.

On New Year's Eve of 1993, some Baptist friends had us over for two reasons: to usher in the new year and to try and save us from our lunacy. We had been studying the early Church for months now, and they saw the effect it was having upon us. They wanted to talk, and talk we did. In the midst of the conversation, I stood up and asked my friend, "Do you realize that if you and I had seen Jesus crucified and risen from the dead we would have never read the Gospel of John?" He retorted, "Why not?" I replied, "Because it wasn't written until about 100 AD, and we would have been dead long before that. Jim, how did the first Christians live and practice Christianity without the New Testament?"

On the way home, I was quiet for a long time. Janet asked, "What are you thinking?" I said, "This is getting very scary; the more we argue against the Catholic Church, the more I realize we are backing ourselves right in the front door!"

The next day was January 1, 1994. It was a delightful day with no phone calls or business. We had no interest in football either. At this point, we were consumed with our quandary — What is the Church? What does God expect of us? Where did the Bible come from? Could the Catholic Church possibly be the Church Jesus founded and promised to build?

We had tackled all the obstacles one at a time: the pope, Mary, purgatory, priests, Confession, the Eucharist, faith alone, Bible alone, and many more, and it was all coming to a head. We had books open all over the living room floor. We were asking questions and reading passages aloud to each other. Then it happened: I began to sob. I closed all my books and sat on the floor, crying like a baby. With great concern, my wonderful wife asked, "Steve, what is wrong?" I responded through my tears, "Nothing is wrong.... I just realized, I am a Catholic!" She responded, "Oh good grief," but she said the same thing as I did less than twenty-fours later.

I called my friend Al Kresta (the same person I had called stupid a year earlier) and said, "Happy New Year, Al. Guess what? I'm a Catholic!"

There was silence on the other end of the phone.

"Al, are you there?"

"Yeah," he replied, "but I don't think I heard you correctly, what did you just say?" After I explained, he replied, "You are the last one I thought would ever say that!"

Then he asked me a question for which I was certainly not prepared: "Steve, tomorrow is Sunday, how would you like to go to Mass with us?"

I stopped dead in my tracks and froze. It had never dawned on me that if I would read my way into the Catholic Church I would have to some day go to a Catholic Mass! Old sentiments die hard, and I had lots of them about the Catholic Mass.

I covered the phone and related to my wife what Al had asked. She responded as cool as a cucumber, "Tell him we will go, but we will leave the kids at home; we want to get there late, sit in the back row, and leave early." (People have jokingly told us we were real American Catholics from our first day.)

Al did not keep his promise, and we ended up arriving at Mass early, and we sat in the front of the church. I will never forget that morning. Tears welled up in my eyes for the second time in two days when I watched an apostolic man process up the aisle. I had never seen a priest up close before, but I knew exactly what he was. Janet was weeping too. We wept at every Mass for the next six years, and still do.

On Pentecost Sunday, May 22, 1994, Janet and I, along with our entire immediate family, were received into the Catholic Church. We have never looked back.

The complete story of Steve Ray's journey to the Catholic Church can be read in his book Crossing the Tiber: Evangelical Protestants Discover the Historical Church, *published by Ignatius Press. To learn more about Steve's work, please visit his website at www.CatholicConvert. com.*

Into Peter's Ark

Thomas Storck

former Anglican

I was raised in a family that considered churchgoing very important. But we were not theologically orthodox, even by the standards of most Protestant denominations. My father was the cause of this unusual combination, for despite being a skeptic in religion, he always valued the social aspects of church attendance.

So in the small and medium-sized Ohio towns where we lived, my family attended services of various Protestant congregations, and at one point, I went to Sunday school at a Methodist church practically next door to us. For a short time, my father even conducted his own Sunday services in our home. Then later, when I was about six or seven, we started to attend a Unitarian congregation in a nearby city, whose teachings were more to my father's liking.

When I was about ten, however, we left the Unitarians — I think because of quarreling among the members and the presence of eccentrics among them, such as flying-saucer devotees. We began to attend the Episcopal Church instead. My father was attracted by the dignity of the service and the music, by the comparatively intellectual character of the clergy and members, and by the undogmatic emphasis of the Episcopal tradition.

Into Atheism and Theism

When I was young, say from about age four to eleven, I had a vague notion of God. On one occasion, I believe, I equated

Him with a large piece of farm machinery that was parked near our house. As I approached adolescence, I began to wonder whether there was a God or not, but had not the slightest notion of how to find out.

By around the age of thirteen, I had concluded that there definitely was not a God, and I considered myself an atheist. During this period, I underwent the Episcopal confirmation ceremony. I had had some hesitation about being confirmed, but my father urged me to do so, because of his belief that it was important to belong to some church, even if one did not believe what it taught.

I remember in the tenth grade, during the moment of silent prayer at the beginning of the school day, consciously not praying, indeed attempting to do homework. But the homeroom teacher told me I had at least to sit there and do nothing if I did not want to pray. (This, of course, was in the public schools!)

Then during the next year everything changed. As far as I can remember, this is the sequence of events.

I read something about the Anglican writer C. S. Lewis in some Episcopal publication that my parents received. Though I remember nothing about the article in question, I remember thinking that since Lewis was both a Christian and an intellectual, perhaps I should investigate whether Christianity might actually be true.

Also about this time, my brother gave me a gift certificate for a local bookstore as a Christmas or birthday present. I used it to buy two books, one of them John Henry Newman's *Apologia pro Vita Sua*. I don't think I had ever heard of Newman before, but I was attracted by the Latin title, since I was studying Latin in school.

Reading this book naturally put into my mind not only the idea of conversion, but the entire question of our relationship with God and of seeking the truth about His revelation. But the first decisive moment came in a different and unexpected way.

I have implied that, though a skeptic, my father had a great interest in religion. His library of several thousand books included a fairly large religion section. In fact, I think it was the one section for which he bought or acquired more new books than any other.

One day he brought home a book of some meditations by a Protestant minister. I took a look at it, as I usually did with whatever new books he brought home. One of the first meditations in the book was about the existence of God.

It included some simplified versions of the traditional arguments for God's existence. But in my state of knowledge at the time, that was enough for me. I can still see myself at the bottom of the stairway, in front of a glass bookcase, reading this book, with the realization suddenly coming to me that God did indeed exist. It was obviously a stupendous event in my life, even if I did not fully realize its importance then.

BECOMING A CHRISTIAN

As significant as this event was, it had not yet made me a Christian, only a theist. I was working part-time after school, and I began shortly afterward to have discussions with a Protestant woman at work. I told her I believed in God, but not in Jesus Christ as His Son. She told me to pray to God, that He would show me the truth of the matter, and I began to do so.

One stumbling block was that I did not understand the idea of the Incarnation — namely, how God could be both Creator of the world and yet present in it in the flesh. I got the idea from C. S. Lewis, whom I had then begun reading, of a playwright writing himself a part in his own drama. Although obviously this analogy is not a proof of anything, at the time it sufficed for me, and I accepted that Jesus Christ was the Son of God and began to consider myself a Christian. This was around January of 1968.

When I was a baby, I had been "baptized" in the Unitarian Church in Brooklyn. But it was impossible to discover what form of words had been used or what the minister's intentions might have been. I realized that I had a duty to be baptized, but I was afraid to ask or do anything about it.

After a few months, however, without even praying (I was too ignorant!), God changed my heart and gave me the courage to approach our Episcopal minister at the parish we were then attending about Baptism. As a result, I was conditionally baptized in July of 1968 in the presence of my family.

About this time, my father acquired another new book on religion, entitled *Liturgy and Worship*, published by the Society for the Promotion of Christian Knowledge, an organization in the Church of England. This book was a high-church survey of the Anglican liturgy and necessarily included a considerable amount of theology. I read it, and, thanks be to God, this work gave a direction to my religious life that ultimately brought me to the true faith.

From reading this book, I got a sense of the Church of Jesus Christ as a visible, corporate, and institutional Body, with a liturgy and sacraments and a faith handed down from our Lord and the Apostles. I never had the common Protestant Bible-only approach to Christianity. As a result, I was put in a position where I could begin to assimilate many Catholic truths.

Besides *Liturgy and Worship*, my father also had several Catholic books in his library, including the *Baltimore Catechism*, Ronald Knox's *The Belief of Catholics*, G. K. Chesterton's *The Everlasting Man*, and others. During this time, I read Knox, a former Anglican minister who had converted and become a Catholic priest and prolific author. I also read much of the catechism, and a bit of Chesterton. These books taught me much Catholic doctrine and helped me think clearly and avoid some of the common errors in religious thought in our culture, such as the notion that religious truth is personal and subjective or that it exists entirely to give us psychological comfort in this world.

Additionally, these books enabled me to avoid misconceptions about what the Catholic Church really taught. I continued to read C. S. Lewis, from whom I learned much, not so much by way of actual doctrine as of an attitude toward religious truth that has always stood me in good stead: Lewis never compromised on the fundamental supernatural outlook essential to any form of Christianity, nor did he allow his reader to forget the ever-present issue of salvation or damnation.

There is no mushy Christianity with Lewis. In addition, he provided me with a sufficient intellectual underpinning for adherence to Christian faith so that I never had any serious intellectual difficulties in college or graduate school.

From the time of my baptism as an Episcopalian until 1976, I lived as an Episcopal layman, attended a college (nominally) affiliated with the Episcopal denomination, was married in the college chapel, and worked as a parish religious education director. I read a considerable amount of high-church Episcopal theology, including the ten-volume series of dogmatic theology written by Dr. Francis J. Hall (1857–1932), sometimes called the Anglican *Summa Theologiae*. From this latter, I learned considerable Catholic theology, though in one important matter, as I will relate below, I was seriously misled.

Although for part of this time, especially when I was an undergraduate, I was involved in several pan-Protestant prayer groups with no particular denominational affiliation, I was careful to keep my theological thinking more or less high-church. I never received communion from a minister I did not consider to be in the apostolic succession.

CONSIDERING THE CATHOLIC CHURCH

I continued in this situation until I was forced to consider carefully the claims of the Catholic Church because of actions by the Episcopal denomination. Specifically, I was disturbed when the ordination of women as "priests" was authorized by the General Convention, the governing body of the American Episcopal Church, in the fall of 1976.

Before discussing this issue, however, I should say something about what I thought of the Catholic Church during my ten or so years as an Anglican. Obviously, from the examples of Newman, Knox, and Chesterton, the idea of conversion from Canterbury to Rome was quite familiar to me during all those years. In fact, for many years, the Catholic Church had been very attractive to me.

I was a high-church Episcopalian who adhered to the so-called "Branch Theory" of the Church. This is the notion that the one, holy, Catholic, and apostolic Church is made up of three more-or-less coequal branches: the Anglican, the Eastern Orthodox, and the Roman, with at most a primacy of honor given to the bishop of Rome. Though I considered myself already Catholic, then, many aspects of the Church of Rome and of Catholic life appealed to me.

In a sense, Rome was a temptation to me, a temptation specifically to accede to her without a sufficient intellectual conviction, because of various cultural or populist reasons. I was attracted, for example, to the Catholic Church because she contains such a wonderful mass of humanity, the poor of so many nations, colors and cultures, not just the upper-middle classes of English-speaking countries.

In 1975, in Santa Fe, New Mexico, I encountered the externals of Catholic culture for the first time. I immediately fell in love with the Spanish culture, with its buildings, its art, its people, its life. Twentieth-century New Mexico could hardly be called a Catholic culture in its fullness, but enough of the externals of the faith remain so that it helped to build up in my mind this image of the Catholic Church.

One of the most memorable things I saw was an exhibit at the Museum of New Mexico of colonial religious art from the seventeenth through the twentieth centuries. Here I saw religious art as a living and popular tradition, for the exhibit included a few paintings done well into this century, pictures depicting answered prayers. One painting, for example, might show someone lying on a sickbed with others praying and perhaps a saint above receiving the petitions. The next panel might show the invalid up and about again. These were paintings done by or on behalf of families living in New Mexico in the twentieth century to commemorate some actual answered prayer. Here was Catholic culture alive and well and part of the lives of ordinary believers.

But something else in Santa Fe, which at the time created perhaps an even bigger impression on me, involved less authentic Catholic art. I mean the rosaries and plastic statues of the Infant Jesus of Prague for sale at the Woolworths on the plaza. Here again was a sign of the matter-of-factness Catholics felt about the faith. Though doubtless for Woolworths it was simply a means of making a buck, for one brought up in a Protestant culture, it was a revelation. I had never seen anything like it, and it delighted me. Here was further evidence — to me, refreshing — that among Catholics religion was not something to be put in a little box, something separate from life, something so special that it was almost unreal.

No, religion was a part of life. Why? Because God, the Virgin, the angels, and the saints were all as real, and as close to us, as the other things Woolworths sold, such as soap, clothes hangers, or underwear. In *The Belief of Catholics*, Ronald Knox speaks of this popular side to Catholic piety:

> There is among Catholic saints a familiarity which seems to raise this world to the level of eternity. There is among Catholic sinners a familiarity

which seems (to non-Catholic eyes) to degrade
eternity to the level of this world. The point is most
clearly demonstrated in connection with that attitude toward religious things which we call "reverence." For good or for evil, the ordinary, easygoing
Catholic pays far less tribute to this sentiment than
a Protestant, or even an agnostic brought up in the
atmosphere of Protestantism. No traveler fails to be
struck, and perhaps shocked, by the "irreverence"
or "naturalness" (call it what you will) that marks
the behavior of Catholic children wandering about
in church. (From chapter XIII, "The Air Catholics
Breathe," online at http://www.ewtn.com/library/
CHRIST/BELIEF.txt)

I found other aspects of Catholic life attractive as well. For
example, while a senior in high school, the reading of Richard
Tawney's *Religion and the Rise of Capitalism* began in me a
lifelong passion for the social teaching of the Catholic Church.
All these things were attracting me to Rome during my years
as an Anglican, although I tried to keep the emotional pull
of Rome separate from my intellectual considerations about
conversion.

APPROACHING CONVERSION

I don't remember how many times I seriously considered
conversion before I actually did convert. But I know there
were at least two times, one in the summer of 1972 and the
second during the subsequent winter. The first time I talked at
some length with a seminarian friend of mine (now a priest of
the Diocese of Toledo, Ohio) and the second time with a priest
resident near my undergraduate college.

This latter priest turned out to be a modernist. His remark
that, now that they had successfully demythologized Scrip-

ture, they would begin to demythologize dogma rather put me off. I didn't speak any further to him.

About this same time, during the first semester of my senior year (fall 1972), I wrote a paper for an English history class on the question of the continuity of the Church of England with the pre-Reformation Catholic Church. I remember being shocked when I discovered that those who had assisted Henry VIII in setting up the Church of England regarded ultra-Protestants such as Calvin as their friends and co-religionists. So much for the Branch Theory in the 1540s!

However, my Episcopal professor suggested that instead of looking at the intentions of the Anglican founders, I should look for how much of Catholicism (as he and I understood it) managed to survive the Protestant Revolt, despite what Cranmer and his colleagues may have desired. This satisfied me and helped keep me in the Episcopal denomination for another few years.

The crisis, as I said, came after the General Convention's authorizing of the ordination of women in the fall of 1976. I knew that this was entirely against Christian Tradition, and for a short time, I even edited and published a little periodical, *The Newsletter on Women's Ordination*, in opposition to the idea. The Sunday after the Episcopal Church voted to allow it, my wife and I attended Sunday services as usual.

This was almost the last time that I attended an Episcopal church as a worshipper. The following Easter we journeyed to Columbus, Ohio, to attend an Episcopal parish that had rejected the General Convention's action, and a few other times in the next year we went to Episcopal churches for special reasons. But my days as an Episcopalian were essentially over.

Many Episcopalians were opposed to what the denomination had done, and almost immediately began organizing breakaway groups. Had there been one convenient to us, we would have joined. We would have also considered attending an Eastern Orthodox parish.

Practically speaking, though, the only parishes of my great Three-Branched church convenient to us were Roman Catholic, and since I believed that it was our duty to attend the eucharistic sacrifice, my wife and I began attending Catholic Mass. This didn't make me a Catholic, but it did allow us to learn about natural family planning (the lack of knowledge of which had in part prevented me from more seriously considering Rome in the past). It also caused me to think that perhaps I should seriously investigate the Catholic faith.

THE QUESTION IS SETTLED

I made the decision to undertake this investigation the following fall when we were living in Baton Rouge, Louisiana. We began instruction at a local Catholic student center, but it was staffed by modernist priests who were later expelled by the bishop from the diocese. However, because of my earlier reading — including some of what I learned from the Episcopalian writer Francis Hall — I was not corrupted by the instruction. In fact, I argued with my instructor, particularly over the teaching in *Humanae Vitae*, which I had come to accept.

I didn't attempt to find a better Catholic parish because I didn't know any existed. I had read so much in the secular press about dissent in the Church that I thought it wasn't worth the trouble to look for one. It wasn't until several months after we became Catholic that we discovered an excellent parish, St. Agnes, not far away from where we lived. And, in fact, a few months after we became Catholics, we left the student center to attend St. Agnes.

Our instruction began in the fall of 1977, but by December, I was still completely undecided. Consequently, the priest recommended that we take our Christmas vacation to more seriously consider the matter.

Though I knew that the key to the entire question was the attitude of the early Church toward the papacy, I actually had read little of the Fathers, except for Augustine's *Confessions*. So, among other things, I did some reading in the Fathers and other early writers, from a book of excerpts of their writings. I was shocked to find the following passages:

> For this church [i.e. Rome] has a position of leadership and authority; and therefore every church, that is, the faithful everywhere, must needs agree with the church at Rome; for in her the apostolic tradition has ever been preserved by the faithful from all parts of the world. (St. Irenaeus, *Adversus Haereses*, 3, I)

> The other Apostles were, to be sure, what Peter was, but primacy is given to Peter, and the Church and the throne are shown to be one. (St. Cyprian, *On the Unity of the Catholic Church*)

> That Supreme Pontiff, that Bishop of Bishops, issues an edict ... (Tertullian, *De Pudicitia*, 1)

(I should note that even though this last quote, written when Tertullian had become a schismatic Montanist, was derisive of papal authority, it does witness that in his time — writing in the early third century AD — such titles and authority were already claimed for the bishop of Rome.)

The above quotes surprised me because none of them had been cited by the Anglican writer that I mentioned, Francis Hall. He had been indefatigable in gathering quotations from the Fathers and others on behalf of doctrines and practices that high-church Anglicans accept, such as the seven sacraments or the Church as a visible corporate body. But on the question of the bishop of Rome, he had been strangely selective, and therefore misleading. He had quoted only a few odd statements that supported his point of view on Rome.

In any case, reading these quotes was enough for me. Under the inspiration of the Holy Spirit, I accepted this fundamental principle of the Catholic faith and thus the entire corpus of Catholic belief.

I still did a little reading after that, but the question was essentially settled. That is, since I now recognized that the true Christian Church was gathered in communion with the successor of Peter, I did not need to debate separately such articles of faith as the infallibility of the pope or Our Lady's Immaculate Conception and Assumption. It was enough to know that those Christians who were grouped in the true Church had authoritatively defined these dogmas.

All this occurred in January of 1978. A few weeks later, on February 12, my wife and I were received into the Holy Catholic Church at Christ the King Chapel.

LOOKING BACK

From my standpoint now as a Catholic, I realize that the "Anglo-Catholic" branch theory of the Church is profoundly contrary not just to the Fathers, but to the New Testament itself.

The kind of unity that St. Paul continually appeals to and, in fact, practices, as he travels among the various small congregations of Catholics in Asia Minor and Greece, has nothing in common with the "unity" supposed in the branch theory. Moreover, as others have pointed out, of the three supposed branches of the Church, both the Roman and the Eastern emphatically reject this theory, while among Anglicans, most are indifferent to it, with only a small group of "Anglo-Catholics" accepting it.

One other point I will mention. Sometimes when people, either Catholics or non-Catholics, ask me what I was before becoming a Catholic, they say something like, "Oh, an Episcopalian; well, that's not very different." And in fact there is something to this. As an Anglican, I did believe most of Catholic doctrine.

But there is one thing that is quite different: All Protestants, including "Anglo-Catholics," basically make up their own religion. That is, those Protestants who profess to believe only the Bible can decide for themselves just what the Bible means or how to interpret a difficult passage. And if they choose to follow a particular pastor or evangelist on some disputed point, still, they themselves choose which pastor or evangelist to follow. The decision is in their own hands.

This is true also for high-church Anglicans. Although as an Episcopalian I professed to follow the Fathers of the undivided Church and the traditions common to Rome, Canterbury, and Constantinople, still I decided exactly which dogmas or moral points were universal and thus binding on all Christians. I decided when the testimony of the Fathers was sufficiently unanimous.

Even if I followed an author I thought was sound, it was my decision which author to trust. Despite the fact that I believed I was following an objective authority outside of myself, I essentially made up my own religion. The ultimate source was still within me.

This was no longer true once I became a Catholic and accepted the authority of the Church's Magisterium — and it was the biggest difference I noticed after becoming a Catholic. My reaction to finding the locus of authority outside myself was like my reaction to having cold water thrown over me on a hot day: a bit of a shock, but very refreshing.

I suppose that some people might regard this last statement as evidence that Catholics are glad to abdicate thinking for themselves and like to be told what to believe and do. Any orthodox Catholic knows that this is not true. The refreshment I felt at no longer having to make up my own religion was the refreshment that comes from beginning to learn a bit of humility, as well as from leaving off a job that was never meant to be mine in the first place.

Of course, this does not mean that I denigrate reason. In fact, among Catholics, reason is likely to be more esteemed than among any other group in the world. But true and genuine authority is in no way contrary to reason, but rather its friend and ally.

Thomas Storck has written widely on Catholic social teaching, Catholic culture, and related philosophical and theological topics. He and his wife, Inez, are members of Holy Family parish in Columbus, Ohio. They have four children and seven grandchildren.

CONFESSIONS OF A
PROTESTANT PEW POTATO

TIM COOPER

former Nazarene

I thought to myself, *Oh, no, here we go again.* Some late-comers had forced us to move into the middle of the pew. There's nothing worse than being in the middle of the pew in a Catholic church if you're a Protestant "pew potato."

You've heard of a couch potato? I was a pew potato. I plunked down in my pew every week but didn't participate a whole lot, other than singing a hymn I recognized or shaking hands with my neighbors during the sign of peace.

So what's the big deal about sitting in the middle of the pew? The problem is with the Communion line.

My choice: I could either go up front with my arms crossed and receive a blessing, or I could stay back in the pew. I hated going up and not receiving the Eucharist. And in a large church like ours, chances are I would get a "blessing" from some teenager serving as a eucharistic minister.

No thanks, I thought. *I'll just stay in the pew.*

Unfortunately, this meant I would end up being a hurdle for some folks in my pew, who would have to climb over me either on the way up or on the way back. I always wanted to sit at the end of the pew so I could avoid the "hurdle" problem — which brings up another pet peeve I had about the Catholic Mass (besides the numerous crying babies in the sanctuary). It seemed to me that half of the parishioners showed up two minutes prior to the start of Mass. The situation made it nearly impossible to guarantee my coveted end-of-the-pew position.

This situation was just one dilemma facing a Protestant pew potato. There were others as well. I wasn't sure what I was supposed to do during the Mass. Was I supposed to cross myself? Genuflect? Kneel?

If I wasn't participating in the Eucharist, was I to kneel during the prayer of consecration? At first, I just sat while others knelt. But I felt awkward sitting while everyone else was kneeling.

So I started kneeling during the prayer of consecration. But I didn't believe in the "Holy Sacrifice of the Mass" or transubstantiation. I didn't want to bear a "false witness" to what was going on. So I finally settled on the "half-sitting, half-kneeling" position.

How I Got into This Predicament

I'd never had these problems as a member of various Protestant congregations. They had passed trays of wafers and tiny grape juice glasses, so there were never any communion lines to deal with, where you might have to trip over somebody who couldn't or wouldn't participate. Deciding whether to take part wasn't an issue, especially in one particular nondenominational congregation that publicized its "open" communion policy every week.

So how did I get myself in this predicament? It's all because of my wife, Sandy. I love Sandy with every fiber of my being. I would do just about anything for her.

I agreed to get married in the Catholic Church because Sandy was Catholic and I loved her so much. I agreed to raise our kids Catholic because I loved her so much. I agreed to go to Mass with her every week so we could worship as a family because I loved her so much.

However, I did draw the line at becoming Catholic myself. Before we got married, I told her I would never, ever, become Catholic. She was fine with that. Even so, she told me she could never become Protestant, either, so we would have to figure out a way to work it out.

I had dated several nice girls before, but there was something different about Sandy. It was hard for me to put my finger on it. She was very quiet about her faith. I think I knew in the back of my mind that I was going to marry her after our first date.

What really "sealed the deal" was my observation of how she treated children and the elderly. When we were dating in college, my wife had an internship at a local club for boys. After graduating, she worked in a nursing home. She treated everyone she encountered, young and old, with dignity, love, and respect. I thought to myself, *I have got to make this woman my wife.* A mixed marriage was the price I was willing to accept in order to spend my life with the woman I loved.

NAZARENE ROOTS

If you had told me only a few years before that I would eventually get married in the Catholic Church, I would have told you, "No way." I was born in Indianapolis, one of six kids in a family that belonged to the Nazarene denomination, which was largely hostile to the Catholic faith. (We later relocated to Fort Wayne, Indiana, where I finished my high school years.)

My mom and dad were, and still are, wonderful Christian role models. We frequently had family devotions, including Bible study and prayer. Our faith was part of the air we breathed.

I asked Jesus to be my Lord and Savior when I was twelve years old. I was baptized at the age of fourteen. I gave several emotional testimonies at church.

I remember saying once that I believed God had a special plan for my life. At the time, I was thinking about missionary work or the ministry. They even allowed me to preach the sermon one Sunday: it was "Youth Day," when young people were allowed to lead the services.

I have many wonderful memories from my youth in the Nazarene Church. Our sense of community was strong, and other members of our congregation were always good to me. I remember one Nazarene minister in particular who taught me much when I was a young man. He and his wife were so humble, kind, and pure that the light of Jesus shone through them. I cannot explain it any other way.

The Nazarene denomination had broken away from the Methodist denomination in the early twentieth century as a result of the Holiness revival movement. The Nazarenes remain part of the Wesleyan tradition, so John and Charles Wesley, the central leaders of the early Methodist movement, were heroes of mine.

I was close to my aunt and her husband, a United Methodist minister, and their children. Their youngest son, whom they named Charles Wesley, was close to me and my younger brother. My cousin would eventually enter seminary and become a wonderful minister himself.

Three of my four great-grandfathers were ordained as ministers in various Wesleyan denominations. Even today, numerous Protestant ministers and missionaries are in my extended family. One family is working in Guatemala, encouraging Catholics to leave their religion and embrace what they call "Bible Christianity" instead. Another family is currently serving in Croatia (a country that's more than ninety percent Catholic) with the same goal.

It may be different today, but when I was growing up in the Nazarene denomination, we considered three particular religious communities to be "off the reservation": the Church of Jesus Christ of Latter-Day Saints (Mormons), the Jehovah's Witnesses, and the Roman Catholic Church. We saw none of these groups as truly "Christian."

We believed that salvation came by faith alone, and that Roman Catholics practiced a religion with the heretical view of justification by faith plus works. Roman Catholic teaching was, we said, full of unbiblical, manmade doctrines, rituals, and traditions such as Mariolatry (the worship of Mary). We believed that the Church had fallen off the rails many centuries ago, but that the Protestant Reformers had restored the Christian faith to its true biblical roots.

PEBBLES IN MY SHOE

When I was young, the issue of Christian unity bothered me. St. Paul told the Corinthians: "I appeal to you, brethren, by the name of our Lord Jesus Christ, that all of you agree and that there be no dissensions among you, but that you be united in the same mind and the same judgment" (1 Cor 1:10). In Romans 12:5, the Apostle teaches that we are "one body in Christ."

St. Paul repeatedly wrote about the importance of unity, even demanded it, throughout his Epistles (See, for example, Rom 12:4–5; 16:17–18; 1 Cor 1:10–13; Eph 4:1–6; Phil 1:27; 2:1–2; Tit 3:9–11). Jesus prayed for our unity: "I do not pray for these only, but also for those who believe in me through their word, that they may all be one" (Jn 17:20).

Nevertheless, we couldn't maintain unity even among Wesleyans, much less the broader Protestant community. The Wesleyans had serious problems with the Calvinists. I remember frequent sermons on the "errors of Calvinism" in our Nazarene congregation. Of course, Calvinists weren't as bad as Catholics. But they still had serious errors in their doctrines. We affirmed free will, which Calvin rejected. We agreed with other Christians who taught a type of assurance of salvation. But we rejected the notion of "absolute" assurance. We did not agree with the "once saved always saved" doctrine.

Every once in a while we would make a little fun of our Lutheran and Anglican brothers and sisters, labeling them "Catholic-Lite." We called them that because they believed in some type of Real Presence in the Eucharist, and their worship was liturgical. (For us, "ritual" was a no-no.) Most of them seemed to live like the Catholic "heathen" we encountered, with habits of dancing, smoking, drinking, cussing — that kind of thing. The so-called "mainline denominations" were viewed in general with scorn, since many had modernist interpretations of Scripture, and their members also lived "worldly" lives.

Meanwhile, we didn't agree with our Pentecostal brothers that the gift of tongues is the sure-fire sign of "baptism in the Holy Spirit." In fact, while we recognized the possibility that the gift of tongues is still today a valid gift from the Holy Spirit, speaking in tongues was not a part of our spiritual practice in the Nazarene denomination.

Given all these denominational divisions, the biblical injunction to Christian unity was like a bothersome pebble in my shoe. I couldn't figure out how we were supposed to achieve unity if we couldn't agree on how to interpret Scripture. How literally were we to interpret certain passages that didn't easily lend themselves to a strictly literal interpretation, such as the Genesis account of creation? Was the world created in six days about six thousand years ago?

Another pebble in my shoe was our Nazarene stand on certain practices such as dancing, gambling, going to movies, and drinking. I understood some of the logic behind the prohibitions, but I didn't see them explicitly stated in Scripture. Didn't Jesus change water into wine as His first miracle?

At the time, these practices were absolutely prohibited in the Nazarene denomination. Internally, I started to question this black-and-white view of some of these so-called "moral" issues. I started to wonder whether some of these issues should be approached with moderation and common sense.

Was it really so evil to see a Disney movie at a theatre just because the same theatre might also show an R-rated movie? How far did we have to go with this approach? Should we just hide ourselves in caves until Jesus comes back to snatch us out of an evil world?

As a young adult, I eventually left the Nazarene denomination, and most of my family did as well. We tried other denominations. For a time, I attended the Missionary Church (which also has some roots in the Wesleyan tradition). That denomination didn't have the legalistic view of some of the prudential questions that bothered me about the Nazarene denomination.

In college, I met with a nondenominational congregation, but I never felt comfortable there. For one thing, their continuous harping on "open" communion seemed to water down the faith too much. They would say it doesn't matter whether you're Protestant, Catholic, or Eastern Orthodox; all are welcome to the table. It sounded as if they were saying, "It doesn't matter what you believe as long as you believe." I thought I might have found the unity I was seeking, but at what cost? Didn't truth matter too?

A SPIRITUAL CRISIS

When I was in college, I experienced a spiritual crisis. I encountered too many competing views of reality, and I couldn't make sense of all the different religions and worldviews. I started to question everything.

While I became something of a skeptic, I never became an atheist. Atheists have no explanation why there is anything at all. I also realized I couldn't be an agnostic. Agnostics still have to make a choice. You either live as if God doesn't exist, or you live as if God does exist. I still believed in God, but I was quite confused about the Christian faith.

Eventually, I happened on a book by the Anglican writer C. S. Lewis that brought me back firmly into the traditional Christian fold. The book was called *Mere Christianity*. In it, Lewis posed the question that all seekers must ask themselves.

Jesus claimed to be the divine Son of God; He said, "Before Abraham was, I AM" (Jn 8:58). So if He isn't our divine Lord, He must have been either an evil liar or a lunatic. Neither of the latter options seemed reasonable in light of the evidence we have about His life, so I reaffirmed the Lordship of Jesus in my life.

Since the time *Mere Christianity* was written, skeptics have proposed a new option for the "Lord, liar, or lunatic" proposition. I would call this the "legend" option. That is, the "divine Jesus" was merely a "legend." This position holds that the early Church leaders, possibly including the Apostle Paul, collaborated to fabricate Jesus' claims to divinity, along with followers' claims that He rose from the dead, for the sake of self-promotion, or for other motives.

The problem with the "legend" conspiracy theory, of course, is obvious. All but one of the Apostles, including St. Paul (along with their successors, the early bishops) faced tremendous persecution and suffered eventual martyrdom for proclaiming that Jesus was the divine Son of God. How could they have been motivated to do so by a desire for self-promotion? And would they actually have been willing to die for making a claim they knew to be a lie?

JOURNEY TO THE CHURCH JESUS FOUNDED

With these convictions, I settled into my own form of "mere Christianity." My wife had proven to me that Catholics could indeed be very good Christians. She maintained a better prayer life than I did. She treated others with more charity than many of my Evangelical friends did. I met many good Catholic Christians and became close friends with them.

Even so, I still wasn't interested in becoming a Catholic. Too many doctrinal hurdles remained. I was still firmly entrenched in the doctrine of *sola scriptura* (the notion that Scripture alone is the authoritative source of doctrine and practice). And I couldn't see the pope or the doctrines about Mary (among others) in Scripture. I eventually became involved in several Protestant Bible studies, while my wife started attending a Bible study at our parish.

I had started a business and was busy building my career. When my daughter received her First Communion in 1999, I started to think about investigating the Church. I thought it would be good to receive Communion as a family.

By the time I finally started RCIA (Rite for the Initiation of Christian Adults) in the fall of 2002, I had been attending Mass nearly every week for twenty-two years. I enrolled in the program in our parish to learn why the Church holds to the doctrines she proclaims. I wanted to get scriptural support for Catholic teachings.

Instead, I received a continuous stream of negative views on the papacy and how the Church was unfair to women. For that reason, today I tell people inquiring about the faith to read the *Catechism of the Catholic Church*. Many RCIA programs are solid, but in some parishes, inquirers have to take what they hear in RCIA programs with a grain of salt. I started RCIA in September, and by Christmas, I was ready to quit because of what I was hearing there.

READING THAT HELPED

Fortunately, my wife gave me a book for Christmas, *Rome Sweet Home*, by Scott and Kimberly Hahn. Dr. Scott Hahn was a Presbyterian minister and seminary professor who quit his ministry to become Catholic. Through his research into Catholic doctrines, history, and Scripture, he decided that Catholics got it right. The account of this couple's journey into the Catholic Church was easy to read and captivating.

This book got me thinking about the validity of *sola scriptura*. Dr. Hahn made a rather convincing case that *sola scrip-*

tura is a theological assumption, not a biblical truth. As I read his insights, everything started to fall into place.

His arguments solved the dilemma that had confronted me in college about unity and truth. Since the Bible needs an interpreter, the *sola scriptura* position guarantees you will have to compromise one or the other, but you can't have both. However, when you add Apostolic Tradition and a living teaching office to Scripture, you have a firm foundation that ensures both unity and truth.

Another question that had challenged me was the New Testament canon. Shortly after reading *Rome Sweet Home*, I read another book about the authority of Sacred Tradition, by Mark Shea, entitled *By What Authority?* Together these two books rocked my world.

The canon of Scripture was in flux for more than four hundred years. It was the Catholic Church that finally defined the New Testament canon that I subscribed to as a Protestant. How could a fallible Church produce an infallible canon? I had no good answer to that question.

I soon realized that another one of my cherished doctrines, the notion of the "invisible church," was also a theological assumption and not a biblical truth. Scripture points to a visible church. In Matthew 18:15–17, Jesus gives the Church the final authority to determine what it means to be part of the Christian community. How can an *invisible* church define its own membership?

These authors, also, introduced me to the Church Fathers. I started to read them for myself. I had read some Protestants' attempts to defend Protestant doctrines by using various quotes from the Church Fathers. However, as I read the same Church Fathers, I was surprised to find a very Catholic understanding of ordination, Tradition, authority, the communion of saints, liturgy (including the Sacrifice of the Mass), Baptism, the Eucharist, and much more.

I learned that Protestants had been guilty of cherry-picking quotes that "sounded" Protestant but were from Church Fathers who were thoroughly Catholic. The Fathers opened Scripture in ways I had never imagined before. Suddenly everything in Scripture started coming up Catholic.

I began to see baptismal regeneration referred to in John 3:3–5 as the Fathers interpreted it. I saw purgatory in 1 Corinthians 3:11–15. I saw the Eucharist in John 6:32–58. I connected the dots between the Passover (the Jews consumed the Passover Lamb) and Jesus as our Passover Lamb. I saw the connection between the offering of bread and wine by Melchizedek on the one hand, and the Last Supper and the sacrifice of Jesus on Calvary on the other, in light of what Paul said about the Eucharist in 1 Corinthians chapters 10 and 11.

The Eucharist is clearly one of the practices Paul was referring to when he repeatedly told the early Church communities to hold on to the traditions he had passed on to them, either by epistle or by word of mouth (see 2 Thess 2:15). The very earliest Christians, such as St. Ignatius of Antioch and St. Irenaeus, confirmed that the Tradition that the Eucharist is truly the Body and Blood of Christ had come to them from the Apostles. In addition, the earliest Christians, including St. Ignatius, understood the connection between valid ordinations and the Eucharist — an issue that raises the question of apostolic succession.

THE POPE

I started to find a teaching office in both the Old and New Testaments. I saw the connection between Isaiah 22:19–25 and Matthew 16:19. Why did Jesus give the keys to only one Apostle? Why didn't Jesus explain what the keys mean? These questions had haunted me.

The account in Isaiah chapter 22 is the only Old Testament passage in which a key is passed between one person and another. We see a king (Hezekiah) in the line of David, who removes the key from one royal steward (Shebna) and gives it to another (Eliakim). The royal steward is the king's right-hand man.

Such authority is given to only one person. Verse 19 in this passage refers to the steward filling an "office." This means that the unique authority does not end at that one person's death; it is passed down through an office. Verse 21 clarifies this authority even further: "He shall be a *father* to the inhabitants of Jerusalem and to the house of Judah" (emphasis added).

I began connecting the dots. Jesus, a royal descendant of David, is our King. He left His earthly kingdom and appointed His royal steward (St. Peter) to be a shepherd for His flock (see Jn 21:15–17) and their spiritual father (Is 22:21). The keys Jesus gave to St. Peter designate an office and succession (Is 22:19). This succession was passed on to bishops through the laying on of hands (cf. 1 Tim 3:1; 2 Tim 1:6).

The early Church Fathers constantly wrote about the office of bishop. St. Irenaeus, bishop of Lyons (now in France), spent twenty years with the bishop and future martyr St. Polycarp, who had spent twenty years with the Apostle John. He once wrote about St. Linus, the first bishop of Rome to succeed St. Peter: "The blessed Apostles, then, having founded and built up the Church, committed into the hands of Linus the office of the episcopate" (*Against Heresies,* 3, 3, 3). Hippolytus, Eusebius, John Chrysostom, Jerome, Augustine, and many others also affirm that Linus was the first to succeed Peter.

St. Irenaeus added: "With that church [the church of Rome], because of its superior origin, all the churches must agree, that is, all the faithful in the whole world, and it is in her that the faithful everywhere have maintained the apostolic tradition" (*Against Heresies*, 3, 3, 2). For this reason, I always get a chuckle when I see Protestants using quotes from St. Irenaeus or other Church Fathers to support the doctrine of *sola scriptura*.

MARIAN DOCTRINES

Mary was my last hurdle. From my perspective (and that of many Protestants), the idea of having a relationship with Mary took away from the proper attention due to Christ, our sole mediator. What I discovered is that Mary brought Jesus to us two thousand years ago, and she continues to bring Jesus to us today through her intercessory prayers. She always points us to her divine Son. She doesn't take away from God's glory, but is an awe-inspiring reflection of it.

When I considered becoming Catholic, I asked: Where are the Marian doctrines (such as the Immaculate Conception and the Assumption) to be found in Scripture? But if Christian truths can be passed on through oral Tradition from the Apostles (and therefore aren't limited to explicit references in Scripture), then I should ask other questions: Are these doctrines reasonable? Do they contradict Scripture? Where do they come from? Why are they important?

What I discovered from my research is this: Yes, the Marian doctrines are reasonable. No, they do not contradict Scripture. They come in part from Scripture (or are rooted in Scripture), in part from Tradition and the natural development of doctrine. This natural doctrinal development isn't new revelation or invention, but rather a deeper understanding of revelation, often achieved by connecting the dots in Scripture.

HOME AT LAST

I was received into the Church at the Easter Vigil Mass in 2003. I have never regretted the decision, and I absolutely love being Catholic. I didn't become a Catholic to please my wife; I became a Catholic because I had found the "pearl of great price" (see Mt 13:45–46).

I've never stopped searching for the holiness that John Wesley, the founder of the Methodist movement, first challenged me to seek. Granted, I still have a long way to go to achieve that goal. But having new channels of sanctifying grace in the sacraments — most especially the Eucharist and Reconciliation — have been a real blessing for me.

Tim Cooper is the software developer for the Faith Database CD-ROM, a searchable library of Catholic writings and multiple Scripture translations. (For more information, go to www.faithdatabase.com.) Tim, his wife, Sandy, and their daughter, Katie, reside in Fort Wayne, Indiana, where they are active volunteers in St. Charles Borromeo parish. Tim also volunteers as a helper for the Coming Home Network International.

A Place to Stand

Dr. Todd Hartch

former Episcopalian and Evangelical

The liturgy at the Episcopal church in Greenwich, Connecticut, where I went every Sunday with my family as I was growing up in the 1970s was beautiful. But it confused me because most of the people there, including the ministers, did not seem to believe what they were saying.

We said the Nicene Creed every week, yet the sermons amounted to little more than "Be nice to each other." When a friend of mine once asked our Sunday school teacher what happened when we died, the teacher responded that he was not sure. When the youth group went on a retreat, we had a lot of fun, but we learned little about God. It was almost as if the church were saying, "We love these ancient rituals, but we're not sure what human beings can ever know about God."

When it was time for me to get confirmed in 1982 as a fifteen-year-old, I knew that I didn't believe what I was supposed to believe. But I stood up before the Episcopal bishop and said the words anyway.

Around that time, I read a book review of Graham Greene's autobiography, in which his assertion that he was a "reluctant Catholic" stuck out. I decided that I did believe in God and was perhaps even a Christian, but a reluctant one. The heart of the matter was that I simply had not been taught what a Christian was or why anyone should believe in Christianity.

Nobody in my liberal theological environment was willing to assert much about God, and nobody had foundations other than reason — certainly not Scripture or Tradition — on which to make strong claims. There were people trying to live a good and holy life in that church, but they had no confidence about the most important issues.

I should mention that throughout my childhood and adolescence I knew many Catholics and took them for granted as part of the religious landscape. But it never occurred to me that the Catholic faith might be qualitatively different from the many Protestant denominations that I also knew.

Meanwhile, I'd been having a difficult time socially at my private boys' school. By seventh grade, my friends were drinking, smoking marijuana, and generally running amuck. Although I lacked strong moral convictions, I feared the wrath of my father enough to decide that I couldn't afford to get caught up in what my friends were doing. I did well in sports and academics, but I slowly fell out of touch with my friends and became a lonely and introverted boy.

When I was in ninth grade, my life changed, largely because of two new students, Bill and Steve. Bill would say, "Hi, Todd!" whenever he saw me, which took me aback. No one else in school acted friendly or displayed straightforward affection, because such actions were considered "gay." I couldn't understand why Bill behaved so strangely.

I was even more intrigued by Steve, who announced his intention of starting a Christian group on campus. During our lunch hour, he convened a group of interested boys and began presenting what I would now call apologetics. Unlike the people in my church, Steve seemed to believe that Christianity had a definite content. He made arguments based on reason, but he also used the Bible.

I didn't quite know what to think. Steve's ideas were strangely attractive, but could they be right? Was there more to Christianity? Could we really know if there was?

Bill and Steve, I discovered, were members of an Evangelical parachurch youth organization. (Parachurch organizations are those that engage in various sorts of Christian ministry but make no claim to constitute a local or denominational "church.") This organization brought the Gospel to private schools and had a summer camp on Martha's Vineyard, an island off the coast of Massachusetts. Soon staff workers began a Bible study on the Gospel of John at my school.

It was as if the scales fell from my eyes. On an intellectual level, I had doubts about why we should trust the Bible, but on a spiritual level, I was soaring. The words of Scripture explained by strong believers and simply taken seriously were giving me a whole new picture of Jesus and of what it meant to follow Him.

Peter, the leader of the study and actually the leader of the organization itself, gave me a strong intellectual defense of the authority of Scripture. Yet even more important was the Word of God itself. It came alive for me and pulled me into the mystery of Christ. At last, I had something I could stand on — the authoritative Word of God.

When I was sixteen, I attended a ski week sponsored by the youth organization and knew it was time to make a decision. I now believed those words that I'd been saying in the creeds all my life: Christ was God; He died for my sins; He rose from the dead; He was calling for my life.

I was afraid of what surrender to Christ might cost me, so I hiked the snow-covered trails around the upstate New York lodge, trying to imagine some way that I could maintain control of my life. But I had to admit that there was no such way. I needed to give my life to Christ, and that's what I did.

The change in my life was dramatic. I went from being sad and introverted to happy and, well, still introverted, but much more engaged with the people around me. That summer someone called me "Smiley," and at first, I thought he was making fun of me. Then I realized that I was, in fact, smiling all the time.

During my senior year in high school, I met weekly with the leader, Peter, to study 1 Corinthians and some devotional material. When I arrived at Yale University as a freshman in the fall of 1985, I was therefore well prepared for the secular and often anti-Christian environment. I dove into the campus InterVarsity Christian Fellowship and actually found Yale quite conducive to my spiritual life.

As an active member of the fellowship, I spent thirty to forty hours per week leading Bible studies, going to various meetings and training sessions, and socializing with other members of the fellowship. We went deep into Scripture, especially on retreats and in InterVarsity's distinctive "manuscript study," in which books of the Bible are printed double-spaced with wide margins and studied intensively for hours at a time. The Bible, I understood more and more, was incredibly deep and entirely trustworthy.

I did have a problem in those days, though, with the issue of leadership. Our campus minister had a strong personality and strong opinions about how ministry should be done. At the same time, he insisted that the executive committee of the fellowship should operate on the principle of consensus and that he was just one member of the committee.

The result of his approach was that the executive committee had very long meetings. After all, we had to agree about every single decision we made, and the Bible that we all took as our rule of faith is not exactly explicit about what night to hold meetings or how to plan the fall retreat. In the end, I noticed, we almost always ended up doing what the campus minister wanted in the first place.

I, for one, didn't agree with all his ideas, but I usually let myself be convinced for the sake of ending a meeting. Why couldn't each of us, I wondered, have responsibility for various aspects of the fellowship, subject to approval of the campus minister? Why did we have to pretend that our organization was a perfect democracy? Wouldn't it be more efficient and truer to what we were actually doing to have a more hierarchical system?

Despite technically being an English major, in reality I spent most of my time as an undergraduate doing ministry. After graduation, I worked for four years as an InterVarsity campus minister at Yale because it was what I was best prepared to do after devoting more of my college career to InterVarsity than to academics. I had a decent time as a campus minister, but I decided to move on for reasons closely connected to my attendance at the local Vineyard Christian Fellowship (a charismatic denomination).

Our pastor took everyone's opinion seriously and spent a lot of time with his board of elders. But it was clear that, in the end, the big decisions about the direction of our church were his to make. On the other hand, small group leaders had flexibility in how they ran their groups.

To me, this was like a breath of fresh air after the endless discussions in InterVarsity. At last I could just relax and do my job in the church without feeling that I had to make or even approve of every decision in the church. I was challenged, though, by the pastor's high view of the local church, which to him was much more important than other Christian organizations.

Organizations such as InterVarsity had their place, he believed. But the real action in God's Kingdom took place in the local church. Missions, for instance, were in his view primarily a matter of church planting.

I was challenged also by the Vineyard's emphasis on the power of the Holy Spirit. In the Vineyard, healing, prophecy, speaking in tongues, dreams, and visions were everyday occurrences. God was active in people's lives, not just in some interior way, but in powerful physical ways.

Ultimately, I accepted what the pastor and the Vineyard were teaching: Christ had come to start churches, not parachurch organizations. Churches ran best under a clear leader and lines of authority. And the Holy Spirit longed to work today as He did in the Book of Acts.

The more I internalized these lessons, the less comfortable I felt, not just with InterVarsity, but with the whole parachurch model. The Catholic Church was still hardly on my radar screen. But I was more and more committed to the idea of "the church," which was hierarchical and powerfully infused with the gifts of the Holy Spirit.

In 1993, I married Kathline Richardson, whom I had met in the Vineyard, and entered Yale Divinity School (YDS). Marriage to Kathline was and continues to be a nonstop source of blessing, but YDS was more of a challenge than I expected.

I was prepared intellectually for the liberal theology for which YDS is famous. Peter, InterVarsity, and my long immersion in the Bible had insulated me from the classic temptation of Protestant liberalism: the elevation of human reason over and even against the Bible. I was not ready, however, for the spiritual desolation that results when the Bible is cast aside and the most "progressive" nostrums are presented as the agenda of the Church.

When seminary professors, for example, support homosexual behavior, they are not just expressing a personal opinion; they are leading their students and those students' future parishioners into untold depths of misery. My YDS years, therefore, confirmed to me that human reason could not be the ultimate authority. Without the aid of Scripture and Tradition, we are simply too weak to recognize or hold fast to the truth.

YDS was not all negative, however. It was there that I developed a great interest in Church history, especially in the classes taught by Lamin Sanneh, a convert from Islam to Christianity. Sanneh's brilliant work on missions and culture opened my eyes to the great importance of Bible translation — it often leads to cultural renewal — and to the amazing phenomenon of world Christianity.

As he made clear, most Christians now live outside Europe and North America. The "average Christian" of today is not a European male, but rather an African woman. During my undergraduate days, I had become interested in Latin American Protestantism, which was growing by leaps and bounds; I decided to continue this interest by pursuing a doctorate in Latin American history and by applying Sanneh's ideas to Latin American Protestantism.

I didn't know it at the time, but Sanneh would soon be received into the Catholic Church. He is now a member of the Pontifical Council on the Historical Sciences and the Pontifical Council on Relations with Muslims.

The boisterous paganism of Yale's graduate school of arts and sciences was a relief to me after the solemn theological liberalism of YDS. Although none of my new classmates were Christians of any type, and most of them had a decidedly negative view of Christianity, I felt much more at home among them than I ever had at YDS because our identities were clear. I was a Christian; they were not Christians. I disagreed with their deepest beliefs; they disagreed with mine. We knew these basic facts about each other, but we could still relate to each other and develop friendships.

For my dissertation, I chose to apply Sanneh's ideas to the work of the Summer Institute of Linguistics (SIL, also known as the Wycliffe Bible Translators) in Mexico. The SIL had started in Mexico in the 1930s and gone on to become the largest independent Protestant missionary organization in the world, with thousands of Bible translators working in Latin America, Asia, and Africa. So my wife and young son, Trevor, moved with me to Oaxaca, Mexico, for eighteen months of research, starting in 1998.

Living in another culture has its challenges, but we had wonderful neighbors, a friendly charismatic church, and a beautiful city to live in. I spent time in the archives of Oaxaca and Mexico City and in the indigenous villages of Mixtec, Otomí, and Huave. I also got to know some impressive SIL translators.

A typical Bible translation project, I learned, could take twenty years: six or seven years to learn a new language, a few more years to create a grammar and orthography (alphabet) from scratch, then as much as a decade to translate every book of the New Testament. Since most indigenous villages are located in the most remote parts of Mexico, these translators, some with children, spend much of their lives without electricity, running water, and the other common aids to modern life.

I couldn't help, at this point, thinking seriously about the Catholic Church. I was surrounded by Catholics and Catholic churches wherever I went. Although the Protestant movement in Mexico was vibrant, I had to admit that it was constantly defining itself against the Catholic Church.

I don't think our pastor in Oaxaca, for example, could give a sermon without criticizing some aspect of Catholic faith. Up to that point, Protestant faith had not been for me a protest; it was simply the biblical form of Christianity. In Latin America, however, this ahistorical notion simply did not make sense.

Almost all Protestants there are either converts from the Catholic faith or the children of converts. They all have their stories of the pain and even persecution occasioned by their choice to become Protestants.

Also, the history I was writing was the story of indigenous Mexicans leaving the Catholic Church as they encountered the Word of God in their own languages. Without in any way condoning the violence that many early Protestant converts encountered, I recognized that the violence was a sign of how seriously Indian communities objected to the destruction of their Catholic or Catholic/syncretistic way of life when community members became Protestants.

It wasn't as if I were thinking about Catholic faith as a personal spiritual matter. I simply felt that I had to take the Catholic Church more seriously as a professional issue. I had investigated the minority phenomenon of Latin American Protestants; perhaps it was time to do some research on the mainstream religion in Latin America.

My first full-time teaching position at Teikyo Post University in Waterbury, Connecticut, seemed like a dream job since it allowed Kathline and me to stay involved in the Vineyard Fellowship and allowed us to see my family and hers on a regular basis. But I soon found out that the college was being sold to a for-profit company that probably would not see history as a profit center. Eastern Kentucky University (EKU) offered me a job, so Kathline and I, now with sons Trevor and Peter, moved to Richmond, Kentucky, in 2003.

At EKU, I began my next research project, an investigation of radical priest Ivan Illich and his think tank in Cuernavaca, Mexico. Looking back, I cannot help but see the hand of God in my choice of research topic.

Initially, Illich had appealed to me because the center he ran in Mexico during the 1960s and 1970s was frequented by a wide range of secular "progressives" and leftists. My field of Latin American history tends to attract mostly secular progressives and leftists as professors and students. Though I'm politically conservative, I thought I could cater to the heart of the field by writing about people popular with my colleagues.

My plan was to focus on radical politics, with the Catholic faith as a secondary issue. But once I started my research, I found that I was actually in the familiar territory of missions, this time of the Catholic variety. Illich, an Austrian who had become an American citizen, pioneered New York City's

Catholic outreach to Puerto Rican migrants in the 1950s, with great support from Cardinal Francis Joseph Spellman.

This period, the 1950s, was also a time when the Vatican became increasingly worried about Latin America. There simply were not enough priests to minister to the rapidly growing population. To make matters worse, the Protestant and Marxist movements were pulling more and more Catholics from the fold.

A solution, Pope John XXIII became convinced, was to send thousands of priests and religious sisters from the wealthy Church in the United States to help the struggling Church in Latin America. Because of his success working with Puerto Ricans, Ivan Illich was named as the director of one of the main training centers for these American missionaries to Latin America.

Illich, I discovered, hated the idea of sending thousands of Americans to Latin America because he believed that they would preach "the American way of life" rather than the Gospel and would do more harm than good. So he turned his missionary training center into a sort of deprogramming center that would convince the missionaries to go home. By the time the American bishops and the Vatican figured out what Illich was doing, it was too late.

Illich almost singlehandedly derailed the American Catholic missionary initiative in Latin America. The radical secular think tank that had initially brought me into the project, I eventually realized, was just the program he developed to continue spreading his radical ideas when the American bishops and the Vatican were no longer sending him American missionaries.

The entire story about Illich took me years of research to piece together. During that time, I grew increasingly familiar with Catholic thought, partially through reading Illich and his critics, and partially through *First Things* magazine, a journal on faith and politics founded by the late Father Richard John Neuhaus, a Lutheran convert to the Catholic faith. Through Neuhaus and other Catholic writers such as George Weigel, I gained a great appreciation for the Catholic mind.

Over and over again, Catholic writers would present Christian views of contemporary issues such as abortion, marriage, and the public square that resonated with my deepest sense of what was right and true. These writers used reason and the Bible, but they also referred to the teaching of the Church's Magisterium, which I came to respect.

Illich's impact on me was more complex because his writing sometimes resonated with me and sometimes infuriated me. But I could see something of the same deep truth in his work as well. That Illich could reach me was startling, since I disagreed with both his political views and his underhanded sabotage of the missionary initiative.

Telling myself it was still a strictly academic endeavor, I began investigating the Catholic faith in a more general sense. I had read a lot of history, but now I was interested in doctrine and practice. Every night as I did the dishes, I found myself, for instance, listening to a podcast by a Catholic who liked to ask converts to the Catholic Church why they had made the jump.

Then I started listening to *The Journey Home* on EWTN and to the *Catholic Answers* broadcast. Pretty soon, I had to admit to myself that my interest was personal. I still didn't think that the Catholic faith was true, but I began to wish that it was.

In the summer of 2008, I started to investigate the Catholic Church seriously. I emailed a former Methodist pastor and convert whom I had heard on *The Journey Home*, and then met with him a few times. He answered my questions and gave me some good books to read.

I bought the *Catechism of the Catholic Church* and read the sections on all the difficult issues for Protestants. Hardest of all, I told Kathline about my interest in the Catholic faith. She was surprised and made me promise that I would not convert for at least a year.

I began RCIA in the fall and continued to investigate issues such as justification, Mary, infant Baptism, and the sacraments. My conclusion on each issue was the same. After researching an issue, I would decide that the Catholic position was a legitimate interpretation of Scripture, but that it was not the only possible such interpretation.

I liked the Catholic faith enough at this point to be encouraged by this development, but I was also somewhat frustrated. How could I tell what was right? Catholic doctrines were not obviously against the Bible, but how could I finally decide what the Bible really meant?

The key issue, I came to see, was authority. If the pope was who Catholic teaching said he was, and if the Magisterium really did have authority, the Catholic faith is the true form of Christianity. If Peter is not the Rock on which Christ built the Church, and if the Petrine ministry does not continue to this day, then the Catholic Church is just one church among many.

The Coming Home Network's *Deep in History* conference in October 2009, which focused on the issue of authority, seemed designed specifically for me. I entered with anxiety and left with peace in my soul. Talks by two former Baptist converts especially made clear to me that Jesus established the papacy as an ongoing office.

From that point on, I knew that the Catholic Church was the true Church of Christ. I had believed before that Christ had established local churches with hierarchical structures and the powerful ministry of the Holy Spirit. Now I knew that Christ had established one Church, with the Holy Father at the top of a hierarchical structure that is more filled with the Holy Spirit than I ever could have imagined.

The first semester of 2010 was a glorious time for me. I was on sabbatical to finish up my Illich project, which involved thinking about the Catholic faith all day, every day. I especially enjoyed reading the Vatican II documents and the papal encyclicals of Paul VI that applied to Illich's work.

For instance, in *Ad Gentes*, the council document on missions, and *Evangelii Nuntiandi*, Paul VI's letter on missions, I found clear and obvious truth that spoke to the depths of my soul. As I immersed myself in the documents of the Church's Magisterium, I came to a new vision of the beauty of truth. I felt that the Catholic Church gave me a place to stand, a way of viewing the world that was not just one way among many, but *the* true and right way to look at all of life.

An economics professor at EKU was a Catholic economics professor, and we began to study the Vatican II documents together. It became apparent to both of us that these documents were not the minutes of a sort of ecclesiastical committee meeting; rather, they were the key to understanding today's world. In them, the Church has spoken on her own nature, on her relationship to the world, and on the most important issues of the day, and her words give us both the proper perspective on reality and a plan of action.

In the summer of 2010, the year that I had promised my wife was up. I met with an outstanding priest in Berea, Kentucky, to go over some of my final questions. On September 12, I was received into the Catholic Church.

I am very much a work in progress. There is so much that I have to learn and so much that I need to do. I have great joy, though, because I have a place to stand.

My search for the proper divine authority, which led me from liberal Protestant faith to Evangelical Protestant faith and then to charismatic Protestant faith, has finally led me home to the Catholic Church. For my Confirmation name, I took Peter, in honor of the papacy that I honor with all my being. I see my vocation now as bringing truth to the university campus: simple historical truth about Latin America; truth about the human person and human society; and most importantly, truth about our Lord Jesus Christ and His one, holy, Catholic, and apostolic Church.

Todd Hartch, Ph.D., teaches Latin American history at Eastern Kentucky University. He is the author of Missionaries of the State: The Summer Institute of Linguistics, State Formation, and Indigenous Mexico, 1935–1985 *(University of Alabama Press, 2006) and* The Rebirth of Latin American Christianity *(Oxford University Press, 2014).*

Born Fundamentalist,
Born Again Catholic

David Currie

former Fundamentalist missionary

The day President John F. Kennedy was shot is one of my most vivid childhood memories. I was in sixth grade playing on the playground when the rumors started. Just before the dismissal bell at the end of the day, the principal made the announcement over the PA system: JFK had been assassinated.

School was dismissed in eerie silence. Tears welled up in my eyes as I walked the half mile home that afternoon. My sorrow was almost overwhelming for a sixth-grader, not only because our President was dead, but primarily because in my heart of hearts I believed that he was in hell.

He was a Catholic, and I was a Christian Fundamentalist.

I was the second child in a family of four children, the only boy. Since my father was a Fundamentalist preacher, I was what people often called a "PK" (preacher's kid). My parents had met at Houghton College after my mother transferred there from Nyack Bible Institute in New York. They returned to Chicago and were married by A. W. Tozer, a well-known Fundamentalist author who was also their pastor. I was born while my father was attending Dallas Theological Seminary. At various times, both of my parents taught at Moody Bible Institute.

I have fond memories of sitting in church every Sunday listening to my father preach. Through him, I had an education in theology before I ever attended seminary. Every Sunday, we attended church for Sunday school, morning worship, evening worship, and youth group. We also faithfully attended Wednesday prayer meeting and Friday youth group each week. Our entire lives revolved around our church.

The only annual religious celebrations our church observed were Christmas and Easter. Other than those two holidays, I had never even heard of a "church calendar" that recognized the events of the Incarnation every year. We did celebrate certain secular holidays, however, such as Mother's Day.

We were called "Fundamentalists" because we believed in the "fundamentals" of the Christian faith. Fundamentalism as a theological movement had been formulated in reaction to the rise of modernism in Protestant theology around the beginning of the twentieth century. We felt that it was important that we be clear on the inspiration and inerrancy of the Bible, as well as the truths of Christ's divinity, virgin birth, substitutionary atonement, bodily resurrection, and imminent second coming to set up His earthly kingdom. (The last of these beliefs is known as "premillennialism.")

Although we believed that Fundamentalist Christianity predated the Reformation, we still accepted the twin pillars of the Reformation: *sola scriptura* (Scripture alone) and *sola fide* (faith alone).

A person became a Christian, we insisted, by believing that Christ died to pay the penalty of sin, admitting that all his own efforts at heaven were useless, and accepting Christ as his personal Savior. A single prayer was the only prerequisite for a "personal relationship" with God.

On a practical level, being Fundamentalist meant keeping oneself separate from the evils of the world. As such, I did not dance, attend movie theaters or the ballet, use tobacco, drink alcohol, swear, play cards, gamble, or date non-Fundamentalists. (Our Southern counterparts also forbade males and females to swim together.) I was almost thirty when I first stepped into a tavern. When I took my own children to see old Walt Disney reruns, I was seeing the movies for the first time.

The adults around me lived up to these standards, and their example made it easier to live this way. I never detected any of the hypocrisy in my parents that the major media tried to portray within Fundamentalism. My parents taught me that commitment to the truth was always worth any sacrifice.

VIEWS ON THE CATHOLIC FAITH

I was taught always to be polite and neighborly to Catholics and other people we considered to be non-Christians. Yet always we had the desire to see them some day become true believers like us. I was trained in how to turn a friendly conversation into one in which I could share the Gospel. When I was in a social situation and failed to accomplish this goal, I felt a twinge of remorse, or even guilt.

Our worldview divided the world into very neat categories. Fundamentalists were the true Christians like those of the early Church. Liberals questioned the fundamentals of the faith. This group included most non-Fundamentalist Protestants. Liberals might make it to heaven, but it was rather unlikely. It was bad to be a liberal, but it was much worse to be a Roman Catholic.

Catholics were not even Christians, we believed, because they did not understand that salvation was by faith alone. We believed Catholics were going to hell because they tried to earn their salvation by good works rather than trusting only in the finished work of Christ on the cross. No one was good enough to earn salvation. We could prove that from the Bible.

Most converts to Fundamentalism were former Catholics. Although they were not saved, at least Catholics could be convinced from the Bible that they needed to be.

The last category was made up of those people who were total unbelievers. There weren't that many of them around. I met my first atheist during my junior year in high school.

All through history, we believed, God had preserved a remnant of people who protected the truth just as we Fundamentalists did now. It was easy to see that the Roman Catholic Church did not contain these believers. All one had to do was look at their beliefs.

Didn't any Catholics ever read their Bible? We were convinced that so much of what they believed was in direct opposition to God's Word. (I had never actually read any Catholic theology for myself, but nonetheless I was sure that I knew what Catholics believed.) We seldom pondered the many areas of agreement we had with Catholics, such as the divinity of Christ, the virgin birth, and the inspiration of Scripture.

It has been said that few people disagree with what the Church actually teaches, while there are multitudes who disagree with what they mistakenly think she teaches. I fit into the second category, finding offensive many teachings that I thought were Catholic.

I thought it was obvious that Mary had not remained a virgin after Christ's birth, since the Bible mentions the brothers of Jesus. I could see no basis for a belief in the Assumption or the Immaculate Conception. The view of Mary as Coredemptrix and Mediatrix seemed to lower the role of Christ as our sole redeemer and mediator.

Catholic prayers to saints and veneration of images and relics also seemed to impinge on the authority of Christ. The belief that our own works were involved in our salvation seemed to fly in the face of Bible verses I had memorized as a child. How could water Baptism be essential to our regeneration? That seemed too physical, too superstitious, too medieval to be true.

Purgatory flew in the face of Christ's finished work on the cross, as did the sacrifice of the Mass. Everyone knew that indulgences had proved to be so susceptible to manipulation. The idea that a mere man, the pope, could be infallible — well, that idea was hardly worth addressing. Even the few Catholics that I did know did not seem to believe that idea.

The practice of adoring a wafer of bread and chalice of wine seemed to be as foreign to true Christianity as anything of which I could conceive. I would never have addressed any non-relative as "Father," especially a priest who had never married and had children of his own. Why would anyone confess their sins to a mere mortal when they could go directly to God and be forgiven with so much less trouble?

Everyone whom I respected was convinced that the Catholics had inserted books into their Bible to bolster these false beliefs. With their traditions, the Catholic Church belittled scriptural authority.

As is evident, there was very little distinctive to the Catholic faith that I had not been trained to reject. But what made things even worse were lukewarm Catholics. It seemed that Catholics lacked any deep commitment to their beliefs. Was it because they did not undergo adult Baptism?

BAPTISM

In Fundamentalism, babies were never baptized. Baptism was not a sacrament that actually changed someone. Nor did it bestow anything. Baptism was merely an ordinance that we did as adults for one reason: to show our obedience to Christ's command. Since a baby could never do that, it was reserved for teenagers and adults.

I remember being baptized at age fourteen by my father. I publicly announced my faith in Christ, and he baptized me in the name of the Father, and of the Son, and of the Holy Spirit. I was then completely immersed in what I recall was extremely cold water.

In the years leading up to my baptism, I had answered numerous "altar calls." An altar call was frequently given at the end of a service. While singing a hymn, people in the congregation were urged to walk down to the front of the aisle and meet with an elder of the church. The elder would then lead any who came down in prayer to receive Christ as personal Savior.

The catch-22 was this: How did you know whether your faith was strong enough to save you? As a child, I repeatedly would hear the altar call and wonder, "What if I was not really sincere last time?" The best solution was to go down again and make sure. Since faith was all it took to be saved, it was important to be sure that the faith you mustered up was genuine!

It was sometime after becoming Catholic that I realized my baptism had been a turning point. Although it was too subtle to notice at the time, in hindsight I realized that my relationship with God had turned a corner at my baptism. Before it, I had continually wondered if my faith was strong enough, and walked the aisle in an effort to make sure. After my baptism, I had a deep assurance that God was my loving Father. I no longer doubted that He wanted me to go to heaven even more than I did myself.

Without knowing it at the time, I had experienced my first sacrament. God had imprinted my soul with His mark. I was His.

It would take me decades before I would appreciate this truth, but God had given me the grace of faith through a sacrament. I did not totally understand the sacrament (who does?), but I did want to be baptized in accordance with Christ's command. In His grace, God had carried me the rest of the way.

Years later, I was amazed that the Church steadfastly refused to rebaptize me after investigating my initial baptism. As a Fundamentalist, I had seen many Catholics rebaptized when they left the Catholic Church. In seminary, I was taught that rebaptizing Catholic converts was necessary.

SEMINARY

The seminary I attended was Evangelical Protestant. Perhaps I should define terms here. Within a few generations after the emergence of the Fundamentalist movement, many Fundamentalists had adopted for themselves the name "Evangelicals" instead. This "Evangelicalism" became in certain ways theologically broader than Fundamentalism and more accepting of modern culture. Many Evangelicals laid aside the strict Fundamentalist rules against attending the theater, playing cards, and the like.

I met some wonderful professors and fellow students at the seminary. I learned a great deal, but some lessons stuck with me even after I left.

First, my Church history class was taught by a devout Presbyterian. I came away from the course with the distinct impression that the Protestant Reformation was very complex. There were important political forces at play that overshadowed any theological disagreements.

This fracturing of Christianity had continued right down into our own day. I had seen congregations split over "theological issues." But when all the facts came to light, a different story usually emerged. There were political disagreements in these congregations that were at least as important as the theological. There would be two strong-willed men, or two groups of men, that simply chose to split a congregation rather than submit to any authority. Theology was many times the public justification, but certainly not the entire reason.

I also discovered that when Protestants study early Church history, they rarely read the primary sources at length. We read a great many comments about what the early Church Fathers believed. But any actual writings by the Fathers were read in snippets.

I later found what I thought might be a large part of the reason why. When I read the Fathers on my own, I came to have the distinct impression that they were thoroughly sacramental and thoroughly obedient to a hierarchy already existent within the Church. In other words, they were not Protestants, Evangelicals, or Fundamentalists. The early Fathers had been thoroughly Catholic.

I found the theological terrain within Evangelicalism to be in crisis. During college, I had majored in philosophy. I had come to the point where I no longer considered myself a Fundamentalist. The rigidity of its theology and the lack of charity were exhibited most clearly in its doctrine of "separation." But overall, I had just come to disagree with too much that Fundamentalists held important.

In seminary, however, I found that Evangelicalism was "all over the map." There were disagreements about everything, even within the seminary itself. Some of the matters of disagreement were perhaps understandable: predestination, premillennialism, the ordinances of the church. But other issues seemed to be basic enough that there should have been some semblance of consistency. There was not.

The most disturbing disagreements centered on the many Bible passages that had no plausible "Protestant" explanation. I had tucked some of them in the back of my mind before seminary. I was sure I would discover the answers to these passages. But rather than finding them answered, I found myself with a longer and longer list as I progressed through my training.

I was surrounded by the brightest and best that Evangelicalism had to offer. My professors came from many different Protestant traditions. But none of them had a satisfying interpretation of these passages — even though these verses were in the one Book that they all agreed contained all they needed for salvation.

SUFFERING

Perhaps two examples might be helpful to illustrate this dilemma.

First, how an all-loving and all-powerful God can allow human suffering has been a topic of discussion since long before the biblical Job suffered. As a college philosophy major, I read *The Problem of Pain* by C. S. Lewis for the first time. It made tremendous sense to me.

Lewis' major point is that suffering is not random. Suffering helps a Christian grow even when no one else knows about it. Suffering teaches unqualified obedience. This perspective made a tremendous amount of sense, but unfortunately it is incomplete when compared with Scripture.

I remember once sitting in our living room with the president of Dallas Theological Seminary when I was a teenager. I had a question. How would he reconcile Colossians 1:24 with the idea of salvation by faith alone? St. Paul had written to the Colossians: "Now I rejoice in what was suffered for you, and I fill up in my flesh what is still lacking in regard to Christ's afflictions, for the sake of his body, which is the church" (New International Version).

Paul's perspective on suffering was much more comprehensive than C. S. Lewis' ideas. Paul attributed salvific merit to his own suffering, even for others. His perspective in this passage was not that people could be saved by "faith alone." Somehow Paul assumed that the Colossians knew that faith must be perfected through suffering — dare I say, through works. He did not justify his statement as though it were a novel idea. He just stated it and moved on, as though no knowledgeable Colossian Christian would have had any doubt about his statement.

I was surprised that the learned, holy, Fundamentalist president of Dallas Theological Seminary had no good way to reconcile this verse in Colossians with his soteriology (theology of salvation). But I could tell that he had obviously thought about it a great deal. Later in seminary, I encountered this phenomenon repeatedly. Verses existed that could not be reconciled with any Protestant tradition by any of the professors I encountered. But it seemed to me that if some of Scripture directly contradicted my theology, it was my responsibility to rethink the theology, not the Bible.

Suffering and its role in salvation did not make sense to me until, long after seminary, I discovered the writings of Pope John Paul II. Somehow I got on a mailing list for a Catholic publisher. I was scandalized that they had somehow obtained my name. But I love books, so I stayed on the list.

One day I saw a book in that publisher's catalog that had organized topically the thinking of Pope John Paul II. The Pope had been so influential in the liberation of Europe that I thought I should read some of what he had to say. It was my first direct encounter with a faithful Catholic author.

The Pope made clear that suffering is not enjoyable. But he insisted that it is essential to salvation. This thoroughly Catholic concept not only makes sense of the verse in Colossians; it infuses suffering with dignity. This was the beginning of my discovery that Catholic literature plumbed a depth of spirituality I had never even dreamed was available in print.

In some mysterious way, Pope John Paul taught, our suffering can even help in the process of other people's salvation. Perhaps I should let him speak for himself:

> In the Paschal Mystery Christ began *the union with man in the community of the Church....* The Church is continually being built up spiritually as the Body of Christ. In this Body, Christ wishes to be united with every individual, and in a special way He is united with those who suffer.... The sufferings of Christ created the good of the world's Redemption. This good in itself is inexhaustible and infinite. No man can add anything to it. But at the same time, in the mystery of the Church as His Body, Christ has in a sense opened His own redemptive suffering to all human suffering. In so far as man becomes a

sharer in Christ's sufferings ... to that extent *he in his own way completes* the suffering through which Christ accomplished the Redemption of the world. Does this mean that the Redemption achieved by Christ is not complete? No ... Christ achieved the Redemption completely and to the very limit, but at the same time He did not bring it to a close.... It seems to be part *of the very essence of Christ's redemptive suffering* that this suffering requires to be unceasingly completed. (*Salvifici Doloris*, no. 24; emphasis in the original)

Suffering's role in our salvation is clearly taught in Scripture. I found no good explanation for this fact until I embraced the ancient faith of the Catholic Church.

THE "END TIMES"

The biblical truth about suffering was only one of many truths I encountered that pressed me to explore Catholic teaching. I came to the firm conclusion that the best way to understand the Bible was to listen to the Catholic Church. Even so, a second example might be helpful.

I had always believed in a version of premillennialism that teaches Christ will return very soon to set up a thousand-year reign in Jerusalem with the Jews. Most American premillennialists also believe this scenario entails a "rapture" that will take "true believers" out of the world. This "rapture" will allow a seven-year "Great Tribulation" that punishes unbelievers and prepares the world for Christ's second coming.

You may have heard of Christians who are striving to rebuild the Jerusalem temple, or seeking to breed the pure red heifer whose ashes, once sacrificed and burned, they believe are necessary to consecrate the temple site (see Numbers 19:1–10). These people are premillennialists.

While in seminary, I pondered how to reconcile Christ's finished work on the cross with any resumption of the Old Covenant animal sacrifices. The Book of Hebrews, for example, teaches that the old cult is no longer necessary and must pass away.

For me, the hardest biblical passage related to this discussion was found in Zechariah. I remember standing in a hallway with a man whose specialty was general eschatology (study of the "end times"). A young man approached us and asked this respected teacher about this verse. His question was this: "If Jesus' sacrifice is final and complete, why will there be sacrifices needed in Jerusalem after the death and resurrection of Jesus?"

The scholar's face momentarily clouded with annoyance. I have never forgotten his next statement. He admitted that he knew of no plausible Evangelical explanation for these two verses.

Zechariah 14:20–21 states prophetically: "On that day ... the cooking pots in the Lord's house will be like the bowls before the altar. Every cooking pot in Jerusalem and in Judah will be holy to the Lord of hosts; and all who come to sacrifice [in Jerusalem] will take some of the pots and cook in them" (NIV). Most premillennialists agree that this passage is speaking of a time after Christ's first coming. Why is it so problematic for them? Because they understand these events to occur during the thousand-year reign of Christ over an earthly kingdom with its capital at Jerusalem.

Here's the rub. After Christ has died and set up His kingdom, why would sacrifices be resumed? There is absolutely no good Protestant response to that question. Evangelicals are adamant about the fact that priesthood here on earth is no longer needed. Sacrifices after the passion of Christ are unnecessary. The crucifixion of Christ was the last sacrifice ever needed. So why rebuild Jerusalem's temple?

This verse had remained an enigma to me for sixteen years, ever since seminary. When I was investigating Catholic Church teaching, I realized that Zechariah was actually talking about a sacrifice offered in Jerusalem every day *now*. He was referring to the Eucharist!

The Eucharist is the only sacrifice that would have any value after the Messiah's passion because of its connection to the passion. The sacrifice of the Mass is being offered every day in Catholic churches, not only in Jerusalem, but all over the world. In other words, the continuing sacrifices of the Church were foretold in the Old Testament. When this reality dawned on me, I got so excited I ran into our living room and gave a "high five" to my thirteen-year-old son.

CRISIS AND RECONCILIATION

We all reach certain critical decision points in our Christian pilgrimage. God gives us a choice: to follow or not to follow. These crisis points are never easy. They always involve sacrifice and suffering. And they are always an occasion of grace.

At the rather late age of forty, I knew that I had approached one of these crisis points. I had been studying Scripture all my life. By this time, I had spent the previous months studying Catholic teaching in relation to Scripture. I had desperately attempted to find a reason not to become Catholic.

I knew my family would lose friends. I knew my wife and children would have to start all over again in a new social circle. I knew that once I "went public" with these convictions, life could never again be the same. I hesitated, wondering if this was the right thing to do.

One day I woke up and knew something for certain. I turned to my wife and said, "Colleen, I know that I believe." We had been investigating and discussing so much that I did not even need to tell her what I believed. After months of study and discussion, she knew that I was referring to the Eucharist.

I believed it really was Christ's Body, Blood, Soul, and Divinity. This faith was a gift from God.

It was not a bolt out of the blue. I had spent months trying to justify to myself what I had always believed: the Protestant interpretation of John 6. Jesus had said, "I am the living bread which came down from heaven; if any one eats of this bread, he will live forever; and *the bread which I shall give for the life of the world is my flesh*" (v. 51, emphasis added).

After studying this text from a Catholic perspective, I knew in my head that the Church was right. John 6 clearly taught that the Body of Christ was the sustenance that I needed for eternity. Zechariah had predicted it. Jesus had instituted it. And only one Church in town taught this truth as Jesus stated it: the Catholic parish five blocks from my house.

But that morning was different. That morning I woke up with the firm conviction in the center of my soul that the Church was correct about the Eucharist. I was certain of this divine truth. This grace was not a gift that I deserved. I do not know why I was singled out to receive it. Someone was obviously offering up prayers and sufferings for my enlightenment.

At this point, God showed me that He had already given me another great gift: my beloved wife. At that crisis point, she simply said, "David, if that is what you believe, then you need to follow your beliefs and join the Church."

Several months later, through another grace of God, I was reconciled to the Catholic Church: not alone, but together with my wife and all six of our children. That was over twenty years ago. Since then, God has blessed us with two more children.

I can honestly say that reconciling with the Church is the best thing our family has ever done. This Church is a wonderful place to raise a family and to travel on our pilgrimage to heaven. In fact, it is the only place God ever intended for us.

David B. Currie is the author of three bestselling books. Born Fundamentalist, Born Again Catholic; Rapture: The End-Times Error that Leaves the Bible Behind; *and* What Jesus Really Said about the End of the World. *David graduated from Holy Apostles Seminary (M.A. Theology) and is a research fellow with the St. Paul Center for Biblical Theology in Steubenville, Ohio. He and his wife, Colleen, have eight children and ten grandchildren.*

I Have Come Home

Dr. Janice Lockwood
former Orthodox Jew and Evangelical

I was born into an ultra-Orthodox Jewish home in Wimbledon, a suburb of London, England, just after World War II. My parents shocked the Jewish community by conning an old priest into baptizing me one July Sunday into the Catholic Church. It happened when I was just eight weeks old.

My dad had been interned in Auschwitz during the latter part of World War II. Should the Nazi menace raise its ugly head again, Mom and Dad could readily deny their Jewishness: After all, they'd had me baptized, hadn't they?

Following my baptism, no one in the family gave even a thought to attending church ever again. Our lives were always centered on the synagogue, where my maternal grandfather was the cantor rabbi.

Yet even though we virtually forgot all about that baptism, God still had His eye on me. In 1961, I was admitted to a local Catholic hospital as an emergency patient. In the bed next to mine was a thirty-year-old Maltese nun. Sister Helen, like me, had appendicitis; we were sick in unison!

Now and again I could hear her speaking quietly, yet there seemed to be no one around. Maybe, I thought, she was some sort of a nut, talking to herself!

"I am praying," she told me, a smile across her face. "I am praying to Jesus Christ."

By 1962, I had discovered Him for myself.

My math teacher, a Protestant and an active member at London's Westminster Chapel, invited me to attend a service one Sunday. Why she'd singled me out from the other students at my school, I had no idea. I was undecided about taking her up on the offer, so I thought I'd talk it over with my family.

"Have you taken leave of your senses?" asked my mother. "Listen! You're a good Jewish girl. Don't get involved, Janice, with this teacher. Why does she want you to go there, anyway, huh?"

I shrugged.

"Well, your father and I don't want you to go to that church."

My dad looked surprised to be involved, for he hadn't uttered a word.

My mother continued as the spokesperson. "We don't want you to go. In fact, you're not going, and that's the end of the matter. Right? Now, we don't want to hear another word."

So I went.

When I arrived, I was filled with a momentary wave of dismay: I hadn't realized the invitation was to a full day's program! After the two-hour morning service and then lunch, I joined my host and some other women for a Bible study.

They all seemed so old to me, for they were definitely all over thirty. Cups of tea and dainty little sandwiches followed. A prayer meeting led up to the evening service, which was as lengthy as the morning service. I was so glad to return to my Wimbledon home!

When I came through the door, Dad peered at me over his *Sunday Times*. He was a man of temperate, even indifferent, belief himself. On the whole, he enjoyed synagogue life, for he'd grown up in it.

"Well, Janice," he said, "I bet you hated the day, eh?"

Gathering myself into a puffed-up importance, I stood bolt upright. Not prepared to admit defeat, I declared: "No. It was great, and I'm going again next week!"

BECOMING A CHRISTIAN

I repeated the morning services, lunches, Bible studies, teas, and evening services Sunday after Sunday. My parents believed I was going only out of rebellion. But my math teacher was encouraged and purchased a Bible for me.

I delved into it, beginning in St. John's Gospel. I also began to read a book about the conversion of John Wesley, the eighteenth-century English founder of the Methodist movement.

Just as I had unwillingly spent an entire day at Westminster Chapel, John Wesley had unwillingly gone to a society in London's Aldersgate Street, where someone was preaching from Martin Luther's preface to the Epistle to the Romans. About a quarter to nine in the morning, while the preacher was describing the change that God works in the heart through faith in Christ, Wesley felt his heart "strangely warmed." John Wesley trusted in Christ. Christ had taken away his sins, he believed, and saved him from the law of sin and death.

What happened to Wesley inspired a longing within me and made me pray with all my might that Christ would come into my life, to "strangely warm" my heart. At 7:22 p.m. on August 22, 1962, He did just that, I believed, for me.

This event took place at Westminster Chapel, London, through the ministry of the well-known preacher and author, Dr. D. Martin Lloyd-Jones. He held strongly Calvinistic positions. Adopting his anti-Catholic doctrines, I was again baptized, this time by total immersion at South Wimbledon Baptist Church in the cold February of 1963.

My parents saw this form of Baptism as an abandonment of my Jewish heritage. Following the ancient Jewish custom of families whose children leave the faith, they refused to allow me into the family home. They observed the traditional rituals surrounding the loss of a loved one: They rent their garments, with buttons popping and dropping to the floor, and a year later, they erected a headstone for me in the Jewish cemetery.

In their eyes, I was dead.

Only seventeen, I was worried about where I would live. But various Christians opened their homes to me, allowing me to complete my education.

Having handed over my life to the Lord, I constantly delved into Scripture, seeking His will for my life. Looking back now, I can declare confidently that all the way my Savior led me.

Believing He was calling me into full-time Christian service, I pursued the rocky path to become a medical missionary. After study at London University and London Bible College, I served in western and southern India, caring for lepers and their babies. Furlough came after four years.

Once home again, I married. I'd met a Methodist minister who preached mostly in West Yorkshire, northern England. Two beautiful sons, Paul and Stephen, were born. Eleven years later, joy of joys, Matthew yelled his way into the world.

During Paul and Stephen's growing-up years, I returned to London University to complete my Ph.D. in theology. The only good school available for them was a private one in Yorkshire run by Catholics. That worried me, for I certainly did not wish the boys to be influenced by their religious teachings.

I made it clear, abundantly clear, to the Catholic staff that neither my husband nor I wished the boys to attend the school assemblies when their parish priest led them. After all, we did not want Catholic teaching brought into our home and their hearts! Our vulnerable boys would get a good all-round education there, but any Christian teachings would be given to them at home and at our chapel. I was still very much the anti-Catholic Calvinist, and I was not slow in making it known.

WEARINESS AND ILLNESS

In the year 2000, however, my life took a whole new turn. I had been busy lecturing in theology in the U.K. and also in Ohio. In the midst of my busyness, I found myself perpetually tired, as if I were always walking through molasses.

I was running a large home as a minister's wife, raising the kids, public speaking, and much more. Even so, the intense weariness I was experiencing was more than something that could be shaken off by a few nights of good sleep. I was convinced I was sick, but the nature of the sickness was enigmatic.

My husband, optimistic as usual, refused to believe I could be so unwell. He decided we should fly to Malta for a relaxing vacation in the sun.

"You've been working unbelievably hard, Janice," Eric said. "Get some Mediterranean sun, and I'm sure you'll feel heaps better. I'm convinced of it. You'll be fine."

"Okay," I said. "Remember the nun I told you about?"

Eric thought for a moment. "A nun?" he asked. "I don't think so." Then suddenly his memory was sparked, and he nodded. "Oh, yes. What about her?"

"Well, Sister lives in Malta now and ..."

"... and you'd like to look her up?"

I felt quite excited about meeting with her again after so long.

Eric wondered why I was so excited about seeing a Catholic nun. Yet he did not oppose me — nor did he encourage me to show any keen interest in her faith. He just shook his head, for we were then still very much against the Catholic faith, or what we thought it was.

During the vacation, I discovered that my weariness became worse. By the end of the trip, I could no longer walk unaided. I also choked throughout the mealtimes, a development that I found more than a little embarrassing. Looking in the mirror, I noticed that my eyelids seemed heavy, and I could not physically lift them to stop them from drooping.

"I'm seeing double," I told Eric, who was now quite worried for me. "Maybe I need my eyes to be tested again."

Back home again, I contacted an eminent consultant neurologist at the Walton Hospital in Liverpool. He was convinced I had a disease known as Myasthenia Gravis. I began a six-year course of aggressive treatments, which made me very sick.

When I did not improve, further tests were performed. A DNA test showed I had never had Myasthenia Gravis, but rather a degenerative condition that was even more rare, and for which there was no known treatment: Oculopharyngeal Muscular Dystrophy (OPMD). I was shocked, especially when I was told I'd soon become much worse.

With a low immune system now, too, I became virtually housebound. Too tired to do much more than sit around and listen to music or watch television, I became an avid viewer of EWTN.

Moving Toward the Catholic Church

I began to watch *The Journey Home* every Tuesday night. I found it fascinating to hear guests share their conversion stories, describing their personal obstacles, doctrinal objections, and attraction to the Catholic Church. I was lapping up every word, yet at the same time I was confused.

I needed to know how it was that these Catholic converts had a personal relationship with Christ. How could this be if they were Catholic? One Tuesday, when some converts from Pentecostalism were testifying, I beckoned to my husband.

"Come and look at this program, Eric," I called. "These people are Catholic and ..."

He shrugged. "Sure, there are born-again Catholics in the Catholic Church. But, as well you know, the Catholic Church itself, with all the worship of Mary and ..."

"I'm not so sure anymore," I interrupted. "Maybe the Catholic Church, as they are saying, is the one true Church. I dunno."

Eric tightened his lips and sighed. "You've been watching too much EWTN," he stated, then walked back into the living room.

I think it was the next morning when my telephone rang. It was Sister Helen phoning from Malta.

"Hello, darling," she began. "I've just had a thought. Why don't you contact a local priest and ask him to pray about your illness — ask him to anoint you?"

Protestant friends had already surrounded me. They strongly believed that our great and wonderful God, who "is able to do far more abundantly than all we ask or think" (Eph 3:20), could heal me. Quoting Isaiah 53:5, "With his stripes we are healed," they believed these words to be an unconditional promise to all those who believe.

Nevertheless, it appeared that the Lord wasn't intervening in the way they would have liked. They blamed me for not having enough faith after they'd anointed me with some cooking oil. They also had the same attitude toward my husband, who had been diagnosed with prostate cancer and was growing worse. When they told him that he did not have a good enough faith, he replied with a quote from St. Paul: "Trophimus I left ill at Miletus" (2 Tim 4:20).

Sister Helen told me not to allow myself to be judged in such a way. "Let God be God," she told me. "Anyway, it can't do any harm to contact a Catholic priest."

I decided to put pen to paper to the priest, explaining to him from beginning to end about our circumstances, a little of my background, along with a preamble concerning my OPMD. It was difficult to scribe, not only because I was seeing double, but also because my hands were affected. I found it difficult to make a fist or hold a pen.

I folded the lengthy epistle and placed it in an envelope. Eric said he would mail it to Father Jones, for he'd found the priest's address.

Eric made for the door, but suddenly I had second thoughts. I shouted to him to bring it back, but he didn't hear and made off to the mailbox.

In response to my correspondence, the very next day a tall, handsome, white-haired man in his sixties stood in the open doorway of our apartment, a broad smile across his friendly face.

"Hello," he said. "I am Father Jones. I got your letter. Sorry you're so unwell with this unusual illness. You'd like me to anoint you?"

"Well, yes, please. I need to tell you, though, that I'm not Catholic. In fact, I've not been all that nice in the past about your church. You'd be shocked if I told you how nasty I'd been."

He responded only with raised eyebrows. He stood over me, praying and quoting from James 5:14–15:

> Is any one among you sick? Let him call for the elders of the Church, and let them pray over him, anointing him with oil in the name of the Lord; and the prayer of faith will save the sick man, and the Lord will raise him up; and if he has committed sins, he will be forgiven.

He anointed me with an oil duly blessed by the bishop. Before he could say any more, I told him that I believed our heavenly Father could heal me in the blinking of an eye.

Father Jones smiled and nodded. "Of course!" he exclaimed, sitting back down on our couch, as if to wait for my reactions. To break the silence, it was then that I told him I had been baptized in the Catholic Church when I was a baby.

"Where was this?" he asked, a frown across his brow.

"Wimbledon. I was brought up near Wimbledon Common." I told him the full story.

The priest leaned forward, his elbows on his knees, his hands clasped. "Well, Janice, that baptism actually makes you a Catholic," he stated. "You're a Roman Catholic!"

Astounded, I found myself repeating: "Oh, wow! Oh, wow!" I babbled on. "Hey! That's really something, huh?" He chuckled at my response.

I surprised myself, for I'd always been so very anti-Catholic, believing the Church of Rome to be the Antichrist. But here I was excited to be told such news.

"Now listen, Janice. If you really want to go ahead, give me a phone call. Think carefully, very carefully, for it's a big step, especially for someone like you."

Before I telephoned the priest to confirm my decision, I thought it wise to talk it over with Eric. I didn't want to upset him, for he had just been told his prostate cancer had spread to his bones. We thought his old cancer had been contained, yet it distressed us to know his poor prognosis.

Looking at him straight in the eye, I asked him, "Eric, what would you think if I became Catholic? How'd you react, huh?"

"Frankly, I thought something like this would happen," he replied. "I'm not surprised, not one bit, what with the Coming Home Network, the Maltese nun, and now the priest. So what's going to happen to my Calvinistic wife, she seeing the Roman Church as the Antichrist, eh?"

"I was watching *The Journey Home*, and they stated that folk came to the Catholic Church only because of their great love for Christ. I have a great love for Him, too. I have to go ahead with it now."

I telephoned Father Jones. "Yes, please," I said, "I really want to go ahead to become a Catholic. When shall you confirm me?"

MARY'S ASSISTANCE

During this time, a religious sister in my parish, told me that the Blessed Virgin Mary's intercession is very powerful. So I put this claim to the test. My husband was no longer eating because his prostate cancer had worsened. Always slender, Eric had now become really skinny.

That night I prayed to Our Blessed Lady. I pleaded with Mary to help Eric eat, even just for one day — to have a breakfast the following morning. I told Eric nothing of my prayer to the Mother of God.

When Eric woke up next day, he said: "I'm so hungry, Janice. Do we have any bacon?"

I stared at him like a cow at a new gate! Mary's power was something I had needed to discover for myself, not as second-hand knowledge.

I told Eric about my prayer. But like most Protestants of his background, even if our loving, heavenly Father had come down and told him about Our Lady, he could only say, "Are you kidding?"

Meanwhile, an appointment had been sent to me from the Walton Hospital in Liverpool. Although there's no treatment, only management, for OPMD, the senior neurologist planned on keeping a close eye on how I was coping with my condition.

Since I was unable now to walk by myself, one of the nursing staff helped me into the neurologist's consulting room. She sat me facing this soft-spoken Scot, whose reading glasses were on the top of his head, hiding the shock of his dark brown hair.

"My, you look different!" he exclaimed. "What have you done to yourself?"

I shrugged. "What do you mean?"

"You've changed your hairstyle."

"Nope. Same as ever."

"I know what it is. You've different glasses. I might be a man, but I notice
these things!"

I shook my head.

"You've had a nip 'n' tuck under your eyebrows without telling me. What did it cost you?"

A second time I shook my head.

"Okay, I give in. Tell me."

I didn't know what he was getting at until he tested my vision and discovered I was no longer seeing double. I still required my glasses, but with them I was seeing well.

"What exactly has happened to you? With this degenerative condition you should be worse, not better."

I gave a burst of rather weak laughter. "My eyelids are still drooped," I reminded him.

"Dr. Lockwood, I have been a consultant neurologist in this hospital for a number of years, and I'm no fool."

"A Roman Catholic priest anointed both my forehead and my hands," I said. I began explaining that, since then, I was no longer seeing double. "If I'm really tired — I mean, very weary indeed — I do occasionally see a little bit of blur. Yet not at all often."

The neurologist sighed and listened patiently. Although a confessed atheist, this scientist did not challenge my Evangelical standpoint. When I showed him my hands, how my fingers, with the exception of the little finger on my left hand, were normal, how I could rapidly make a fist without pain, he only paused my explanation to say, "Well, I never!"

He asked me to explain about why I'd named my little finger my "Jacob's hip." I told him the biblical story of Jacob, and how, when he wrestled God, God touched his hip. Ever after, Jacob was left with a limp as a reminder of his encounter with the Lord (see Gen 32:24–32).

"So, you see, my crooked little finger is a constant reminder of what the other seven fingers and two thumbs were like before the priest anointed me with oil!"

The consultant neurologist replied that my beliefs could never see their way into his life. Even so, he was gracious enough to worm his way out of the situation by saying, "He must be a very special priest."

Since that time, my medical condition has remained remarkably good, considering the typical consequences of OPMD. Though I haven't been fully cured, I know that God has shown Himself gracious to me, and He holds me in His hands.

HOME AT LAST

The day I'd waited for, longed for, since the first afternoon I had encountered my priest, finally arrived. I was becoming a Catholic. For this Protestant, it was a miracle! I believed I had truly "come home" because of God's great love for me, because of mine for Him.

In 1961, I discovered just who Jesus is. A year later I asked Him to come into my life, to become my Savior and Lord, loving Him, loving His Word. No turning back! Then in 2007, I was confirmed a Catholic, deep in faith, deep in Scripture, deep in the Magisterium. And I loved it — every nanosecond.

Following my Confirmation, I telephoned the Coming Home Network International and declared: "I'm a Catholic!"

My husband bought me a surprise gift for the occasion. He purchased The CTS New Catholic Bible, wrapped it in pretty paper, and wrote inside: "Presented to my beloved wife, Janice, by her loving husband, Eric. 'The God of all grace who called you to the eternal glory in Christ will see that all is well again; he will confirm, strengthen, and support you. His power lasts for ever and ever. Amen'" (1 Pet 5:10–11).

Eric, weighing only eighty-four pounds, struggled on for another eleven months, battling hard against his prostate cancer, which had spread to his boney chest wall, his pelvis, and his legs. Soon he was unable to swallow much more than liquids, and his pain was way out of control. We tried to care for him well at home, but he begged to be admitted to a nearby hospice.

Always declaring he had lived as a Protestant, he would die an Evangelical Methodist. Yet he amazed me by asking: "Do you think Father Jones would visit me, Janice? I'd like him to anoint me." Father Jones made a number of visits, anointing him on more than one occasion.

In October 2008, Father Jones sat with Eric, having anointed him again. "Would you hear my confession, Father?" Eric asked. "Bless me Father …" he began, with tears streaming down his thin face.

My priest then sat with him for about an hour, helping this frail man to write a note to Matthew and me, telling us how much he loved us.

A few days later, Eric left behind a communication stating he truly wished he'd become a Catholic. Then he slipped away to be with his Lord — the Lord he had loved and served for over fifty years from Japan to the U.K., always as preacher and evangelist.

In the following days, I was thrilled to be Catholic. In the past, I'd rarely found it difficult to take a stand as a Christian, but now I was somewhat apprehensive about telling those truly hardened Evangelical friends that I had come home to the Catholic Church. Was I to be in for a tough time? How would I cope?

Then one evening I turned on *The Journey Home*. The guest was a former missionary to China and well-known evangelical author. Listening to her story, I realized that if this gracious person, with her Evangelical Protestant background, could take a stand, then so could I. As a result, twelve of my Protestant friends also came home, and in turn, they witnessed to their friends and relatives, too. The effect has snowballed!

So I thank God for her witness, for unknowingly giving me courage to spread the word, to tell others of how, when I asked God for pure gold, He gave me the Catholic faith.

Janice Lockwood, Ph.D., was born into an ultra-Orthodox Jewish home in England and became a Christian as a teenager. She served for four years as a medical missionary, working with leprosy patients in India. After returning home, she married a Methodist pastor, earned a Ph.D. in theology, and became a lecturer and speaker in the U.K. and the U.S. She entered the Catholic Church in 2007. Recently widowed, Janice lives in North Wales, where she attends the Catholic Church in Llandudno. She is the author of Costly Roots *(under the pseudonym Sarah Cohen).*

A PROTESTANT HISTORIAN DISCOVERS THE CATHOLIC CHURCH

DR. DAVID ANDERS

former Evangelical professor

I grew up an Evangelical Protestant in Birmingham, Alabama. My parents were loving and devoted, sincere in their faith, and deeply involved in our church. They instilled in me a respect for the Bible as the Word of God, and a desire for a living faith in Christ. Missionaries frequented our home and brought their enthusiasm for their work. Bookshelves in our house were filled with theology and apologetics. From an early age, I absorbed the notion that the highest possible calling was to teach the Christian faith. I suppose it is no surprise that I became a Church historian, but becoming a Catholic was the last thing I expected.

My family's church was nominally Presbyterian, but denominational differences meant very little to us. I frequently heard that disagreements over Baptism, the Lord's Supper, or church government were unimportant as long as one believed the Gospel. By this, we meant that one should be "born again," that salvation is by faith alone, and that the Bible is the sole authority for Christian faith. Our church supported the ministries of many different Protestant denominations, but the one group we certainly opposed was the Catholic Church.

The myth of a Protestant "recovery" of the Gospel was strong in our church. I learned very early to idolize the Protestant Reformers Martin Luther and John Calvin, because they supposedly had rescued Christianity from the darkness of medieval Catholicism. Catholics were those who trusted in "good works" to get them to heaven, who yielded to tradition instead of Scripture, and who worshipped Mary and the saints instead of God. Their obsession with the sacraments also created an enormous impediment to true faith and a personal relationship with Jesus. There was no doubt. Catholics were not real Christians.

Our church was characterized by a kind of confident intellectualism. Presbyterians tend to be quite theologically minded, and seminary professors, apologists, scientists, and philosophers were frequent speakers at our conferences. It was this intellectual atmosphere that had attracted my father to the church, and his bookshelves were lined with the works of the Reformer John Calvin, and the Puritan Jonathan Edwards, as well as more recent authors like B. B. Warfield, A. A. Hodge, C. S. Lewis, and Francis Schaeffer. As a part of this academic culture, we took it for granted that honest inquiry would lead anyone to our version of Christian faith.

All of these influences left definite impressions on me as a child. I came to see Christianity as somewhat akin to Newtonian physics. The Christian faith consisted in certain eminently reasonable and immutable laws, and you were guaranteed eternal life provided you constructed your life according to these principles. I also thought this was the message clearly spelled out in the official textbook of Christian theology: the Bible. Only mindless trust in human tradition or depraved indifference could possibly explain anyone's failure to grasp these simple truths.

There was one strange irony in this highly religious and theological atmosphere. We stressed that it was faith and not works that saves. We also confessed the classic Protestant belief that all people are "totally depraved," meaning that even their best moral efforts are intrinsically hateful to God and can merit nothing. By the time I reached high school, I put these pieces together and concluded that religious practice and moral striving were more or less irrelevant to my life. It was not that I lost my faith. On the contrary, I absorbed it thoroughly. I had accepted Christ as my Savior and been "born again." I believed that the Bible was the Word of God. I also believed none of my religious or moral works had any value. So I quit practicing them.

Fortunately, my indifference lasted only a few years, and I had a genuine reconversion to the faith in college. I found that my need for God was deeper than simple "fire insurance." I also met a beautiful girl with whom I started going to Protestant services. Jill had grown up nominally Catholic, but failed to keep up the practice of her faith after Confirmation. Together, we found ourselves growing deeper in our Protestant faith, and after a few months, we both became disillusioned with the worldly atmosphere of our New Orleans University. We concluded that the Midwestern and Evangelical Wheaton College would provide a more spiritual environment, and we both transferred in the middle of our sophomore year (January 1991).

Wheaton College is a beacon for sincere Evangelical Christians of various backgrounds. Protestants from many different denominations are represented, united in their commitment to Christ and the Bible. My childhood had taught me that theology, apologetics, and evangelism were the highest calling of a Christian, and I found them all in plentiful supply at Wheaton. It was there that I first thought of committing my life to the study of theology. It was also at Wheaton that Jill and I became engaged.

After graduating, Jill and I were married and eventually found our way to Trinity Evangelical Divinity School in Chicago. My goal was to get a seminary education, and then eventually to complete a Ph.D. I wanted to become one of those theology professors who had been so admired in the church of my youth.

I threw myself into seminary with abandon. I loved my courses in theology, Scripture, and Church history, and I thrived on the faith, confidence, and sense of mission that pervaded the school. I also embraced its anti-Catholic atmosphere. I was there in 1994 when the document "Evangelicals and Catholics Together" was first published, and the faculty was almost uniformly hostile to it. They saw any compromise with Catholics as a betrayal of the Reformation. Catholics were simply not brothers in the Lord. They were apostates.

I accepted the anti-Catholic attitudes of my seminary professors, so when it came time to move on in my studies, I decided to focus on a historical study of the Reformation. I thought there could be no better preparation for assaulting the Catholic Church and winning converts than to thoroughly understand the minds of the great leaders of our faith — Martin Luther and John Calvin. I also wanted to understand the whole history of Christianity, so I could place the Reformation in context. I wanted to be able to show how the medieval church had left the true faith and how the Reformers had recovered it. To this end, I began Ph.D. studies in historical theology at the University of Iowa. I never imagined that Reformation Church history would move me to the Catholic Church.

Before I began my studies in Iowa, Jill and I witnessed the birth of our first child, a son. His brother was born less than two years later, and a sister arrived before we left Iowa (we now have five children). My wife was very busy caring for these children, while I committed myself almost entirely to my studies. I see today that I spent too much time in the library and not enough time with my wife, my infant sons, and my daughter. I think that I justified this neglect by relying on my sense of mission. I had a high calling — to witness to the faith through theological study — and an intellectual view of the Christian faith and my Christian duty. For Evangelical Christians, what one *believes* is more important than how one *lives*. I was learning how to defend and promote those beliefs. What could be more important?

I began my Ph.D. studies in September of 1995. I took courses in early, medieval, and Reformation Church history. I read the Church Fathers, the Scholastic theologians, and the Protestant Reformers. At each stage, I tried to relate later theologians to earlier ones, and all of them to the Scriptures. I had a goal of justifying the Reformation, and this meant, above all, investigating the doctrine of "justification by faith alone." For Protestants, this is the most important doctrine to be "recovered" by the Reformation.

The Reformers had insisted that they were following the ancient Church in teaching "faith alone," and for proof they pointed to the writings of the Church Father Augustine of Hippo (354–430). My seminary professors also pointed to Augustine as the original wellspring of Protestant theology. The reason for this was Augustine's keen interest in the doctrines of original sin, grace, and justification. He was the first of the Fathers to attempt a systematic explication of these Pauline themes. He also drew a sharp contrast between "works" and "faith" (see his *On the Spirit and the Letter*, 412 AD). Ironically, it was my investigation of this doctrine and of St. Augustine that began my journey to the Catholic Church.

My first difficulty arose when I began to grasp what Augustine really taught about salvation. Briefly put, Augustine rejected "faith alone." It is true that he had a high regard for faith and grace, but he saw these mainly as the source of our good works. Augustine taught that we literally "merit" eternal life when our lives are transformed by grace. This is quite different from the Protestant point of view.

The implications of my discovery were profound. I knew enough from my college and seminary days to understand that

Augustine was teaching nothing less than the Roman Catholic doctrine of justification. I decided to move on to earlier Church Fathers in my search for the "pure faith" of Christian antiquity. Unfortunately, the earlier Church Fathers were even less help than Augustine.

Augustine had come from Latin-speaking North Africa. Others hailed from Asia Minor, Palestine, Syria, Rome, Gaul, and Egypt. They represented different cultures, spoke different languages, and were associated with different Apostles. I thought it possible that some of them might have misunderstood the Gospel, but it seemed unlikely that they would all be mistaken. The true faith had to be represented somewhere in the ancient world. The only problem was that I could not find it. No matter where I looked, on whatever continent, in whatever century, the Fathers agreed: salvation comes through the transformation of the moral life and not by faith alone. They also taught that this transformation begins and is nourished in the sacraments, and not through some individual conversion experience.

At this stage of my journey, I was eager to remain a Protestant. My whole life, marriage, family, and career were bound up in Protestantism. My discoveries in Church history were an enormous threat to that identity, so I turned to biblical studies looking for comfort and help. I thought that if I could be absolutely confident in the Reformers' appeal to Scripture, then I essentially could dismiss fifteen hundred years of Christian history. I avoided Catholic scholarship, or books that I thought were *intended* to undermine my faith, and focused instead on what I thought were the most objective, historical, and also *Protestant* works of biblical scholarship. I was looking for rock-solid proof that the Reformers were right in their understanding of Paul. What I did not know was that the best in twentieth-century Protestant scholarship had already rejected Luther's reading of the Bible.

Luther had based his entire rejection of the Church on the words of Paul, "A man is justified by faith apart from works of the law" (Rom 3:28). Luther assumed that this contrast between "faith" and "works" meant that there was no role for morality in the process of salvation (according to the traditional Protestant view, moral behavior is a *response* to salvation, but not a contributing factor). I had learned that the earliest Church Fathers rejected that view. I now found a whole array of Protestant scholars also willing to testify that this is not what Paul meant.

The second-century Church Fathers believed that Paul had rejected the relevance of only the Jewish law for salvation ("works of the law" = Mosaic Law). They saw faith as the entrance to the life of the Church, the sacraments, and the Spirit. Faith admits us to the means of grace, but is not itself a sufficient ground for salvation. What I saw in the most recent and highly regarded Protestant scholars was the same point of view. From the last third of the twentieth century, scholars like E. P. Sanders, Krister Stendhal, James Dunn, and N. T. Wright have argued that traditional Protestantism profoundly misread Paul. According to Stendhal and others, justification by faith is primarily about Jew and Gentile relations, not about the role of morality as a condition of eternal life. Together, their work has been referred to as "The New Perspective on Paul."

My discovery of this "New Perspective" was a watershed in my understanding of Scripture. I saw, to begin with, that the "New Perspective" was the "Old Perspective" of the earliest Church Fathers. I began testing it against my own reading of Paul and found that it made sense. It also resolved the long-standing tension that I had always felt between Paul and the rest of the Bible. Even Luther had had difficulty in reconciling his reading of Paul with the Sermon on the Mount, the Epistle of St. James, and the Old Testament. Once I tried on the "New

Perspective," this difficulty vanished. Reluctantly, I had to accept that the Reformers were wrong about justification.

These discoveries in my academic work were paralleled to some extent by discoveries in my personal life. Protestant theology strongly distinguishes belief from behavior, and I began to see how this had affected me. From childhood, I had always identified theology, apologetics, and evangelism as the highest callings in Christian life, while the virtues were supposed to be mere fruits of right belief. Unfortunately, I found that the fruits were not only lacking in my life, but that my theology had actually contributed to my vices. It had made me censorious, proud, and argumentative. I also realized that it had done the same thing to my heroes.

The more I learned about the Protestant Reformers, the less I liked them personally. I recognized that my own founder, John Calvin, was a self-important, arrogant man who was brutal to his enemies, never accepted personal responsibility, and condemned anyone who disagreed with him. He called himself a prophet and ascribed divine authority to his own teaching. This contrasted rather starkly with what I was learning about Catholic theologians. Many of them were saints, meaning they had lived lives of heroic charity and self-denial. Even the greatest of them — men like Augustine and Thomas Aquinas — also recognized that they had no personal authority to define the dogma of the Church.

Outwardly, I remained staunchly anti-Catholic. I continued to attack the Church and to defend the Reformation, but inwardly I was in psychological and spiritual agony. I found that my theology and my life's work were founded on a lie, and that my own ethical, moral, and spiritual life were deeply lacking. I was rapidly losing my motivation to disprove Catholicism, and instead I wanted simply to learn the truth. The Protestant Reformers had justified their revolt by an appeal to "Scripture alone." My studies in the doctrine of justification had shown me Scripture was not as clear a guide as the Reformers alleged. What if their whole appeal to Scripture was misguided? Why, after all, did I treat Scripture as the final authority?

When I posed this question to myself, I recognized that I had no good answer. The real reason I appealed to Scripture alone was that this is what I had been taught. As I studied the issue, I discovered that no Protestant has ever given a satisfactory answer to this question. The Reformers did not really defend the doctrine of "Scripture alone." They merely asserted it. Even worse, I learned that modern Protestant theologians who have tried to defend "Scripture alone" do so by an appeal to tradition. This struck me as illogical. Eventually, I realized that "Scripture alone" is not even in Scripture. The doctrine is self-refuting. I also saw that the earliest Christians knew no more of "Scripture alone," than they had known of "faith alone." On the issues of how-we-are-saved and how-we-define-the-faith, the earliest Christians found their center in *The Church*. The Church was both the authority on Christian doctrine as well as the instrument of salvation.

The Church was the issue I kept coming back to. Evangelicals tend to view the Church as simply an association of like-minded believers. Even the Reformers, Luther and Calvin, had a much stronger view of the Church than this, but the ancient Christians had the most sublime doctrine of all. I used to see their emphasis on Church as unbiblical, contrary to "faith alone," but I began to realize that it was my Evangelical tradition that was unbiblical.

Scripture teaches that the Church is the Body of Christ (Eph 4:12). Evangelicals tend to dismiss this as mere metaphor, but the ancient Christians thought of it as literally, albeit mystically, true. St. Gregory of Nyssa could say, "He who beholds the Church really beholds Christ."1 As I thought about this, I realized that it spoke to a profound truth about the biblical meaning of salvation. St. Paul teaches that the baptized have been united to Christ in His death, so that they might also be united to Him in resurrection (Rom 6:3–6). This union literally makes the Christian a participant in the divine nature (2 Pet 1:4). St. Athanasius could even say, "For He was made man that we might be made God" (*De incarnatione*, 54.3). The ancient doctrine of the Church now made sense to me because I saw that salvation itself is nothing other than union with Christ and a continual growth into His nature. The Church is no mere association of like-minded people. It is a supernatural reality because it shares in the life and ministry of Christ.

This realization also made sense of the Church's sacramental doctrine. When the Church baptizes, absolves sins, or, above all, offers the Holy Sacrifice of the Mass, it is really Christ who baptizes, absolves, and offers His own Body and Blood. The sacraments do not detract from Christ. They make Him present.

The Scriptures are quite plain on the sacraments. It you take them at face value, you must conclude that Baptism is the "bath of rebirth and renewal by the Holy Spirit" (Titus 3:5 NAB). Jesus meant it when He said, "My flesh is true food, and my blood is true drink" (Jn 6:55 NAB). He was not lying when He promised, "Whose sins you forgive are forgiven them" (Jn 20:23 NAB). This is exactly how the ancient Christians understood the sacraments. I could no longer accuse the ancient Christians of being unbiblical. On what grounds could I reject them at all?

The ancient Christian doctrine of the Church also made sense of the veneration of saints and martyrs. I learned that the Catholic doctrine on the saints is just a development of this biblical doctrine of the Body of Christ. Catholics do not worship the saints. They venerate Christ in His members. By invoking their intercession, Catholics merely confess that Christ is present and at work in His Church in heaven. Protestants often object that the Catholic veneration of saints somehow detracts from the ministry of Christ. I understood now that the reverse is actually true. It is the Protestants who limit the reach of Christ's saving work by denying its implications for the doctrine of the Church.

My studies showed this theology fleshed out in the devotion of the ancient Church. As I continued my investigation of Augustine, I learned that this "Protestant hero" thoroughly embraced the veneration of saints. The Augustine scholar Peter Brown (born 1935) also taught me that the saints were not incidental to ancient Christianity. He argued that you could not separate ancient Christianity from devotion to the saints, and he placed Augustine squarely in this tradition. Brown showed that this was no mere pagan importation into Christianity, but rather tied intimately to the Christian notion of salvation (see his *Cult of Saints: Its Rise and Function in Latin Christianity*).

Once I understood the Catholic position on salvation, the Church, and the saints, the Marian dogmas also seemed to fall into place. If the heart of the Christian faith is God's union with our human nature, the Mother of that human nature has an incredibly important and unique role in all of history. This is why the Fathers of the Church always celebrated Mary as the second Eve. Her Yes to God at the annunciation undid the No of Eve in the garden. If it is appropriate to venerate the saints and martyrs of the Church, how much more appropriate is it to give honor and veneration to her who made possible our redemption?

By the time I finished my Ph.D., I had completely revised my understanding of the Catholic Church. I saw that her sacramental doctrine, her view of salvation, her veneration of Mary and the saints, and her claims to authority were all grounded in Scripture, in the oldest traditions, and in the plain teaching of Christ and the Apostles. I also realized that Protestantism was a confused mass of inconsistencies and tortured logic. Not only was Protestant doctrine untrue, but it bred contention, and could not even remain unchanged. The more I studied, the more I realized that my Evangelical heritage had moved far not only from ancient Christianity, but even from the teaching of her own Protestant founders.

Modern American Evangelicals teach that Christian life begins when you "invite Jesus into your heart." Personal conversion (what they call "being born again") is seen as the essence and the beginning of Christian identity. I knew from my reading of the Fathers that this was not the teaching of the early Church. I learned studying the Reformers that it was not even the teaching of the earliest Protestants. Calvin and Luther had both unambiguously identified Baptism as the beginning of the Christian life. I looked in vain in their works for any exhortation to be "born again." I also learned that they did not dismiss the Eucharist as unimportant, as I had. While they rejected Catholic theology on the sacraments, both continued to insist that Christ is really present in the Eucharist. Calvin even taught in 1541 that a proper understanding of this Eucharist is "necessary for salvation." He knew nothing of the individualistic, born-again Christianity I had grown up with.

I finished my degree in December 2002. The last few years of my studies were actually quite dark. More and more, it seemed to me that my plans were coming unhinged, my future obscure. My confidence was badly shaken, and I actually doubted whether or not I could believe anything. Catholicism had started to seem like the most sensible interpretation of the Christian faith, but the loss of my childhood faith was shattering. I prayed for guidance. In the end, I believe it was grace that saved me. At that time, I had a wife and four children, and God finally showed me that I needed more than books in my life. Quite honestly, I also needed more than "faith alone." I needed real help to live my life and to do battle with my sins. I found this in the sacraments of the Church. Instead of "Scripture alone," I needed real guidance from a teacher with authority. I found this in the Magisterium of the Church. I found that I *needed* the whole company of saints in heaven — not just their books on earth. In sum, I found that the Catholic Church was ideally formed to meet my real spiritual needs. In addition to truth, I found Jesus in His Church, through His Mother, in the whole company of His saints. I entered the Catholic Church on November 16, 2003. My wife also had her own reversion to the depths of the Church, and today my family is happily and enthusiastically Catholic. I am grateful to my parents for pointing me to Christ and the Scriptures. I am grateful to St. Augustine for pointing me to the Church.

Dr. David Anders was born and raised in Birmingham, Alabama. He began college at Tulane University in New Orleans, Louisiana, where he met his wife, but they both completed their degrees at Wheaton College in Wheaton, Illinois. Dr. Anders earned a B.A. from Wheaton (1992), an M.A. from Trinity Evangelical Divinity School (1995), and a Ph.D. from the University of Iowa (2002), where he studied Reformation history and historical theology. Dr. Anders taught history and religion in Iowa and Alabama. He currently resides in Birmingham, Alabama, with his wife and five home-schooled children. His website is calvin2catholic.com.

FROM THE DESERT
TO PARADISE

REV. DEACON TOM CABEEN

former Jehovah's Witness elder

M y parents became Jehovah's Witnesses in April 1954, shortly after my fourth birthday. My father had grown up unchurched; my mother was a nominal Methodist. They embraced the Watchtower version of Christianity enthusiastically. In 1955, believing the end of the world to be imminent, they volunteered to move "where the need is great" and sold their new home in Phoenix, Arizona. Dad was appointed to oversee the Cottonwood, Arizona, congregation, which at the time consisted only of our family of three and one other elderly woman. By 1960, it had grown into a small but zealous group of about a dozen families.

Dad brushed up on his high-school Spanish and started a small Bible study among a group of Mexicans in the area. In 1961, at the Watchtower Society's request, we moved to El Centro, California, where he served as overseer of a Spanish-speaking congregation. My mother and I started to learn Spanish. I learned it rather easily, but she had much more difficulty. She never learned to speak it fluently. In 1963, we were again asked to move, this time to a small Spanish congregation in Casa Grande, Arizona.

I graduated high school in 1967 and became a full-time door-to-door preacher, or "Pioneer." As a result, I was classified 4-D (Minister of Religion) by my local draft board and exempted from military service. In the summer of 1968, I applied to serve at the world headquarters of Jehovah's Witnesses in Brooklyn, New York. I was invited to serve at "Bethel" starting November 14, 1968. This was the start of a long spiritual pilgrimage.

Shortly after I left home, my parents, encouraged by my example, also began "Pioneering." Dad was invited to become a traveling minister or "Circuit Overseer." He worked with Spanish-speaking congregations in the southwest and northeast of the United States for about a decade.

SUCCESS IN BROOKLYN

At Bethel, I was determined to learn as much as possible about Watchtower teachings. I studied hard and applied myself diligently to my work. That, along with a natural aptitude for the duties assigned to me, resulted in my being given much more responsibility than usual for someone my age.

In 1969, I was assigned to the printing department, working on the press which produced *The Watchtower* magazine. Within three years, I was a foreman over several presses. In 1977, I was appointed Pressroom Overseer, with supervision of more than a hundred men and forty large printing presses.

When not working, I cultivated friendships with mature, responsible members of the Bethel staff, many of whom worked in offices where the most respected, loyal, and mature Witnesses were assigned. I had many in-depth discussions with them about the Society's teachings and the functioning of the organization.

Late in 1973, I began dating another Bethelite, a lovely young woman named Gloria, whom I had met shortly after she arrived in 1971. We were married on May 25, 1974. Gloria was also a zealous believer and a hard worker. We had both decided to dedicate our lives full-time to what we believed to be the few remaining years before "Armageddon," the end of this age and the beginning of a new one.

In my local Brooklyn congregation, Greenpoint Spanish, I was first appointed an elder in 1971, when I was twenty-one. The following year I was appointed a "Bethel Elder." As such, I often spoke as an official Watchtower Society representative at summer conventions in English, Spanish, and French. (I was the featured speaker at a District Assembly in Roanoke, Virginia, at age twenty-six.) Gloria and I both learned French and were assigned to a French-speaking congregation, composed mostly of Haitians, in Newark, New Jersey.

DISTURBING QUESTIONS

I was baptized as a Witness in 1959, but had never read through the Bible. I was required to do so as a new member of the headquarters staff. The more I read, the more inconsistencies I found between plain statements in Scripture and Witness beliefs. At first, I attributed the problem to my youth and inexperience. But in time, as I began to be more respected and trusted, I discussed my Bible questions privately with older, well-placed headquarters staffers, and was surprised to discover how many of them had the same kinds of questions and how openly they discussed them.

The publication of *Aid to Bible Understanding*, a Bible dictionary, in 1971, initiated major organizational changes for the Watchtower Society. For many, including me, this opened the door to a reexamination of other teachings. I wondered, "If we have been wrong in our understanding of arrangements we formerly thought to be solidly based on Scripture, why couldn't we be wrong about doctrines, too?"

During the 1970s, a growing number of sincere Bethelites began to read other Bible translations in addition to the Watchtower's own *New World Translation*, as well as Bible commentaries. Some gathered in private groups to study and discuss things without the "assistance" of Watchtower publications. By 1979, I was convinced that there could be no reconciling of some key Watchtower teachings with the Bible. I still believed, however, that God was guiding the Watchtower organization and that the end was near, so I expected big changes to come. I awaited them with eager expectation.

Gloria, on the other hand, was unhappy. She wanted us to leave Bethel and start a family. Since I firmly believed the Watchtower chronology upon which their end-times predictions are based, I could not imagine why anyone would want to leave with the end so close. I brought the matter up with a trusted friend on the Watchtower's Governing Body. He gave me a copy of a letter sent to the Watchtower Society by Carl Olof Jonsson, a Witness elder from Sweden. Jonsson presented indisputable historical evidence that Watchtower chronology was seriously flawed. His logic was solid and his documentation scholarly. I read and reread the evidence. Finally, I was convinced. I was also heartsick.

What was hard to accept was not so much the error but its corollary. "Bible chronology" is absolutely essential in establishing the Watchtower Society's claim to be God's "channel of communication" to mankind in the "time of the end," just prior to the end of this wicked world. If the chronology is wrong, so are all the Watchtower claims. I began to seriously consider the possibility that the Watchtower leaders were misled at best, hypocrites and false prophets at worst. At this point, there was no reason to postpone our desire to have a family. Gloria and I resigned from Bethel service effective July 15, 1980, and moved to Lancaster, Pennsylvania, where Gloria had grown up.

I was not ready to simply walk away entirely from my religious community. Our whole lives were tied up with Jehovah's Witnesses. Still, our lives were to change greatly. We had absolutely no money, for we had spent the previous twelve years working as unpaid volunteers. I had studied hard and had both extensive job experience and technical expertise, but no college degree. (I could have attended college on a full scholarship, but Witnesses are strongly discouraged from higher education. As a "true believer," I followed their teaching in that matter, too.)

Although I had worked in good conscience and thoroughly enjoyed my service with the Watchtower Society, and loved my Witness brothers and sisters dearly, it appeared virtually certain that there would be an even more significant parting of the ways. I simply lost my desire to actively support a belief system in which I no longer believed. We would have to start over, both spiritually and financially.

DISFELLOWSHIPPED AND SHUNNED

We had left the headquarters of our own volition, and I was still officially in good standing with the organization. So I was appointed an elder in the Lancaster congregation. Although I had doubts about Watchtower teachings, I did not discuss them openly, and saw no reason to withdraw from Jehovah's Witnesses as long as my association with them did not require me to violate my conscience. However, the main focus of Watchtower publications for many months was warnings against and condemnation of "apostates," defined as those who disagree with Watchtower teachings. I could not support that perspective, but I was often asked to do just that. Early in February 1981, I resigned my eldership. Later that year, on August 9, 1981, our first son Matthew was born.

In the spring of 1982, the elders asked to speak with Gloria and me after one of the regular congregation meetings. I was questioned (in Gloria's presence) for an hour or so about "doubts." The elders asked if I believed the Watchtower Society to be God's exclusive organization (a key Watchtower teaching). I replied that although I thought that God had worked through Jehovah's Witnesses, I was not willing to state that He works through them exclusively. The meeting ended with no action taken. The same elders asked us to attend a second brief meeting a few weeks later. In this meeting, they announced their decision to disfellowship us. This official action meant that every Witness member of our family and friends would be required to completely shun us or face the same consequences. Nearly three decades of association with Jehovah's Witnesses were over. Our families and our religious community had rejected us. We were on our own.

DOES GOD WORK THROUGH AN ORGANIZATION?

What I needed was some reliable way to determine which Watchtower teachings were true and which were false. I had discovered error, but what I needed was truth. Because of the centrality of the Witness idea that God uses the Watchtower organization as an exclusive channel to communicate with His people, that was the first focus of my study. Using a concordance and Bible dictionary, I began to carefully search the Scriptures for evidence as to whether or not God had consistently worked through an organization as an official instrument to communicate with or direct humans. I concluded that He did not, and published my research in an article entitled, "Does God Work through an Organization?" It was eventually translated into several languages and became popular among exiting Witnesses, particularly after the Internet came into wide use.

Although I wrote in good conscience, I am somewhat sad now at the degree of success I had. I had "thrown the baby out with the bath water," concluding that all religious structures are basically alike. A few years later, I revised my article to show that Christ was joined organically with His Body, and that it is not like human organizations. But I did not yet grasp the significance of that truth. I had much to learn about the visible Church.

"Organized Religion" Revisited

For several years, Gloria and I did not join any organized Christian fellowship. We read and studied the Bible only on our own or with other former Witnesses in a small support group. We formed strong social bonds with these dear friends, but our spiritual growth was slow. Usually our discussions were negative, centered on things we once believed but now rejected. We covered much of the same ground every time we met. Finally, Gloria said, "I am tired of going over and over these same old things. I want to learn something *new* and *true* about Jesus Christ!"

Our second son, James, was born November 22, 1986. As our two boys began to get older, we felt a growing need to find Bible-believing Christians with whose children ours could associate. We visited a local Christian and Missionary Alliance fellowship and became friends with the pastor and his wife. When I told him about my background, he asked me to teach an adult Bible class. He did not ask me for details of my actual beliefs, but I always taught "orthodoxy" as I understood it. I always supported my teaching from passages of Scripture and respected Protestant commentaries. Neither Gloria nor I ever officially joined that fellowship. We were still reluctant to become associated with "organized religion." After about a year, the pastor reluctantly asked me to step down as a teacher, since I had still not officially joined. I didn't blame him.

We looked for a place to worship that was "kid friendly" and eventually settled into an independent Evangelical Baptist fellowship. There we met many fine Christian people, and quickly got involved in religious activities. A few months after we began attending there, I was again asked to teach an adult Bible class, which I did almost continuously for nearly fourteen years.

History Lessons

In 1998, I started working on another article, entitled "Where Is the Body of Christ?" My intention was to help former JWs find and associate with other believers in the community. I wanted to highlight the similarity between Evangelical worship and that of first-century disciples. I wanted to show that practical Christian living rather than uniformity of structure and doctrine is what matters most, and encouraged my readers to find and join a "Bible-believing" Christian fellowship of their choice.

I started my research using only the Scriptures, but soon discovered how little I actually knew about the early Christians. I realized that I was "reading into" the Scriptures what I wanted to find. I honestly could not reconstruct the early Church in much detail simply from what is written in the New Testament. So I ended up buying history books — dozens, eventually — and started reading. I published the article. But my research had raised a whole new set of interesting questions.

During my research, I kept running across references to the "early Church Fathers." Practically every scholarly source I knew of respected them highly. But I knew very little about these writers, so I bought a set of the ten-volume Ante-Nicene Fathers and began to read, starting with the writings of those who had known and conversed with the Apostles.

What first surprised me is how they applied the Scriptures. There was no official collection of Christian Scripture when these writers put pen to parchment, but they did quote from writings that later became part of the Christian canon. Often they applied a familiar passage in a way that was completely new to me. I was intrigued by the implications of this fact.

I began to see that the Bible is not self-interpreting. Most passages can be understood in more than one way. The problem is not resolved even if one is familiar with the original languages, as were all the ancient writers. Clearly, some parts of the sacred writings are to be taken literally, some metaphorically, others allegorically or figuratively. How do we sort out which is which? I had paid a lot of money for excellent commentaries, yet often I was surprised at the variety of explanations of a given passage I found among respected commentators from differing Christian traditions or denominations.

Slowly, I came to understand that there is simply no reliable way to determine if a particular Christian teaching is true based only on whether or not it is logical, reasonable, and seems to be supported by "proof texts" from Scripture. Some other source of authoritative interpretation is needed. Some Christians expect to receive individual interpretational guidance from the Holy Spirit; others rely on scholarship, historical sources, or reason. But none of these methods produces general consensus among all commentators or interpreters.

I finally realized that this is why every single denomination uses written materials in addition to the Bible, whether a catechism, commentaries, books, tracts, or other publications. No one just hands a Bible to a potential convert and says, "Read the book, and you will understand the Christian message completely and clearly." *Every Christian teacher must add explanation to Scripture* in order to communicate the full Christian message.

About this time, we began attending the Episcopal Church. We loved the Anglican liturgy, music, and overall approach to worship and theology. Although widespread liberalism was a problem in many parishes, our parish was warm, friendly, and quite orthodox.

A GREAT APOSTASY?

Nearly twenty years had passed since I had left the Watchtower Society, but I still believed that, sometime shortly after the end of the first century, the faithful, early, apostolic Church had become the corrupt Roman Catholic Church. Most Protestants, I later learned, have a somewhat similar view, except that they date the falling away from orthodoxy into the fourth or fifth century or even later. Both Luther and Calvin, however, believed that the ante-Nicene Church taught authentic Christianity.

I began to think about the implications of the "great apostasy" idea. If true, one corollary is that for some period of time, Jesus had no authentic congregation of faithful followers, no visible body of believers, or church, on earth. But if that is true, and if the Bible is not self-interpreting, once the correct interpretation got lost, it could never be restored.

Scripture says that Christ revealed many things to His disciples that were not written down (Jn 21:25). It also says that "the *church*" (not the holy writings) is the "pillar and foundation of the truth" (1 Tim 3:15). The teachings Jesus taught His disciples orally were not "added to Scripture" by the Apostles. They were taught orally to the new disciples they made. The writings that later became Scripture were composed *within a fully functioning church setting in which every member had been taught orally for decades*. When the Apostle Paul wrote epistles to congregations, he had usually spent much time with them prior to that, teaching them orally. So, his letters often left many things unstated. They primarily dealt with exceptions, not normal teachings and practices everyone already knew.

AN INVISIBLE CHURCH?

For many years after I left the Witnesses, even as an Evangelical Protestant, I believed that the members of the "true Church" were scattered among all the world's Christian denominations. This "invisible church" was composed of believers in any Christian community who take their faith seriously and attempt to live by the Scriptures. They were the "wheat" of Jesus' "wheat and weeds" parable (Mt 13:24–30). I began, however, to see problems with that perspective.

An invisible church composed of scattered individuals who are not in contact with each other, and who are not under any common leadership, in fact, has no outward, visible characteristics at all, for it is *invisible*! We can never know anything for sure about such a church: where it is, what its members believe, or how they worship. It looks like whatever we want it to look like, for there is nothing real with which to compare it. It is, *and will always remain*, a "church" of our own construction.

More importantly, it doesn't look at all like the Church described in the New Testament, which was full of real people, saints and sinners alike, a living, structured community, under the leadership and tutelage of bishops, elders or presbyters, and deacons, to whom the believers submitted. Every Christian congregation of God's people described in Scripture is not only visible, it is human, with all the problems which exist in any family, group, or community of humans anywhere. How can an invisible church be "salt and light" in the community? How can unbelievers see its good works and give glory to God? Even the Reformers, though they rejected the authority of Rome, recognized the need for and existence of leadership and structure within the body of believers. I rejected the idea of an invisible church once and for all.

SACRAMENTS

I continued reading history books, along with the early Christian writings. I was surprised that so many concepts and teachings I had once rejected had been presented incorrectly, even dishonestly, in both Watchtower and Evangelical Protestant literature, then explained away as illogical or unscriptural. The early Christians' presentation of these concepts usually made more sense and fit the Scriptures better than the explanations of Christian teaching I had read in Protestant commentaries. As I became convinced of their validity, gradually my understanding of Christianity began to change. "Problem passages" of Scripture with which I had struggled for years slowly began to disappear. A new "big picture" was starting to fit together for me. I was learning things that were entirely new to me. They were to completely transform my understanding of how Christ reconciles sinners to a righteous God.

A prime example is the early Christian belief that bread and wine, when blessed by the Christian presbyter officiating at a Eucharist celebration, actually *become* the Body and Blood of Jesus Christ. Of course, this is exactly what Jesus actually says in the narratives of the Last Supper, but the idea was still startling. Most Protestants take Jesus' words to be symbolic. (There's that interpretation problem again!)

I knew that Christians, in some mysterious way, actually *are* the Body of Christ. I once took that to be merely a metaphor. But I learned that Christ's disciples are joined in a very literal way to Christ when they consume His Body and Blood. This action corresponds with the ancient Jews consuming the Passover lamb and is intimately connected with salvation. In fact, "unless you eat the flesh of the Son of man and drink his blood, you have no life in you" (Jn 6:53). What a concept!

This was my introduction to the "sacraments" or "mysteries" of the Christian faith. God extends graces to His people *through* and in connection with material objects or actions: the water of Baptism, the oil of consecration, and hands laid on in Ordination. I had never heard these things from Witnesses or Evangelical Christians. At first, I thought the idea to be totally unscriptural, but I began to see it everywhere. I noticed how many powerful works done by Jesus and the Apostles involved physical acts like touching or breathing on the recipients, or objects like bread, fish, oil, or wine.

Material objects, when blessed and used by the Apostles and their successors as Jesus taught, become both signs of and instruments *through* which God's grace is given to humans. They play an important role in healing and restoring sinners to full fellowship with Him. God works through His creation, not around or in spite of it.

At that time, I still knew virtually nothing about the Catholic Church. So when I noticed a copy of the *Catholic Catechism* at a used book sale, I bought it and started reading. I was shocked at what I found! The Catholic explanation of Christian faith and morals, including salvation, Baptism, and redemption, and my investigation into the historical early Church had allowed me to adopt a Catholic perspective without my strong anti-Catholic prejudice getting in the way.

POINT OF DECISION

I began to read Catholic writings enthusiastically. Catholic explanations of Christianity fit the Scriptures, the real world, and the human heart. I still had much to learn, but every single teaching I investigated rang true. The deeper I looked, the better they looked. At some point, the evidence became conclusive for me. I shared the things I was learning with Gloria, who is deeply spiritual. (She had been baptized Catholic as an infant, but raised as a Witness.) She read, reflected, and prayed. We discussed some issues, but I did not pressure her into a decision. I just prayed and waited. She did the same, reading and praying; then one day, she simply said, "We should become Catholics." Her openness to the Holy Spirit's guidance confirmed to her that the Catholic Church is what we had been searching for.

What we have found Catholic teaching to be is astounding: deep, scriptural, historically supportable, elegant, logical, and coherent. I honestly believe that anyone who follows these teachings faithfully will become a godly man or woman. This is where we have belonged all these years. We were received into the Roman Catholic Church on Friday, June 9, 2006, and are completely happy within the ancient Church of Jesus Christ. Most importantly, we are home.

Tom, Gloria, and their son Matt were received into the Roman Catholic Church in 2006. Their son James entered the Church in 2009. Tom was ordained to the permanent diaconate of the Archdiocese of Hartford, Connecticut, on June 7, 2014.

From Hatred to Hope: One Man's Twenty-Year Journey into the Catholic Faith

Daniel Burke

former Southern Baptist and Anglican seminarian

M y first exposure to Catholicism was through an abusive step-father. A few key memories include our home being destroyed end-to-end in a drunken rage, and forensic photographs of my mother after a brutal encounter. My most prominent memory is of gunfire in our home during a shouting match between him and my mother. I was only nine years old. Not the greatest introduction to the faith.

As a young boy, these and a seemingly endless string of dark trials led me to frequently consider suicide. However, a few of these experiences, particularly my mother's dabbling in the New Age movement, resulted in the idea that there was something more to life — there must be. There was a spiritual reality behind the gray haze of my existence. In my late teens, I began an energetic and deliberate search for God.

During my quest, I encountered a coworker at a pizza restaurant who was unusually kind. Upon inquiry about his motivations, he revealed that he was a Christian. Christ had lifted him out of drug addiction into a life of grace, and the transformation was obvious. Though I did not follow through on his invitations to Bible study and church, he illumined a path that I have wandered now for some twenty years.

Years later, my first church experience came at Glenn Memorial Baptist Church in Covina, California. I had been listening to the "Bible Answer Man" on the radio for some time, and the host indicated that he was a Southern Baptist. So, one Sunday on my own, I slipped into the back row of the nearest Southern Baptist church I could find. My hope was to go unnoticed as I anonymously checked this "Christian thing" out. Well, the first five rows were soon packed, and I found myself all alone in the back with about twenty empty pews between us.

The pastor couldn't help but notice me and approached me after the service. By the end of our conversation, he had committed to a few hours every Thursday night to answer my questions and talk about life. Over the next year, we spent most of our time studying the scriptural and historical evidence for the life, death, and resurrection of Jesus Christ. In the end, it became clear to me that the Bible was a reliable document and that Christ was who He claimed to be. I prayed the "sinner's prayer," made my public profession of faith, and was baptized.

The anti-Catholic bent of this church fit well within the grooves of the emotional scars of my youth. I devoured anti-Catholic literature, memorized Scripture, witnessed door-to-door, taught Bible studies, and became a deacon. Though I carried much of the pain and weight of sin into my faith, my encounter with Christ was real and life-changing.

Constant Scripture reading and study, however, resulted in a nagging discomfort and doubt regarding the teachings of my denomination. I was fascinated by Church history and enamored by the idea of being able to see God's hand at work in time. Even so, Church history, even slanted Reformation-side, served to fuel my unease.

Meanwhile, my pastor was obsessed with the idea of getting back to the purity of the early Church. This also drove me deeper into history, and deeper into struggle, not with Christ, but with the Protestant view of the Church. Before I continue, I must say that I am deeply grateful for my Protestant heritage. It was a Protestant pastor who introduced me to Christ and the richness of His Word. I have worked daily for almost fifteen years among Evangelicals, and I could not imagine working among better people. They have a passion for Christ and the family that has changed my life. To them, I owe far more than I can ever repay. That said, an early encounter with a Jehovah's Witness and a Catholic woman at work set the trajectory of my faith toward the Catholic Church.

The Jehovah's Witness was passing through my neighborhood and initiated a conversation. He introduced me to the idea that the Emperor Constantine had corrupted the Church and that political power had overcome the true Christian faith (Arianism). My instinct was to take him at face value; after all, I already "knew" that the Catholic Church was a corrupt institution. I decided to research his claims and assumed that some documentation of this event (the Council of Nicaea) was available for scrutiny. To begin my studies, I purchased, among other books, a collection of the early Church Fathers.

The second trajectory-setting encounter was with a Catholic coworker whom I hassled regularly. In my mind, she was not a Christian and thus was a target for evangelism. Worse yet, she was a wolf among sheep (we worked together in a prominent Evangelical ministry). After a year of patient replies to my constant prodding, she announced that she was leaving. At her going-away party, she asked five of her coworkers to sit on high bar-stool-like chairs prominently placed at the front of the department meeting area. She then, one by one, recounted how each person had positively impacted her life, gently removed their shoes and socks, and then washed their feet. I was one of the five. It was clear to me that day who had a more substantive Christian life and relationship with Christ.

These events behind me, I continued to study Church history (Reformation and beyond), the early Church Fathers, their lives, and their writings. I was astonished at the depth of the faith of the Fathers as demonstrated by their steadfast suffering. Several ideas became prominent as I studied. First was the idea of *proximity* to the disciples of Christ — the Apostles themselves. Many of their writings overlapped the time frame of the New Testament authors. It was an easy extension of sound reasoning to assume that this proximity granted them a view into the meaning and context of Scripture that could not be replicated through a *sola scriptura* lens. I concluded that it just might be wiser to listen to their counsel than to those two thousand years later who had no real interest in the context out of which the New Testament was birthed.

The second powerful realization was that of the *piety* of these men. Like the Apostles, they lived and often died for their faith. The most prominent and bold radio preachers and pastors of my early Christian experience had never suffered a hair's breadth in comparison with these men. Whose witness and perspective was more credible?

As I continued to read, however, I began to notice nagging patterns, common beliefs that began to change my views of the early Church. The Church these noble Fathers described was *nothing* like the Protestant "back to the early Church" perspective I was surrounded by. At first, I dismissed these ideas as an attempt to manipulate and control people within the context of persecution and dispersion. In one of the texts, I have comments in the margins arguing with the authors and their obvious "Papist Bias."

However, as my readings continued, I was confronted with the need to make life-altering decisions. Did I truly believe that these men, because of their proximity and piety, should be taken seriously? If I did, what would happen to my faith and life as a Christian?

Regardless of the daunting prospect of bending to the teachings of these men, I decided to ask one simple question, "What is the most obvious teaching that seems to be held in common by the Apostolic Fathers?" I set to reading the texts again. What immediately surfaced for me was the idea of apostolic succession. Given the momentum of my study, I could not get around this idea. The implications? My pastor did not have the authority that I had once assumed. This caused a huge dilemma for me because by this time I was solidly Reformed theologically (a firmly TULIP'd Calvinist). I believed that justification by faith *alone* was abundantly clear in the New Testament. Where could someone turn who believed in apostolic succession *and* justification by faith? The only answer was the Anglican Church.

At that point, I began the shift into the shoes of a 39-Article-believing-Anglican (someone who assents to the entire codified beliefs of the Anglican Church, a rare thing in the U.S.). I began to search for an Episcopal church that I could attend. Still holding fast to the doctrinal Articles and apostolic succession, I persisted until I found the Orthodox Anglican Church. Because I already had aspirations to ministry, when I contacted them, they encouraged me to consider studying for the priesthood. I promptly enrolled at St. Andrew's Theological College and Seminary in North Carolina.

As I began my affiliation and studies, I discovered the depth and richness of ancient traditions of prayer and liturgy — I was permanently hooked. To this day, I consider the earlier versions of the Book of Common Prayer to be unparalleled in beauty. It was obvious to me that the worship and beliefs of the traditionally rooted corner of the Anglican Church were far more closely aligned to the world of the Apostolic Fathers than I had ever experienced in other areas of Protestantism. However, the issue of the claims of Rome regarding Peter, the papacy, and the Magisterium continued to nag at me. I could not escape the clarity of the primacy of Peter in the New Testament, and the primacy of the see of Peter in the early Church. I was faced with more difficult choices than I had ever imagined.

A friend of mine who had preceded me to Rome confronted me with the most difficult choice I faced. "When are you going to recognize that there are only two options? You either submit to the Church and the authority that Christ established, or you rule yourself on the basis of your own judgment" – which, he reminded me, was the fundamental choice that had spawned over thirty thousand denominations since the Reformation. His question resonated with me and brought it all down to a very simple equation; I would either trust in my own limited judgment, or in two thousand years of consistent teaching of the Catholic Church.

Though extremely difficult on an emotional level, the intellectual decision was easy. I left seminary shortly thereafter. I was received into Christ's one, holy, Catholic, and apostolic Church on the Feast of Our Lady of Mount Carmel in July of 2005. Aside from my first submission to Christ, it was and still is the best decision I have ever made in my life.

Dan Burke is the executive director of EWTN's National Catholic Register, *co-host of Register Radio, president and founder of the Avila Institute for Spiritual Formation, an international speaker, author of the award-winning book* Navigating the Interior Life — Spiritual Direction and the Journey to God, *frequent radio and television guest, retreat master, and founder of the award-winning site dedicated to authentic Catholic spirituality,* Roman Catholic Spiritual Direction. *Dan lives in Birmingham, Alabama, with his wife and children.*

Three Treasures of the Church: My Journey Home

Allen Hunt

former Methodist pastor

M y friend, Sean, watched his father, Henry, die. Henry had been a WWII hero, a flying Tiger. Henry radiated Yankee independence, frugality, and self-sufficiency. He built his own house in Connecticut. He loved time in the woods. He raised his children well. But now he was gone.

Sean's mother, Mary, continued to live in their family home for the next few years, until she chose to move to Florida. My friend, Sean, helped her clean out the decades of belongings and collections from the family home so she could sell it and relocate. Fifty years of memories had accumulated in that old house.

On the last day of moving out of the old house, Sean took one last walk-through, just to reminisce on years gone by and also to look for any possessions that had been missed in the packing. In his parents' bedroom, Sean noticed an odd screw in the ceiling, an object that had never before captured his attention. Sean knew his dad and knew that the screw surely had some purpose, so he stepped on a stool to look at the screw in the ceiling. When he removed the screw, a panel slipped out of the ceiling. Behind the panel rested two Folger's Coffee cans, each of which was filled with cash. The thought occurred to Sean that, if his father had hidden cash in one place, there might be others, so Sean soon discovered screws, panels, and coffee cans in holes in the wall all around that old house. By the end of the hunt, Sean had found more than $5,000, hidden years before in the old house by a Depression-era man who knew what we all now know: you cannot always trust banks. Instead of using banks, Henry had carefully hidden his treasure in the ceilings and walls of his old house.

For the first thirty-plus years of my life, the Catholic Church was just an old house. To someone who had grown up Methodist, the descendant from at least five generations of Methodist pastors in the South, the Catholic Church existed in my world simply as an old house. The Catholic Church was old and historic, often architecturally remarkable, but never something that attracted my attention in any real way.

Even in my nearly twenty years as a Methodist pastor, I neither liked nor disliked the old house of the Catholic Church. It meant nothing to me; I had no reason ever to notice its existence. It was just an old house, with some old rituals, old buildings, and old ideas. Along the way, however, God began to reveal to me the treasures hidden in the life of the old house known as the Catholic Church. Over time, as I discovered those hidden treasures, they proved so powerful and meaningful that they led me home to the Catholic Church.

Six hidden treasures, in particular, I discovered in the Catholic Church, but three stand out most of all. And I found them in various parts of the house.

THE DINING ROOM:
THE TREASURE OF THE EUCHARIST

I found a hidden treasure in the dining room of the old house, but it took fifteen years for me to realize it. This discovery began my journey home and also proved to be the climax of that journey.

After I completed seminary at Emory University in Atlanta, my family and I moved to New Haven, Connecticut, to enable me to pursue a Ph.D. in New Testament and Early Christian Origins. Of the four students admitted to the degree program that year, one was a Presbyterian, one a Jesuit, one a Dominican, and, of course, I was a Methodist. The Dominican friar, Father Steven, and I immediately became close friends in our first week at Yale, and he opened the doors to the Catholic Church for me for the first time.

In our second year at Yale, Father Steven arranged for the two of us to give Lenten lectures to a group of cloistered Dominican nuns in North Guilford, Connecticut. In their monastery, God planted the seeds for my conversion, seeds which took nearly sixteen years to come to fruition, and seeds which I did not even realize were being planted at the time.

Father Steven and I enjoyed a wonderful time with the nuns at the Monastery of Our Lady of Grace. I discovered later that I had been the first male who was not an ordained Catholic priest ever to instruct the sisters behind their enclosure. It was a rare privilege and blessing. Our lectures focused on Thomas Aquinas, John Wesley, sanctification, and the places where our beliefs intersected far more than we had anticipated. We enjoyed great interaction and conversation with the nuns. After our last lecture, we reserved time for questions and answers. For many of the sisters, I was the first Methodist pastor they had ever met.

One sister, whom I call "Sister Rose," raised her hand and said something like, "Allen, thank you for having come these past few weeks. We've enjoyed your teaching. You sound so Catholic. After hearing you, I can't help but wonder, why aren't you a part of the Church?" The question startled me. "I AM a part of the Church," I responded. It had never occurred to me to use that kind of language: a part of THE CHURCH.

It took me a moment to realize what she was saying. Then I responded that there were a handful of reasons why I was Methodist as opposed to being Catholic. I mentioned one reason was the Eucharist. I told her, "It just seems obvious to me that, when Jesus said that He was the Bread, He was speaking metaphorically. I mean, it is bread and juice. I really do not understand why you all take it so literally. It is a symbol."

Sister Rose then came right back at me, kindly but directly. "Well, you are a New Testament scholar, right? So why does Jesus say ..." She then began to walk me through John 6 and Jesus' teaching on the Bread of Life. She then moved to 1 Corinthians 11 and pointed out where Paul uses the language of Jesus, "This is my body ... this is my blood." She schooled me for about five minutes! Then she concluded, "What don't you understand, Allen?" We all laughed, I shrugged it off, and we moved on.

Looking back, however, God planted a seed at that moment. That seed, in the end, led to my conversion.

In the years that followed, God continued to water that seed, often in unseen ways. For example, when my family and I would vacation, I usually worshipped at a Catholic church, which may seem unusual for a Methodist pastor. As a Protestant pastor, I normally had about four Sundays off per year. I always wanted to worship somewhere since those Sundays were precious occasions when I did not have the responsibility of leading worship. However, worshipping in towns where I knew no Protestant pastors meant that I would be "rolling the dice" since most Protestant worship experiences usually revolve around the pastor's sermon rather than the eucharist. I did not want to squander the handful of Sundays where I could worship on my own by attending a church where I had no idea what the quality of the sermon would be. So I usually worshipped at a Catholic church where I knew exactly what I would get — not so much a sermon, but a timeless liturgy centered on the Eucharist, the Creed, and the sacrifice of our Lord. Frankly, I never thought much about it other than when our family was on vacation.

As time passed, however, I grew increasingly uncomfortable with my role as pastor and the emphasis on the sermon as the centerpiece of worship. As the pastor of the largest Methodist church in the Southeast at that time (in terms of average worship attendance on a normal Sunday), I found that discomfort put me in an increasingly awkward position. Only then did I begin to examine why the Catholic Church felt like home when I was on vacation. It was because of the altar as centerpiece and the Eucharist as focal point.

Again, this transformation occurred over time, not in some midday epiphany. God put pieces of the jigsaw puzzle together in my spirit one at a time over many days and years. But as I reflected on the early Church Fathers and how they saw the Real Presence of Jesus in the Eucharist, and on the early martyrs who went to their deaths accused by earthly authorities of being cannibals for their consumption of the Body and Blood, God changed my heart.

Such a change of heart was only confirmed by the art of Salvador Dali and then in my reading of Flannery O'Connor and Thomas Aquinas. O'Connor, in her famous comment in a letter to a friend, says regarding a Protestant's dismissal of the Eucharist as merely a symbol, "Well, if it is just a symbol, all I can say is to hell with it…. It is the center of existence for me; all the rest of life is expendable." And Aquinas, while celebrating Mass himself at the altar, had such a moving experience of the Real Presence of Christ that he reflected, "All that I have written seems to me like straw compared to what has now been revealed to me."

Ultimately, I realized I had nothing to "protest." Why was I a "Protestant"? I had no real reason to dissent from Mother Church, and when you have no reason, you go home. So I did. I came home because I had discovered the treasure of the Real Presence of Christ in the Eucharist, served in the dining room of this old house all over the world every day at the Mass.

THE KITCHEN:
THE TREASURE OF HOLINESS

During our three years in New Haven, my family and I encountered suffering and struggle unlike anything we had ever experienced before or since. I battled ulcerative colitis, a battle that culminated two years after its onset with the removal of my entire colon. My wife suffered two painful miscarriages. We already had two daughters and were delighted to receive more, but that plan failed to materialize. Shortly after the removal of my colon, I was diagnosed with melanoma. Fortunately, the diagnosis came early enough that the cancer was not life-threatening. Nevertheless, for our little family of four, these three years proved to be a crucible of suffering and purification that we had not anticipated, being a thousand miles away from home, with no family anywhere in the vicinity.

To make matters worse, for the first time in my life, I was at the bottom of my class. Of the four of us in the Ph.D. program, I clearly was the weakest when it came to academic preparation. My weakness revealed itself most plainly in our coursework in classical Greek. Each day that class presented the greatest struggles I have ever faced in a classroom.

Fortunately, my good friend, Father Steven, was far better prepared than I was. So I usually stopped by the priory where he lived each day on my walk home from classes. He could offer wisdom and guidance to help me. I entered the priory from the rear door, which led into the kitchen. I would sit and chat with the cook, Mary, until Father Steven came downstairs to work with me for a few minutes at the kitchen table.

Nearly every time I entered the kitchen, I met Father Cajetan Sheehan, O.P. Father Caj was eighty-nine when I met him. He stood about 5'2" and weighed perhaps 120 lbs. A wisp of a man. With a fiery spirit. And an aura.

Father Caj had "retired" from more than a half-century of pastoring, and retirement had evolved into a new ministry of prayer. Each morning and each evening, he and the other priests gathered for prayer. Some attended as they could; Father Caj was *always* there. Prayer permeated Father Caj's life.

Without fail, each time that I saw him, Father Caj asked about my health. He asked about my wife, and he asked about my children. Every time. Without fail. And each time, without fail, he would say in his curmudgeonly New-England-Catholic-priest kind of way, "Well, I've been praying for all of you." I knew those were not empty words. Prayer permeated Father Caj's life.

When he retired, the secretary at his new home, St. Mary's Priory, always knew that if someone in the parish needed a pastor in an emergency, Father Caj was the one to call. He stood always ready and always eager to go. At age eighty-nine, Father Caj stood ready to do the right things rather than merely the easy things.

When I met him, Father Caj still wore the same clothes he had been wearing for nearly thirty years. He took his small pension each month and placed it in its entirety in the Poor Box, the small box at the front of the church where believers could give to help ease pain and hurts of others. The parish where he lived provided all that he actually needed, and Father Caj figured that was enough. So he gave all that he had. At eighty-nine.

I will always remember the day that I stopped by the kitchen and ran into Father Caj. I knew that he had been in continuous prayer for a friend of ours. When I saw him, his head was swollen with a large bruise on it. "Father Caj, what happened?" I asked. His matter-of-fact reply came, "Oh, I was in the prayer chapel, and I was praying for you. And I fell asleep and hit my head on the railing." He bowed up with just a touch of pride, the first time I had ever seen someone with a red badge of prayer courage.

I experienced, in a way I had never experienced before, that Father Caj had a deep aura of holiness that comes only with time. Father Caj possessed a holiness, probably without ever realizing it, that most of us will never attain. A life of faithful prayer, generous and sacrificial giving. A life of eager, willing, and joyful service. Caj and Jesus were good friends. The Spirit of God flowed so deeply in Caj's veins that it nearly oozed out of his pores. Caj was walking closely with Jesus — seeking to do that which would be helpful and to avoid that which would be harmful.

That holiness never landed him on any magazine cover; it never made him wealthy beyond compare. It just made him a whole lot like Jesus.

And that holiness made an impression on me. An impression that never left me.

Why had I never encountered anyone this holy before? The question just turned over in the back of my mind for years, slowly cooking in my spiritual crockpot.

Then, I encountered Pope John Paul II, a man from whom holiness emanated, even through a television. His holiness attracted me like a magnet.

As a Methodist, I knew the theology of John Wesley and his emphasis on holiness. I believed that theology, and I yearned for holiness in my own life. But I had never encountered holiness like that which I observed personally in Father Caj Sheehan in the kitchen of St. Mary's Priory or vicariously in Pope John Paul II through my reading and viewing.

God put these odd jigsaw pieces together for me through the writing of Thomas Merton. While serving as a Methodist pastor, I normally took my monthly daylong retreats at the Cistercian monastery on the east side of Atlanta. The silence and solitude moved deeply within me. Oddly, I had never considered why I chose a Catholic monastery for my monthly retreats, although it seems a bit obvious now, huh?

One afternoon, I was reading Merton's *Seven Storey Mountain*, while sitting in the library at the monastery. The words leapt off the page.

First came the words that captured what I had been considering for years but had never been able to articulate. "Professor Hering was a kind and pleasant man with a red beard, and one of the few Protestants I have ever met who struck one as being at all holy; that is, he possessed a certain profound interior peace …"

Merton was right. Holiness comes with a profound interior peace, and in the busyness of Protestantism, much of which produces Kingdom fruit, I had rarely encountered anything like the holiness I had encountered in several Catholics. In fact, in the monasteries and other settings, I had even encountered whole pockets of holiness. In Father Caj, Pope John Paul II, not to mention the witness of the Dominican sisters, Brother Lawrence, and countless others, there resided a holiness that I yearned to experience for myself in some measure. A holiness rarely found in my experiences as a Protestant. A holiness that flows from God through the Eucharist in His Church to us.

That holiness is God's calling and promise for each believer, even me. It is a sure thing in 1 Thessalonians 5:23–24 where the Apostle Paul writes, "May the God of peace himself sanctify you wholly; and may your spirit and soul and body be kept sound and blameless at the coming of our Lord Jesus Christ. He who calls you is faithful, and he will do it."

I experienced that deep level of holiness in the kitchen of this old house. And in many ways, that treasure called me home.

The Storage Shed:
The Treasure of God's Family

My grandmother died in Ohio in 1991. She had lived in the same house for nearly sixty years, a small, four-room house near the Ohio River.

When she died, my brother's family and my own joined my parents in Ohio for the funeral and to settle the simple estate. My mom, who is an only child, coordinated the affairs and asked my brother and me to clean out the storage shed in the back yard.

In the shed, we found a large footlocker, looking eerily like a treasure chest. It was locked but not heavy. No one had the key, nor did anyone know the key's whereabouts, so my mind instantly began to flash with the idea of a hidden pirate's treasure that my grandmother had stored for years and never revealed to anyone. A treasure of jewels and gold only to be discovered after her death, a treasure that was going to make me rich beyond my wildest imagination and dreams!

My brother and I pried open the treasure chest with a screwdriver, eagerly anticipating the riches that would soon be ours. As we opened the footlocker, we discovered it was filled to the brim with … old pictures. Old, black-and-white photos. Hundreds, perhaps thousands, of them. All kinds of people in all kinds of poses. These photos clearly captured my grandmother's family members, whom I had never met, and friends who had filled her life with joy.

We sifted the pictures through our fingers, and then turned them over, only to discover that none of them contained any writing or identification whatsoever. Sadly, we realized we were in possession of countless photos of people who were important to us, but we had no idea who the people were. It was almost like being an orphan. You know you have relatives; you just are not sure who they are.

As a Protestant, I had always known "of" the saints. I just really did not know who they were. I was like a spiritual orphan who had photos of thousands of relatives in the family of God, but had no names or identification for the photos.

In fact, on one journey to England to attend the World Methodist Conference, I visited holy sites like St. Paul's Cathedral, Westminster Abbey, and Canterbury. The event frustrated me to no end because I realized how little all we Methodists had in common other than the name "Methodist" and a loose claim to the paternity of John Wesley. However, while attending the conference and traveling England, I encountered St. Thomas More and St. John Fisher, old relatives whom I had not encountered before. When I heard their stories, and gazed at their "photos", I saw men of great courage. Men who had lost their lives (by losing their heads) for standing for truth against King Henry VIII.

Again, it is my own fault. As I had never really considered teachings on the Eucharist, I just never had really given much thought to where the Methodist Church had come from and its origins in the Church of England. The Methodist Church had always been an assumption for me. My family had been saturated in Methodism for as many generations as we could trace. My relatives had launched Methodist colleges, edited Methodist newspapers, unified Methodist denominations, and led Methodist congregations. I myself had been a pastor and leader in the Evangelical realm of the United Methodist Church. Still, I had never seriously considered the origin and authority of my own spiritual home.

St. John Fisher emerged as the chief supporter and trusted counselor of Queen Catherine when Henry sought his divorce. He declared himself ready to die on behalf of the Church and her teaching on the sanctity of marriage. Fisher spent time in prison, lost all his property and possessions, suffered countless indignities and humiliations, and ultimately lost his life for his stance.

In May 1535, Pope Paul III, made Fisher cardinal priest of St. Vitalis. King Henry replied to the pope, telling him not to send the cardinal's hat to England, saying that he would send Fisher's head to Rome instead. Fisher was beheaded on Tower Hill, and his head was stuck on a pole on London Bridge for all to see. Fisher became one of the fifty-four English martyrs of the Church during the Reformation.

Fisher had much to protest. He stood between truth and error, defending truth at any cost. Somehow, I had never absorbed that story before, and it sank deeply into my spirit. I had a bold relative in the faith who called into question the lineage and authority of my own tradition. The questions became clear in my mind: Did I stand in the way of King Henry or in the way of St. John Fisher and the Church? What am I protesting? I could find no justifiable reason to be separated from the Church. Again, I discovered that God was calling me home.

Becoming Catholic has filled my life with the names and faces of countless saints and relatives in the faith. The New Testament uses "family" as a description of the Church more than any other term. I now have a very large family. Family members who walk alongside me, cheer me on, pray with me, encourage and inspire me. Family members from whom I had been distanced in my Protestant formation. Family members who once lay unidentified in the storage shed of the old house but now make themselves known in marvelous ways. Family members who welcome me with gladness into the greatest family of all!

"Therefore, since we are surrounded by such a great cloud of witnesses, let us also lay aside every weight, and sin which clings so closely, and let us run with perseverance the race that is set before us" (Heb 12:1).

In the Atlanta airport, a three-story escalator leads you from the underground tram system up to the baggage claim area. At the top of that steep escalator is a waiting area where moms and dads, sons and daughters, friends and family, stand eagerly awaiting the arrival of their beloved family member who is arriving from a faraway land. The waiters stand with signs, with balloons, and with eager faces teeming with anticipation. They stand waiting and peering at the top of the escalator as each passenger pops into view. "Will the next one be our family member?" "I hope so." "Is that him?" "Isn't she supposed to be here by now?" The waiting area literally tingles with anticipation. Each passenger arrives to squeals of joy, roars of laughter, tears, embraces, and twirling around in the arms of the family.

That is how I envision heaven. Each of us arrives one by one into the presence of God, appearing on the horizon like travelers from a faraway land. Our family members and "heavenly greeting team" stand waiting, tingling with delight and joy as they anticipate our arrival.

I do not think that I get to pick, but I can hope that my greeting team includes not only my father and grandmother, but also John Fisher and John Paul II, Teresa of Avila and Catherine of Siena, Father Caj, Sister Rose, Mary, and Jesus Himself. All waiting to receive me as the newest arrival into the family of God once and for all. Waiting to show me around the newest renovations of this old house. Waiting to say, "Welcome home!"

Allen Hunt served as a United Methodist pastor for nearly twenty years. He now partners with Matthew Kelly at Dynamic Catholic. Allen was received into the Church on the Feast of the Epiphany, January 6, 2008. He and his wife, Anita, have two daughters. Allen is the author of several best-selling books, including Confessions of a Mega-Church Pastor, Everybody Needs to Forgive Somebody, *and* Life's Greatest Lesson. *You may contact Allen at allen@dynamiccatholic.com.*

More Than Enough

By Kathy McDonald

former Lutheran

Our third son was ten days old on "Reformation Sunday" 1998. The preacher that Sunday at the local Lutheran church we attended was a retired Lutheran school principal, a man in his seventies with a great shock of white hair. He ascended the pulpit and held up a book, a book he proclaimed "the work of the devil!" The book was by a Catholic author on justification. The preacher offered this book as evidence that "the Reformation must go on!" To me, he came across as so angry and fearful, so unreasonably opposed to the Catholic author, that I leaned over and whispered to my husband, Joe, and said "Sounds like a book we ought to read."

Though we were Lutheran, my husband was on the faculty of a Catholic college in a small town to which we had moved just two months before our son was born. Joe found the book in the college library and brought it home for me to read. That was the beginning of the end of my life as a Lutheran.

Sound beginnings

I was born and raised in a conservative German Lutheran family (Lutheran Church Missouri Synod or LCMS), the third of five children; I was baptized as an infant, as were all my siblings. We attended church and Sunday School every Sunday without fail even when traveling. My happiest childhood memories are from church, particularly Christmas and Easter. I always had a lively faith and took to heart everything I could grasp at church. The messages of Advent and Lent, delivered through the Wednesday night services our family faithfully attended, left deep impressions on my heart. One year, I was quite surprised to wake up one Christmas morning to find Jesus had not returned yet, because so vividly and urgently had our pastor proclaimed His second coming that Advent! I loved singing the beautiful, strong hymns of our church and participating in the liturgy even though I couldn't understand why we told God we were "hardly" [heartily] sorry for our sins in the Confession of Sins each Sunday. I regularly and devoutly read my treasured book of Bible stories, the only religious book in our home, which I had won for perfect Sunday School attendance.

By the time of my Lutheran confirmation when I was in the eighth grade, I was concerned I didn't have "real faith." I had questions about the Bible: "How do I know someone didn't just make this up?" and "How can anyone know the truth?" Typical adolescent questioning, but I was tortured by these threats to my faith. I was afraid I was an atheist when I was confirmed and prayed God would just "zap" me with unwavering faith at the moment of confirmation. It didn't happen. I wasn't zapped. But I did get a wonderful gift of a prayer book for the event and settled on a "Prayer for Faith" that has sustained me since that day. "Lord, I believe," the prayer goes, "Help Thou mine unbelief. Strengthen Thou this weak and flickering faith."

I prayed that prayer often through high school as I struggled with doubts. Truly I sought God but didn't know where to find Him.

I got involved in *Young Life* (a Christian ministry for middle school through college age students) for a while, which was an eye-opening experience. It was there I first experienced extemporaneous prayer. I had wanted just to "talk to God" but had never been shown how. I was introduced to Christian books (I had never known Christian bookstores existed until then) and read exciting stories of courageous men and women of faith, like David Wilkerson (*The Cross and the Switchblade*) and Brother Andrew (*God's Smuggler*). I wanted to be like them, giving my life for God. Finally, I had found something I had been searching for — people who boldly lived the faith they professed.

My parents had not been happy with my foray into *Young Life*, not understanding why I didn't want to go to our Lutheran youth group. After three years with *Young Life*, however, I did not sense the depth of the faith I was seeking. I couldn't define it at the time, but it seemed to me "just not enough." By my senior year, as I prepared to attend a Lutheran college, I felt compelled to return to our Lutheran church youth group (the "bloom where you're planted" idea). I had one goal for my life now: to find God, to know Him and love Him, and to give my life to Him. I wanted to be a missionary, but it appeared the only way for a woman in the LCMS to do that was to marry one.

To a Lutheran, the Word of God is of primary importance. It is one of the two "means of grace" (the means by which God creates and increases faith in us); the other being the sacraments of Baptism and the Lord's Supper, or Holy Communion. I reasoned if I wanted the heroic faith I yearned for, I must commit to studying God's Word. In Lutheran colleges, though, that track was found in "theology," not Bible study. The only reasonable course to follow, in my mind then, was to study theology. The only career option for women at that time which called for a theology major was deaconess.

THE LONG SEARCH

Theological studies were a huge disappointment. None of it was about the personal relationship with God I sought, only intellectual talk about God, and much of it called into question the foundational Christian truths I had been taught. Despite its noble-sounding motto — "Faith and Service in Christ"

— the deaconess preparation program was my first encounter with feminism; serving the feminist cause, not Christ. I sought immersion in life with God, but was being groomed toward breaking open the male-only ministry in the LCMS to include women. The LCMS fractured while I was in college. The conservative faction, which retained the name LCMS, still has only male pastors today. The "liberal" faction later merged with other Lutheran groups to form the Evangelical Lutheran Church of America (ELCA), which ordains women as pastors and bishops. Upon graduation from a Lutheran university with degrees in theology and Greek, I hadn't come any closer to finding God but, rather, was left discouraged and confused about what to do.

My search for God continued for several years through a series of church occupations: a deaconess internship (after which I abandoned the whole deaconess track), director of Christian education in a Lutheran church, and then a Lutheran schoolteacher. I looked for God in Israel pursuing graduate studies and later as an elementary school teacher in Jerusalem. I was impressed by many of the Catholic shrines in the Holy Land, particularly the Church of the Holy Sepulcher in Jerusalem which encloses the traditional sites of our Lord's crucifixion, burial, and resurrection. The beauty of it all left a deep impression on me, but I didn't yet have a context for appreciating Catholic history or worship.

Back in the U.S., I worked for the LCMS in mission education, traveling around the country promoting LCMS missions. This work took me around the country and even to Nigeria. The beauty and simplicity of the Nigerian people and their worship touched me deeply. Here, I sensed I was getting a little closer to God.

Paving the road

During these years of searching for God, I had several encounters with "real Catholics." I had not thought Catholics were "real Christians;" I thought they just went to church because they "had to" but did not have "saving faith." During that time, though, I met some Catholics who made me question this presumption. One was a woman whom I had known as a child in our Lutheran church. She had converted to Catholicism and told me about her devotion to Mary (I was *not* ready for that!). Her story was the first I had heard in which someone converted to Catholicism out of conviction, not just for marriage.

Another was a Catholic fellow I dated for a while who took me to my first Mass. Something struck me at that Mass, although I didn't know what. I wanted to go back, again and again, and even attended a few classes with the priest who gave me my first book on Catholicism. I was dumbfounded reading through that book — there was so much in there that I believed! But there was also much I couldn't touch yet and so I set it aside. Looking back, I can see how the Holy Spirit was paving the road for my own conversion through these encounters with faithful Catholics.

First light

So I continued in the Lutheran Church, married, and had children. I was content enough with the Lutheran church where we lived, which was certainly on the "orthodox" end of the Lutheran spectrum and with a solid liturgy. I was occupied with family matters that my burning quest for the deeper things of God was tempered.

But then, shortly before our third son's birth, we moved to the town where my testimony began. My husband, Joe, and I were uncomfortable with the local LCMS church from the beginning. The Baptist-style services and preaching tended in the opposite direction of the orthodox Lutheranism we knew, but we weren't in the position to go looking elsewhere at that point. However, our experience on "Reformation Sunday," not only catapulted us out of that church, it eventually landed us in the arms of the Roman Catholic Church. More on that journey later, but now I'd like to address some of the difficult theological issues that had to be overcome before I could embrace Catholicism.

LUTHER AND HIS DOCTRINES

The Catholic book Joe checked out of the library dealt with the cornerstone of Lutheranism. To have the doctrine *sola fide* ("faith alone") fall, meant Luther's foundation was fatally fractured. What I had learned and held as a Lutheran came crashing down when I squarely faced what the Bible said about faith and works. I had blindly accepted what I had been taught, memorizing "proof texts" for Lutheran doctrines from childhood, never questioning whether or not they actually proved the truths of Lutheran teaching.

Occasionally, it seemed there were inconsistencies between the Bible and Lutheran doctrines; for instance, the doctrine of *sola scriptura* ("Bible alone") came in conflict with New Testament passages. I had trouble reconciling the doctrine of "faith alone" with James' passages on the importance of works (but we had learned that Luther had called the Book of James "an epistle of straw," so we didn't hold it very highly either). However, there was another inconsistency: who was Luther to say what should and should not be in the Bible? That thought was pretty close to blasphemy, I was sure, so I dismissed it.

We had never been taught any Church history between the time of the Apostles and Luther. I first heard of the "Church Fathers" in a Greek class in college. As I translated Irenaeus' writings from the Greek, the truth of what he had written amazed me. I wondered why I had never been told of him before. None of my theology courses in college ever mentioned the Church Fathers. We were never given any devotional readings beyond what Luther wrote. I did begin to read some of Luther's larger works in college and was indeed troubled by his anti-Semitism and hatred of the papacy and Catholic Church. However, that was explained away by saying, "that's how people wrote and spoke in that time" and "he was German" (and having been raised in a very German family, Luther's "German" personality made sense to me).

Now, after "Reformation Day," I faced a book that challenged the most fundamental of all Lutheran doctrines. I shut the book hard several times, afraid of what I was reading. "If this is true," I surmised, "everything I have believed in my whole life as a Lutheran is in question. If this is true, what else have I wrongly believed?" I did finish the book and I was scared. I was embarking upon the greatest adventure of learning of my life.

I happened upon an online Catholic forum, which became my greatest help for understanding Catholic doctrine in the context of my Lutheran understanding. In these early days of probing Catholicism, I first thought we, as Lutherans and Catholics, were all talking about the same thing, just in a different way. We all believe in justification by faith, but emphasize different aspects. The biggest shock for me came when I learned that the Catholic Church does not teach, as Lutherans do, that man is totally corrupted through Original Sin, totally incapable of cooperating with God in any way, that God only covers our sins, or that when God looks at us, He does not see us but only Christ.

I was also confronted by something that has taken me years to grasp, and still I am afraid I cannot explain the Catholic doctrine of justification well. It is not simple or single-stranded, but involves the doctrines of sin (original and actual, mortal and venial), grace (actual and sanctifying), the sacraments (all *seven*), and runs so deep it can never be fully grasped. What confronted me was a completely new, non-linear way of thinking. I would have to empty myself of everything Lutheran and learn the Catholic faith on its own, not in comparison or in relation to anything I had known as a Lutheran.

I was beginning to see Catholicism not as a set of doctrines, as I had understood the Lutheran faith, but more like a tapestry where every thread of truth is bound up with all the others: pull out one thread and the whole thing unravels; held together, you have a magnificent picture. I had begun with thinking I just needed to translate my Lutheran understanding into Catholic language, but I was looking for cognates in a language where there were none. This was going to be much more like learning Hebrew than Greek.

If I admitted that the Catholic Church was right on justification, which would be borne out in its consistency in all other doctrines, I believed I was compelled to become Catholic. The scandal of Christian disunity deeply troubled me. The least, and best, I could do would be to join the Church Christ Himself founded. But how to get from here to there was nowhere clear to me.

MORE LIGHT ON THE PATH

The next book my husband brought home from the college library was *Rome Sweet Home* by Scott and Kimberly Hahn. I could not believe what I was reading! Here were real people, devout and educated Protestants, who chose to become Catholic. They addressed many of the common Protestant obstacles to the Catholic Church in ways that made sense. I was starting to get an inkling of the process of conversion.

I couldn't talk to any non-Catholics (which included all my family and friends at the time) about my Catholic musings, because I could not yet explain it. I had no words, no defenses, no context for any of it. I wouldn't know how to answer their objections, but just knew in my heart I had come upon the truth. The most I could say was what I had told a Lutheran pastor who asked before we joined his church, "What are you looking for in a church?" I replied, "I am looking for a church that will help me live as a Christian and die as a Christian." All I could say to my horrified Protestant family and friends was, "I have found the Church I've been seeking."

I continued reading and asking questions of my online Catholic friends. I devoured convert stories and somehow got connected with the Coming Home Network International, probably through the online Catholic forum I had found. CHNetwork provided me with a wonderful mentor, a woman who was formerly a Lutheran pastor. I will be forever thankful to her and CHNetwork for the help I received on my journey to the Catholic Church.

My husband did not yet share my enthusiasm for the Catholic Church and I had to learn that while we were one in marriage, God has His plans for us as individuals. He calls us and works with us according to our individual natures and only God knows the time and manner that is best for that call. It was certainly a challenging time for our marriage, but I know even these struggles were part of God's way of preparing us both to enter the Catholic Church.

THE LAST FRONTIER

A couple years later, we moved again, this time to Alaska, now with four children, having added a daughter eight months earlier. I had continued my Catholic reading and correspondence and was growing more restless about continuing in the Lutheran church. My restlessness came to a head when I began planning for the new school year.

We had begun homeschooling two years earlier when our eldest child was in the third grade. Raising our children in the Christian faith was the central tenet of our homeschool and choosing the right religion curriculum was the first thing on my teacher's to-do list each year. I looked over the Lutheran books in front of me and compared them with some Catholic curriculum a Catholic friend from our former homeschool group had shared with me. I was a convinced Catholic by this point and could not in good conscience teach our children what I did not believe. I chose the Catholic curriculum.

Another dilemma presented itself: I would be teaching the Catholic faith to our children while we still worshipped in the Lutheran Church. I talked with my husband and said I could not have one foot in the Lutheran Church and the other in the Catholic Church. Our children needed to have a consistent message. We agreed that day to begin attending the Catholic Church with the view toward becoming Catholic.

LEARNING TO BE CATHOLIC

Deciding to become Catholic was one thing; learning how to be Catholic would be something quite different. Actually realizing what we sought — that is to enter the Catholic Church fully and completely — proved a very difficult journey, fraught with many obstacles. Perhaps ironically, this is one thing I appreciated about the Catholic Church: that it's so hard to get in! It seemed the devil was very interested in keeping us out, so we must be on the right track, I surmised. Looking back over my journey to the Catholic Church, I can see God's love and providence in allowing every obstacle, every challenge, along the way. How true it is that the harder we work for something, the more we appreciate it!

The first thing I did to learn "how to be Catholic" was to begin a Catholic prayer life. I purchased *Manual of Prayers* and began an early morning routine of prayer and reading, rising before my family was up. I believe this was the single most important step I took on my journey to Catholicism. After I found a pamphlet on praying the Rosary in our church's "tract rack," I started taking it with me on my daily "prayer walks," forcing myself to memorize the prayers and mysteries.

It was hard to warm up to this devotion, I admit, but convinced of its importance to the Catholic life, I persevered. By the time I had memorized all the mysteries, I found I was looking forward to my daily Rosary. I have received so much consolation and help through praying the Rosary that now I can't imagine a day without it.

In the fall of 2001, my husband and I enrolled in RCIA to begin the process of formal reception into the Catholic Church. Unfortunately, RCIA proved to be a trial rather than an aid on the way; not at all what I envisioned the Catholic Church to be. We endured it, went to Mass faithfully, and began preparing our 10-year-old son, Gabe, for his First Holy Communion. Our priest gave us permission to prepare Gabe at home using the materials I had purchased for our homeschool. This turned out to be a great way for me to learn about the Catholic faith as we studied together. Gabe became the first "official" Catholic in our family when he received the Sacraments of Penance and Holy Communion the following spring.

Though my husband and I had completed RCIA, we had another obstacle to overcome before we could enter the Church; we needed to have our marriage blessed and for that we would both need to seek annulments of prior unions. The annulment process took two and a half years. Many criticize the Catholic Church's annulment process. I am not one of them. It is a gift the Church gave us that provided tremendous healing. It required great patience to endure incomprehensible delays with no guarantee of a positive outcome. It afforded a great opportunity for growing through prayer and study, learning what it means to be Catholic. In the end, our annulments were granted and our marriage was blessed at a beautiful ceremony with our children and Catholic friends around us. The following Sunday, my husband (who chose "Augustine" as his Confirmation saint) and I ("Mary, Queen of All Saints" — why not go for the gold?) received the Sacraments of Confirmation and Holy Communion.

I am amazed at how God works! I am thankful for my solid Lutheran upbringing that first brought me to faith and taught me the Scriptures. Growing up Lutheran, I gained a great foundation in and appreciation for sacred music, something I probably would have missed in the Catholic Church during that time (I was raised in a conservative Christian church at the time the Catholic Church was undergoing its "identity crisis" following Vatican II). Now our family is assisting our Catholic parish with its sacred music ministry.

I join so many others God has called out of strong Protestant churches and into the Catholic Church who are now realizing the fullness of the faith. When I first met with our priest telling him of my desire to become Catholic, I told him I believed I would be bringing many more with me. That remains my hope and I pray daily for my extended family, that they, too, will realize the fullness of the faith.

My search is over. I have enough — more than enough to last my lifetime!

ADVICE FOR THOSE ON THE WAY TO BECOMING CATHOLIC

Begin a Catholic prayer life as soon as you are convinced you are on the way to the Catholic Church. Get a "lifetime" prayer book like *Manual of Prayers* and make this a habit for the rest of your life.

If you are married to a non-Catholic spouse, recognize that although you are one flesh in marriage, you remain individuals spiritually. God does not call couples; He calls individuals. Your call is not your spouse's call. Be patient with yourself and with your spouse. Pray, pray, pray! Let God do the work of conversion in you both.

Kathy McDonald lives with her husband, Joe, and their children in rural Tennessee. They are members of Holy Cross Catholic Church in Paris.

PLUMBING THE TRUTHS OF CHRIST'S CHURCH

ROB EVANS

former Evangelical Pentecostal

One day, on a bank application, my wife wrote that my "form of employment" was that of a "Singing Plumber." To me, that conjures an image of a man in a tuxedo, cleaning drains as he sings opera. I do sing, not opera, but Christian songs to kids under the name "The Donut Man," because I end every concert by "repairing" the hole in a donut to remind everyone that God sends His love to fill up the empty place in our hearts.

BOTH SIDES OF MY BRAIN

I tell you this to let you know that both sides of my brain, the musician and the plumber, had to be convinced to become Catholic. You've heard from the scholars, theologians, and educators on the *Journey Home*. Now it's time to find out why a blue-collar, ex-hippy, musician-type like me would "cross the Tiber." But first, some instructions are needed.

Plumbing Rules and Tools. To be a plumber, I had to master some very practical things, such as: sewage runs downhill; cold water is on the right, hot is on the left; payday is on Friday; and don't chew your fingernails. And then there are the tools. Let me tell you, plumbers have tools for their tools! We've got "goes-inta" tools and "goes-outta" tools. There are twisting, cutting, cleaning, bending, burning, gluing tools, and of course we always want more tools. Why? Because we've got a job to do! Truly successful plumbers have to find the shortest, straightest line between two points and run their pipe accordingly. Water comes down the tower, through the main, into the house, and out the tap. In order to work, it all has to be connected to bring refreshment and cleansing to the occupants, and then safely conduct the waste to where it can be appropriately handled. Just think of the diseases that plague cultures that don't do it!

If you're not really excited by my story yet, hang in there. Because if good plumbing is important in the natural realm, think of how much more important it is in the spiritual!

"Spiritual Plumbing" is something I think the Catholic Church does remarkably well. Not that my Protestant experience was sorely amiss, but it was just not employing all of the "tools" Christ has supplied. This was especially true on the issue of dealing thoroughly, and appropriately, with sewage. By sewage, I mean sin.

In with the Good, Out with the Bad. Both Catholics and Protestants agree that all sin is pardoned by Christ's finished act on Calvary. Some Protestants, however, tend to consider Baptism as only a symbolic act, whereas Catholics embrace and employ the promise found in 1 Peter 3:21, that "Baptism … now saves you." The Sacrament of Baptism actually sets us apart to God, and as a daily reminder, we can bless ourselves with holy water, and reappropriate, by faith, the power of our Baptism every time we walk through the doors of the church. That is good plumbing. And, it gets better.

A Protestant is far more on his own when it comes to confessing sin within the church. In all of my years of support groups, small groups, venting groups, and spiritual-help groups, I never, ever had anyone look me in the eye and say unequivocally, "Through the ministry of the Church, may God give you pardon and peace, and I absolve you from your sins in the name of the Father, and of the Son, and of the Holy Spirit."

That is what a Catholic priest says to us when he administers the Sacrament of Reconciliation. (Ahhh. What a wonderful-sounding "flush" that makes)!

Connected. Plumbing systems don't work if they are not connected! Yet the Catholic Church is the only church that sees the "apostolic connection" as a must. Apostolic succession, Holy Orders, is found in the Roman Catholic Church because before Peter died in Rome, he handed off the Church to the next guy, and that guy to the next guy, and then the next guy, and so on. In other words, when a priest distributes the Eucharist under the appearance of the bread and the wine, he is "piping-it-in" all the way back to Peter, Jesus, and the first Eucharist! This is a marvelous, miraculous, historical connection (more about the Eucharist later)!

Plumber's Key. Most plumbers carry a shut-off key in their truck. It has a "T" handle with a long stem that goes way down into the street to access the supply to your house. Let me tell you, when you need that key, you really need it! Therefore, I appreciate the keys that Jesus gave to Peter in order to operate this "supply and waste system" otherwise known as the Catholic Church. Protestants believe that Peter took the keys with him to the grave. The Catholic Church does not (check out the first chapter of Acts where the disciples gave Judas' empty office to Matthias). My point is, the pre-eminent office of Peter still functions today, with a wonderful teacher named Jorge Mario Bergoglio, otherwise known as Pope Francis, keeping an eye on those incredible keys!

Rust. Now in a system this old, you might find some rust in the pipes. But anything else two thousand years old would have shut down a long time ago if God wasn't in it. I used to be "put off" by the traditional liturgy, the pomp and circumstance of the Catholic Church. Some of its style strikes me as a bit "rusty." But as a plumber, if you told me that the first water mains here in Philly were made of plastic, I would know you are no plumber! The first water mains that Ben Franklin and company set in the ground were hollowed-out logs. I've seen some in the museums around town. In front of the display, the "plumber-in-me" calls my family over to admire what I find to be so exciting, "Wow, look at this hollowed-out log with metal bands on the ends!" And my kids pat me on the shoulder and say, "That's nice, Dad."

I recognize an original when I see one. They see a log. I see this old wooden pipe as a seminal invention, obviously the real McCoy. So, too, do I now see Catholic ritual and liturgy. Yes, it can seem tedious, culturally speaking — not modern, to say the least. But if you are looking for the real, historical Church that Jesus handed off to Peter and the disciples, wouldn't you expect something two thousand years old to have a few things that look and act a bit strange? Perhaps even a bit anachronistic? But when we do encounter "rust" (and we will), let us pray for the fresh water of the Holy Spirit to cleanse every bit of corrosion from the vital function of the Catholic Church today!

NOW FROM THE OTHER SIDE OF MY BRAIN

I'm a musician, a singer, a songwriter, poet ... dreamer. I love a good story, and can recognize when a story is fully realized or not. As the "Donut Man," I have sung Bible stories from the first-person perspective with great effect. "Daniel in the Lion's Den" is sung by the lion. The "Parable of the Mustard Seed" is sung by the mustard seed, and so on. This "first-person" style of storytelling has allowed me to view things from a fresh perspective.

For over forty years now, my life has been rocked by the greatest story of all: the story of the Messiah, Jesus Christ. When I was introduced to Jesus at the Gospel Temple of Philadelphia in 1972, it was accompanied with the pastor's personal attention and discipleship as we sought to apply God's Word and promises to my life. I remember him exhorting me to allow God to address my need for what he called the "Three Ms" of life: master, mate, and mission.

"Jesus is your master," he said. "Now, let's pray about the other two."

The Prayers of the Saints. There began a long-standing prayer relationship with Jesus and me. As I prayed, and as we worshipped later with our worship band in church, the overhead projecting the words upon the wall, I closed my eyes and imagined Christ on the cross, Christ rising from the dead, and Christ now on a marvelous chair there in His throne room. I must tell you that over the years, as I considered the "manifold witnesses" and "the spirits of those made perfect" surrounding us in our approach to Mount Zion, I found it odd that Christ was always portrayed in the throne room surrounded by everyone thanking Him, praising Him, worshipping Him, but not praying to Him. Not that "The Master" let me down. He certainly did answer my prayers. For a "mate," he gave me Shelley, my wife of forty years. And the "mission"? Well, that is still being revealed! But I came to realize that Catholics had it right when they asked the saints in heaven to pray for them.

The Ultimate Mom. Perhaps it was the storyteller/writer in me that started to think that something or someone else was missing in my spiritual life, in my understanding of heaven. But it wasn't until I started to go to a Catholic church that the missing persons in that throne room were identified. Of course! A great King would not be sitting on the throne by Himself. Rather, He would be surrounded by His Bride, the Church, the mighty men and women comprising it, and most prominently, there would also be by His side … His Mother. In Mass, I have found various feast days to be inspiring and revelatory, because now I pray that these saints in glory would pray to the Lord our God for me, that the virtues they enjoyed would be created by the hand of almighty God in me as well.

I love the fact that in any given Mass, a saint who has been dead for fifteen hundred years can be recognized and his or her prayers requested. That is heavenly stuff! I also ask that the first and ultimate disciple of all would pray for me as well, since she is the finest reflection of God's glory ever found in a created being. That, of course, is Jesus' mother, who is now our mother: Mary.

The Eucharist: Symbol or Heaven Itself? The same Protestants who dismiss Baptism as the real impartation of grace usually also dismiss the possibility of the Real Presence of Christ being imparted in the Eucharist. It follows that if you deny the power of the Sacrament of Baptism, you would likewise deny the power of the Eucharist. I therefore raise a flag of truce and ask for a parlay of both camps! Come hither, let us talk peacefully! Here, as Protestant and Catholic camps gather under the white flag, we agree on many points.

We all agree that the God-who-created-everything-by-the-words-of-His-mouth so humbled Himself, that He was born of a Virgin. And when this child became a man, He humbled Himself even more, to be tempted by every temptation common to man. We also all agree that this Man-born-of-the-Virgin humbled Himself yet again, to the point of dying on a cross. But then, after His resurrection, the Protestant says God would never continue to humble Himself to the point of becoming bread and wine! The Catholic says, "Why would He stop humbling Himself at this point?!" The storyteller in me shouts, "The Catholics have it right!"

Jesus said, "Lo, I am with you always." The Protestant says, "That means that Jesus is with us by His Holy Spirit." The Catholic says, "Today, at Mass, Jesus was physically present to me in the Eucharist, and spiritually present by His Holy Spirit, and in the community of saints." Why would the sending of the Holy Spirit at Pentecost countermand Jesus' declaration found in John 6? God, the ultimate iconoclast, smashes the barrier of heaven and earth, time and space, when He says that when we eat the Bread of His flesh, and drink His Blood that it is indeed real food and drink. The limits of heaven and earth, of time and space, are like putty in the hands of Jesus, the Creator-made-flesh.

Now from the Heart. So far, I've given you some practical plumbing tips, songs about "repairing" donuts, reflections on the sacraments, apostolic succession, the keys of Peter, the communion of the saints, and the Eucharist. I have two more things, but these are from my heart. You see, I am a child of divorce. My heart was broken when my mother divorced several times, and both of my parents remarried, providing me with two half-brothers, a half-sister, and a myriad of step-siblings. Of course, I am happy that I got siblings out of the deal. But our family unity was scattered to the wind, and I had to adjust to a whole new framework for my identity. My agonies prepared me to receive the Gospel.

When I became a Christian, I was told that this would be my "forever family." That was true for about three years, until the senior pastor committed adultery, and our church went on to split several times in several ways. That was when Shelley and I moved on; out to Los Angeles, then to Nashville, and then back to Philadelphia. Over the next thirty years, we belonged to a variety of Protestant churches. Of the eight churches that we were members of during that time, four of them split and divided for a variety of reasons. The closest emotion that I can equate with a church split, especially in our younger years, is the pain in my heart when my own parents divorced. It was an agony to see friends shattered and scattered. I actually pulled the car over several times during that period to weep. I have to admit, by the time the last church split, we saw it coming and "ducked."

Now that I am a Catholic, I have learned that the "denominations" that I had taken for granted in my Protestant experience had not always been there. To study Church history is to discover that about five hundred years ago, people known as "The Reformers" split away from the Catholic Church to form a brand of Christianity that did not include the "See of Rome" in the equation. It was, essentially, a divorce, a split driven by sincerity and the need for reform, but resulting in the great divide that we see today. I found that it forced me into choices that are very difficult.

As a child of divorce, I found that I had to choose between my father's lifestyle and my mother's lifestyle. I found that choice to be impossible, untenable, and emotionally debilitating. Now I have to make a choice between two spiritual families.

If you are struggling with the style differences between modern Protestant seeker-friendliness and solemn Catholic liturgy, I can empathize! I love contemporary music, clapping and singing, but I have a deeper need for solemnity and the awe that accompanies worship in the communion of the saints. That is why I now go to the Catholic Church. I appreciate the many biblical contributions that the brilliant teachers of Protestantism have to offer about every aspect of life: marriage, finance, faith, child-rearing, and so on. But I prefer a homily followed by the Real Presence of Christ that is found in the Eucharist.

Marriage: A Shadow Cast from Heaven. As I reflect on my two trades, music and plumbing, I forgot to mention the obvious: I learned these trades in order to provide for my family. My driving force has always been that my loved ones would be provided for. But now I have been pointed toward a mystery that makes me peer over every cloud and look eagerly beyond the horizon to heaven itself. Here's why: in my years now as a Catholic, the most profound teaching I have found is the "Theology of the Body," and it is, in my humble estimation, one of the highpoints from the teaching of the great Pope St. John Paul II. He observed that "all analogies of heaven are imperfect, but the spousal analogy for the Kingdom of God is the least imperfect."

In short, I am living in a sacrament called "Marriage." My marriage is actually a veil for heaven itself. The light source is the Trinity, shining through the throne room of heaven, and earthly marriage is the shadow this light casts. The "Theology of the Body" observes that all created things point toward their Creator, but Christian marriage, Catholic marriage, is the "crown of God's creation."

For a child of divorce, with such dysfunctional experiences and shattered memories, to "get back on the saddle" and ride off into the sunset with my wife Shelley at my side is a miracle of sorts, don't you think? Shelley is also a child of divorce. We met in church, and then thirty-four years later we came into the Catholic Church together. We both absolutely agree that the sacraments are now an indispensable agent of grace within this grace we know as our marriage. We both agree that the two key sacraments that keep us going are Confession and the Eucharist. Modern man's pessimism claims that you can never give what you never got. As Catholics, we disagree. The Godhead, the Trinity, is the eternal source of all unity. And the marriage of Jesus, the Son of God, the Second Person of the Trinity, to His Bride — the Church — with Mary by His scarred side, and with St. Joseph standing nobly in attendance, is the heavenly model that we earnestly emulate and call upon for prayer.

I leave you with this "spousal analogy." On my wedding night, I did not take the keys from my bride. Rather, I gave them to her. Shelley got the keys to the house, keys to the car, and keys to our bank account brimming with $640. She did not need to ask me every time she used the keys. I "endowed her" with full authority to use them, anytime, as my bride, as she saw fit. So it is with Jesus giving the keys to Peter. When He gave the keys to Peter, He endowed the Church (His "Bride") with all authority necessary to conduct earthly affairs in His name, until His return. I thank God that my home is now under Peter, who is under Christ. This "Singing Plumber" has a lot of work to do, and a lot of songs yet to sing. But I can rejoice to call myself a Roman Catholic.

Rob Evans and his wife, Shelley, live in Merion Station, Pennsylvania, a suburb of Philadelphia. They have six children, and nine grandchildren. Rob travels worldwide encouraging young families with his Christ-centered music and videos. To find out more about Rob Evans' Donut Man Apostolate, go to his website: www.donutman.com.

CHRIST IN HIS FULLNESS

BRUCE SULLIVAN

former Church of Christ preacher

I will begin with a statement that I made to a Catholic friend of mine back in 1993. In complete seriousness — and with absolute confidence — I said, "Look, Sharon, if you or anyone else can show me from the Bible that the Catholic Church is the Church that Christ established, I'll become a Catholic tomorrow." With that bold challenge, I had hoped to goad my devoutly Catholic friend into a serious, evangelistic Bible study. Instead, she handed me a copy of Karl Keating's *Catholicism and Fundamentalism*, and so began the end of my career as a Fundamentalist preacher.

I was raised in the South as a Southern Baptist. Attending church three times each week was standard fare in our home. I am eternally grateful to the Southern Baptist Convention, and to my family, for rooting me in the Scriptures, for introducing me to Christ, and for instilling within my soul the conviction that what this world needs more than anything else is Jesus. But it was not until I went off to college that I began to examine what I believed and, more importantly, why I believed it.

Throughout my college years, I interacted with members of various Protestant denominations and listened to a wide variety of campus preachers. I knew that my own theology had several loose ends, and I was searching intently for what could tie it all together. My searching eventually led me to a relatively small denomination known as the Church of Christ.

The Church of Christ is a denomination that sprang out of what some historians refer to as the American Restoration

Movement or the Stone-Campbell Movement (so named for its two most prominent historical figures, Barton W. Stone and Alexander Campbell). Launched in the early nineteenth century, the movement was originally conceived by its proponents as a means of transcending denominational divisions and uniting all believers in Christ on universally accepted essentials of the faith. Because of the difficulty in establishing the precise content of "universally accepted essentials," the movement soon became a very divisive one and eventually split into three separate denominations: the Christian Church (Disciples of Christ), the independent Christian Churches, and the Churches of Christ. The modern-day Disciples of Christ emphasize the movement's early theme of Christian unity, whereas the independent Christian Churches and Churches of Christ tend to emphasize the theme of "restoration." Together, these three denominations can claim approximately four million members.

The Churches of Christ attracted me by what they would call "nondenominational Christianity." They had several neat-sounding "credal" statements that I found nothing short of enthralling. These included such declarations as: "We are Christians only, but not the only Christians"; "We speak where the Bible speaks, and we're silent where the Bible is silent"; and "We call Bible things by Bible names." These concepts were mighty attractive for me in view of the denominational chaos surrounding me. So in 1985, I was baptized at the Auburn Church of Christ in Auburn, Alabama, and began a ten-year association with the denomination.

The Churches of Christ had an enormous impact on my life. For one thing, they introduced me to my wife Gloria, who was a fifth-generation follower of the Stone-Campbell Movement and an active member of the Auburn Church of Christ. They also introduced me to ideas that were very much at odds with my Baptist upbringing — ideas that would dramatically impact my spiritual journey.

First of all, the Stone-Campbell Churches of Christ introduced me to the biblical basis for believing that Christ established a visible, identifiable, and institutional Church. That is a very Catholic idea, and one that is not usually associated with Evangelical Protestantism. Secondly, they showed me — from the Bible — that Baptism is for the remission of sins. Likewise, this may be a distinctly Catholic idea, but it is not a very Baptist idea. Finally, they also presented me with the scriptural evidence for believing that justification is not by faith alone and that one can, indeed, fall from grace (as opposed to the Calvinist teaching of "once saved, always saved). Again, these ideas were definitely not in line with Baptist teaching, but as I was to learn later, these were solidly in line with Catholic teaching. Though I didn't realize it at the time, the Churches of Christ were to become something of a stepping-stone from my Evangelical Protestant upbringing to the Catholic faith.

After graduation from Auburn in 1986, Gloria and I were married and departed for studies at the Sunset School of Preaching in Lubbock, Texas. We chose Sunset because of its reputation for academic intensity and missionary zeal. For two years, we were the privileged pupils of men who had given their lives in missionary service all around the globe. Their examples served to heighten our own desire for missionary service. We became charter members of a missionary team that was bound for Brazil — the largest Catholic nation in the world. We selected Brazil because, at the time, we believed that more than anyone else, Catholics stood in need of the true Gospel of Jesus Christ.

It goes without saying, but my view of Catholicism at the time was somewhat less than complimentary. I did not believe that Catholics should be considered Christians in the proper sense of the word. In my mind, they were idolatrous, Mary-worshipping, children of the Whore of Babylon, who had embraced a soul-damning false gospel that came straight from the pits of hell! I must hasten to add, however, that it was not mean-spiritedness that animated me in my posture towards Catholics and Catholicism. Rather, I was compelled by sincere conviction and, sadly, gross ignorance.

The plan was for each of the mission team families to work with a sponsoring congregation for a period of two years prior to embarking on a five-year service commitment in Brazil. So upon graduation, Gloria and I moved to Kingsport, Tennessee, to work with a congregation that had agreed to be our sponsor. Those two years were intended to provide team members the opportunity to gain practical ministry experience, study Portuguese (the language of Brazil), and develop a working relationship with their sponsoring congregation. It was a solid plan formulated by a group of veteran missionaries. Within less than a year, however, our mission team disbanded.

The disruption in our missionary plans left us in a tough spot financially. With Gloria and I both determined to keep her at home with our daughter Mary, I decided to seek employment outside of the ministry. Since my degree from Auburn was in agriculture, I applied for — and received — a position with the University of Kentucky College of Agriculture's Cooperative Extension Service. I was given the appointment as County Extension Agent for 4-H & Youth Development in Hart County, Kentucky (only thirty miles from Gloria's home in Metcalfe County). We continued to actively serve in our local congregation of the Church of Christ. I continued to preach and teach on a regular basis. And true to the vision instilled in us at Sunset, we continued to look for the opportunity to join a mission team bound for South America.

It was after moving back to Gloria's home in Kentucky that our conversion to Catholicism began in earnest. It began when a large Catholic family — the family of Art and Sharon Antonio — moved into our area.

Art had just retired from the Navy. He and Sharon were drawn to Kentucky by affordable land and the prospect of raising their children in a wholesome, rural setting. We became acquainted through my work in the county Extension office. Upon learning of their devotion to the Catholic faith, I set out to do the most charitable thing I could think of: introduce them to the "true" Gospel of Christ as presented by the "true" Church of Christ.

For many months, I tried to "evangelize" the Antonios. In turn, they gave me a three-pronged introduction to the Catholic faith. This three-pronged introduction took the form of the Couple to Couple League, Karl Keating, and Father Benjamin Luther.

First, let me mention the Couple to Couple League. Gloria and I had always been very pro-life on the issue of abortion but were unaware of the connection between contraception and abortion. Through the Couple to Couple League, we learned the scriptural, historical, and rational support for the Catholic Church's moral teachings regarding artificial means of contraception. In response to this, we immediately changed our practices in this area of life. And, believe it or not, what I had thought would drive a wedge between husband and wife — namely, the Church's teaching on marital chastity — proved instead to be a most sublime blessing. Ironically, this teaching that is so often dismissed out of hand by those born into the Catholic faith, has been shown, time and again, to actually draw people into the Church.

But while the impact of this introduction to the beauty of the Church's moral teaching was profound and life-changing, we were far from convinced that the Catholic Church was the true Church of Christ. As we say in Kentucky, "There was still a long row to hoe."

The second part of our introduction to the Catholic faith came in the form of a book by Karl Keating, the president of Catholic Answers. After months of getting nowhere in my attempts to get Mrs. Antonio to study the Bible with me, I decided to engage in a little bit of charitable baiting. It was after one particularly frustrating exchange that I looked at her and said, "Look, if you or anyone else can show me from the Bible that the Catholic Church is the Church that Christ established, I'll become a Catholic tomorrow." The next day, she handed me a copy of Karl Keating's *Catholicism and Fundamentalism.* I could not have been more thrilled. As I saw it, in giving me that book to read, she was also giving me license to critique it and expose to her the manifest errors that I knew it had to contain. In other words, I took it as a sign that we were finally getting somewhere.

I went home and looked at the book. On the back cover, I read a statement by Sheldon Vanauken: "I strongly advise honest fundamentalists not to read this book. They might find their whole position collapsing in ruins." I laughed. I think I may have even laughed out loud. But I didn't laugh for long.

Keating's book did at least three things for me. First, he provided numerous examples of the ways in which anti-Catholics distort the Catholic faith and obscure the truth about Catholicism. Second, he exposed the flimsy nature of the assumptions underlying my own Protestant faith (particularly those assumptions pertaining to the Bible and authority). And last, but surely not least, he did something that I thought no one could do: he provided a compelling biblical presentation of the Catholic doctrines that are most often opposed by Fundamentalist Christians. By the time I had finished reading the book, I knew that I was in trouble. I realized that I had far more questions than answers.

The questions that troubled me the most were those pertaining to authority. I was particularly perplexed by the issue of canon. How could I claim that the Bible alone was all that I needed when the Bible itself does not identify its own canon? After all, there were literally dozens of writings that had circulated throughout the early Church that claimed to be inspired. On what basis did I accept the canon of New Testament Scripture upon which my faith depended? How could I know with infallible certitude that the twenty-seven books in my New Testament comprised the true canon? Maybe there were supposed to be twenty-nine books in the New Testament, and the two that were missing contained keys to understanding the other twenty-seven. Maybe there were supposed to be only twenty-five books in the New Testament, in which case our present canon would have two too many. What if those two extra books contain false doctrine? After all, Martin Luther struggled with this notion and actually suggested that the Epistle of St. James be removed from the Bible!

Were I to gloss over the problem of determining canon, I was still left in the unenviable position of claiming that all I needed was the Bible when, in fact, the Bible itself teaches no such thing. Actually, it indicates the contrary. For example, St. Paul expressly underscored our need for oral Tradition (cf. 2 Thess 2:15) and the Church (cf. 1 Tim 3:15). Moreover, virtually every New Testament Epistle was written with the assumption that the writer and his intended recipients shared a body of common knowledge — the deposit of faith (cf. Jude 3). In other words, the recipients understood what was written in light of the teaching they had already received. Oral Tradition was therefore the context through which what was written was understood and put into practice. Or, to put it yet another way: God inspired members of the Church to write to other members of the Church about matters of concern to the Church — thereby underscoring the teaching that the Church, Sacred Tradition, and the Bible are truly inseparable. Yet as a

Protestant, I downplayed — if not denied — the role of both Sacred Tradition and the Church.

The more I struggled with the issue of authority, the more I became convinced that it is the ultimate Protestant "pickle." As a Protestant, I had claimed that the Bible alone was all that I needed. Yet the Bible itself indicated otherwise. Without an infallible certitude of canon, the best I could do was stand in the pulpit and proclaim, "Thus sayeth the Lord ... I think." I could offer only my own, admittedly fallible, opinions about the interpretation of writings that I thought to be inspired.

While these realities served to expose the inadequacies of my Protestant faith, they did not necessarily mean that I was ready to accept the Catholic faith. There remained a seemingly endless list of standard objections to Catholicism that needed to be addressed. To help us address those issues, Art and Sharon encouraged us to contact Father Benjamin Luther, a priest from the Diocese of Owensboro, Kentucky, who also happened to be a convert from the Stone-Campbell Churches of Christ.

Father Luther drove nearly four hours to meet with me at a roadside diner near my home. That first meeting lasted six hours. When we parted company, Father Luther assured me that he would keep in touch — and he proved to be a man of his word. From that point forward, it seemed as if our mailbox was hardly ever empty. I am quite convinced that he impoverished himself sending me a veritable library through the mail and taking my collect phone calls nearly every Saturday morning. He proved immeasurably helpful as we worked through the issues in our efforts to separate fact from fiction regarding the Catholic faith.

Early in the course of our studies, we came to the realization that most of what we had been told about Catholicism had been grossly distorted. That realization itself was a tremendous grace. It helped us to see that before we could decide whether or not the Catholic Church teaches the truth, we had to know the truth about the Catholic Church and her teaching. With that realization to guide us — coupled with the knowledge that our former approach to authority was hopelessly flawed — we delved into a thorough, and at times anxious, study of Catholicism.

I characterize our studies as "anxious" because, coming from a Church of Christ background, we had some rather serious convictions regarding truth, judgment, heaven, and hell. We feared not only for our own souls but also for those of our children if, inadvertently, we led them astray. We wanted desperately to do the will of the Lord by embracing the truth, the whole truth, and nothing but the truth. At times, it seemed as if we could argue both sides of the issues. At times, we wondered if there would ever be any clear-cut answers. We knew we could never go back to our former denomination, but that did not mean that we were at ease with Catholicism. A lifetime of prior teaching, coupled with the ghosts of false caricatures of Catholicism, seemed to have a death grip on us intellectually and emotionally. But our Lord is the One who has conquered death. Thankfully, through time, prayer, and study, He freed us from the deadly grip of error and gave to us the grace to embrace our holy Mother, the Catholic Church.

A watershed event in this process came in December of 1993 when Father Luther and I attended the first Coming Home Network retreat on the campus of Franciscan University of Steubenville. On the second day of the retreat, I awakened early in the home of my host family and went downstairs while everyone else was either asleep or occupied with the start of a new day. I could not help but notice a small "prayer closet" off to the side of the living room. It was a rather small niche with a kneeler, various holy images, and candles. In the dark solitude of that moment, I was drawn to prayer. This time, however, my prayer would be different than any prayer I had offered before.

For months, I had found myself arguing both sides of the issues almost to the point of despair. In the quiet of this moment, I knew that I had come to the end of my rope and needed help. I remember thinking to myself, "If what the Catholic Church teaches about the communion of saints is true, then maybe this is the time to enlist the prayers of the saints in heaven." Kneeling in that little niche, I approached the Father's throne of grace, asking for the grace of clarity and understanding. This, of course, was nothing new. I had done so more times than I could count over the preceding six months of struggle. What was new was this: I concluded by asking the saints in heaven to pray for me. Specifically, I solicited the prayers of Peter, Paul, and Mary (not to be confused with the popular 1960s' singing group). Interestingly enough, I was also quick to ask God to forgive me if such an action was offensive to Him. I did this because, while my studies had sufficiently demonstrated the veracity of the Catholic teaching on the communion of saints, the outward, concrete expression of the teaching ran against the emotional grain of my Protestant upbringing. What was about to follow during the next hour, however, would assure me that Sts. Peter, Paul, and Mary had indeed heard my plea and that, in response to their prayers, God was pouring out His grace.

Back on the campus of Franciscan University, our retreat resumed with all of us participating in the early morning Mass in the campus chapel. I had been to Mass a couple of times before, but could never get past the knee-jerk reactions that I seemed to have at nearly everything that was said or done. This time something was different. I was seated in the back of the chapel, simply observing the proceedings. But instead of nitpicking and criticizing, I found myself contemplating questions that were slowly taking shape in my mind. *What if that man (the priest) is who they say he is? What if he is really doing what they say he is doing? What if what they say is happen-*

ing is actually happening? As I considered these questions in the light of what I had learned from the Scriptures and early Christian writings pertaining to the Real Presence of Christ in the Eucharist, I was left quite literally speechless (which, for those who know me well, comes awfully close to a confirming miracle in my conversion to Catholicism).

Please keep in mind that, as a former Church of Christ preacher, this was all a bit difficult to swallow. Church of Christ members are generally very leery of subjective experiences. As a rule, they demand cold, hard, objective facts with the accompanying "chapter and verse" from the Scriptures. Yet the Scriptures themselves testify to the marvelous ways in which God works in our hearts — ways that many might call "subjective." Would I become a Catholic based merely upon a fuzzy, subjective, emotional experience? Hardly. That is not what occurred that morning. What did occur was this: God took all of the "cold, hard, objective facts" that I had learned concerning the Eucharist, tied them together, and removed my self-imposed barriers to understanding. In a word, He gave grace. And with that grace, I knew that I would one day be Catholic.

I was received into the Church during the Easter Vigil of 1995. Shortly thereafter, I went away on a business trip. In the course of a casual conversation, a coworker asked me, "What did you find in the Catholic Church that you did not find in Protestantism?" It was a sincere question and a good one as well. I mulled it over for quite some time and finally settled on a short answer (something quite unusual for me). In Catholicism, I had found Christ in His fullness.

As Protestant Christians, Gloria and I did know and love Christ. We did not, however, experience Him in His fullness. Without realizing it, we had inadvertently rejected many of the gifts He wanted to give us — gifts that could be received only through full incorporation into His Mystical Body, the Catholic Church. Looking back, we are both truly amazed at what God has so graciously given to us in the Catholic Church: He has given Christ in all of His fullness — the fullness of His Word, the fullness of His sacraments, the fullness of worship, the fullness of His family, the fullness of vocation, and the fullness of salvation.

"Now to him who by the power at work within us is able to do far more abundantly than all that we ask or think, to him be glory in the Church and in Christ Jesus to all generations, for ever and ever. Amen" (Eph 3:20–21).

Since being received into the Catholic Church in 1995, Bruce has served as a catechist in his local parish and a lecturer and speaker on topics related to Catholic apologetics. He has been a guest on EWTN's Mother Angelica Live, The Journey Home, Deep in Scripture, *and* Bookmark. *He is the author of* Christ in His Fullness *and* A Layman's Primer of Liturgical Latin *(both published by CHResources). He and his wife, Gloria, are both graduates of Auburn University and reside with their five children on a family farm in Kentucky.*

There & Back Again

Rev. Deacon Joseph A. Pasquella

former Pentecostal pastor

On October 20, 1956, I was born in Paterson, New Jersey, the son of George and Gloria Pasquella. I was baptized on October 28, 1956, at St. Michael's Roman Catholic Church in Paterson. My father died when I was only four years old in December 1960. He was a young man of only forty. A year later, my mother remarried outside the Church.

My family was not particularly religious, but at the age of nine, I wandered into a Catholic church and knew I wanted to be a part of it. In spite of her reluctance, my mother allowed me to attend Mass and receive First Communion. I was confirmed when I was about thirteen at St. Anthony's Roman Catholic Church in Paterson. Soon after, my mother began worshipping as a charismatic Evangelical Christian. She had been Protestant before I was born, and in spite of my First Communion and Confirmation, she compelled me to join her church. I was sad and confused, as if I was abandoning my faith. The pastor of my mother's Assemblies of God congregation took it upon himself to chastise my choice of Catholicism. He told me I had been worshipping idols and that the Catholic Church was a cult and the "Whore of Babylon." He proceeded to indoctrinate me with Pentecostal beliefs. I was only thirteen years old, and very impressionable. Not knowing how to defend my faith, I went along with the program and embraced my mother's church as best I could. My mother had an emotional illness, and life at home was difficult as a result, yet I always knew that God was present in and around me, protecting me at all times.

Perhaps it is too strong to say that I had been "brainwashed" against the Catholic Church, but at the time of my high school graduation, I was convinced that it was not the true Church. With my heart nonetheless devoted to the service of Christ, I moved to Reno, Nevada, to do some missionary work. I ran Christian fellowships out of my home, while working as a mechanic. I eventually entered a four-year Christian Leadership Training Program at the Way College of Biblical Research in Rome City, Indiana. I graduated with an associate's degree in theology on July 8, 1983. Two days later, I was married to my wonderful wife, Cathy, whom I had met at the Christian Leadership Training Program. She was a practicing Protestant at the time, working as a staff member at the college.

Our first assignment was to establish a mission church in Norwalk, Connecticut. We started the mission out of our home and in two years had eighty-five families. We were then asked to go to Sparks, Nevada, to coordinate some other fellowships and start another mission. The outcome was again successful. Throughout the course of both these ministries, I maintained full-time secular employment in addition to my work for Christ. Cathy and I worked hard as a team in our spiritual endeavors. We believed God had given us a place in which His glory and power could be witnessed.

But when the leadership of the International Ministry, referred to as "The Way," began to endorse erroneous doctrines, we spoke up. Their teachings became quite contrary to certain facts in Holy Scripture, such as questioning the divine nature of Christ. We protested vehemently and were shunned by the community.

We settled in Cape Cod, Massachusetts (Cathy's home state), on December 5, 1987. The move was necessary because we had resigned our previous ministry to follow our Christian beliefs. It took two years before we started to seek out a new church. My wife and I had daily Bible fellowship meetings and prayed together with our two children. These two boys (then aged four and six) are a blessing from God in every way. I say this in spite of the fact that they are both disabled and have some emotional difficulties. These challenges have only enhanced our love for each other, and for God the Father.

While we lived with my mother-in-law, a faithful Irish Catholic, she encouraged us to have our children baptized. The priest who agreed to baptize the boys said we first needed to have our marriage convalidated. In 1990, purely in deference to my mother-in-law's wishes, we had our marriage blessed in the Catholic Church, and our boys were baptized Catholic.

As I continued my journey of faith, in March 1992, I met a former Evangelical minister whom I had known. He had converted to the Antiochian Orthodox faith. We talked for hours. In many ways, I was reminded of the Catholic faith. Having had such a distorted image of Catholicism from my Pentecostal background, I was more receptive to Orthodoxy. The Orthodox Christians I met also shared some of the derogatory views of Catholicism that the Protestants had, so I felt comfortable with Orthodoxy.

It came upon me that with all the infighting between the Pentecostal churches, the true Church must exist somewhere! All I had witnessed in the Pentecostal faiths were individuals who interpreted the Scripture as they saw fit. They had no hierarchy, no history, no roots, and no Eucharist. Due to my further research, I began to understand that the Eucharist should be the linchpin of Christianity. My friend eventually put me in contact with an Orthodox priest, and thus my journey to the Orthodox Church had begun.

There was no Antiochian Orthodox Church where I was living on Cape Cod. The few Orthodox Christians who lived near me had to travel far to go to church. It became evident that we needed to start an Orthodox mission church and set our minds and hearts upon the task. We were fortunate to have an Orthodox priest who was on sabbatical, living on the Cape when we started. He provided us with sacramental services and Divine Liturgy on Sundays. In June 1992, I was received into the Orthodox Church at the second Liturgy.

Once fully in communion with the Antiochian Orthodox Church, I soon applied for acceptance into the St. Stephen's Course of Orthodox Theology. The Antiochian Orthodox Archdiocese of the U.S. and Canada sponsors these classes for those who cannot attend seminary but who want to serve the Orthodox Church as deacons or priests. The course was initially instituted for those who were previously ministers in other Christian denominations, wishing to receive Holy Orders in the Orthodox Church.

While taking my courses, I continued to serve in the local Orthodox Church as a reader and cantor, and helped with the pastoral needs of St. Michael the Archangel Antiochian Orthodox Mission of Cape Cod. At the same time, I was doing the required practicum field projects under the supervision of the Orthodox priests assigned to help with the mission. Eventually, I successfully completed this three-year course of study, was ordained a subdeacon. We had a priest available to us only every four to six weeks. When we didn't have him, I would conduct a reader's service, known in the faith as a "Typica Service."

On December 8, 1996, His Eminence Metropolitan Philip Saleeba, the Primate of the Antiochian Orthodox Archdiocese covering the United States and Canada, ordained me a deacon. I was assigned as the administrator of St. Michael's. We still only had a priest visit us about once a month, so I ran Communion services and preached the sermons when there was no one available.

Then in August of 1997, I was diagnosed as having chronic Lyme disease. Due to the residual effects of this illness (severe debilitating headaches, joint pain, short-term memory loss), I was no longer able to keep up my full-time secular work in the nursing field or as a barber. I informed my bishop of my illness and its effects, and asked for his assistance. I was given a leave of absence.

Because of the illness and my inability to work a full-time job, I spent a lot of time studying the early Church Fathers, especially St. John Chrysostom. He wrote something that struck my heart: "Schism is worse than heresy, for it divides the body of Christ." This sparked an unquenchable desire in my soul to closely examine why the Eastern and Western Churches were not in full communion.

The more I studied, the more questions I had. Finally, I came across a book called *Jesus, Peter, and the Keys*, by several authors, including a Byzantine Catholic deacon. This book explains the role of the Petrine office, making a strong case for the Holy See's universal jurisdiction over the entire Church. I found the deacon's phone number and called him. He was instrumental in my gradual conversion and was the major catalyst behind my return to the fullness of the Roman Catholic Church. Then one day I was watching our Holy Father on television, and he said something that amazed me: "The Church has to breathe with both lungs, the East and the West." He was referring to the Catholic and Orthodox Churches. Those words still burn deep within my soul. I began to see that for me to be whole, I would have to be in full communion with Rome under the guidance of the Holy Father.

The beautiful home I had built on Cape Cod was quickly becoming a place that we could no longer afford. We had many debts. My wife and I are not quitters, so I continued to work out of my home as a barber as much as I could.

Meanwhile, I had met a Catholic friend by the name of Michele in Buffalo, New York, through an Internet chat group of all places! She was helping me with my movement towards Catholicism. Michele put me in touch with the pastor of a Ukrainian Catholic Church in Lancaster, New York. I called him, and he helped me to discern many things, including where God was leading me. Not once did he tell me to return to Catholicism. He allowed me on my own to discover where the Holy Spirit was leading. He traveled a number of times to visit us in Massachusetts.

When I made the final decision to convert to the Catholic faith in July 1998, I wrote to my bishop, Metropolitan Philip, and informed him of my plans. It was not well received. He informed me that because I had abandoned the "True Orthodox Faith," I was an apostate. Furthermore, by his apostolic authority, he was suspending me as a deacon. In writing, he stated that I was in effect "un-ordained." I subsequently lost all the Orthodox customers that I had in my barber business, putting us in an even more desperate situation.

With the encouragement of my wife and through my own study of other books on the Catholic Church, I asked the pastor of St. Anthony's Church in Falmouth, Massachusetts, to receive me back into the Catholic Church. Deep in my heart, I had experienced an epiphany: that the Church should not be divided in two. In July 1998, I made a profession of faith and received the Sacrament of Reconciliation, thus returning to full communion with the Holy Roman Catholic Church.

The Catholic Church was more amenable to unity than Orthodoxy. Catholicism had grown with Vatican II and set itself upon reaching the modern world with the Gospel. With the Council's document *Lumen Gentium,* the baptized were all equally prophet, priest, and king! For me, the average layperson, the Catholic Church provided ownership of those offices. Catholicism seemed so dynamic to me; Orthodoxy, so stagnant and clericalized. Catholicism has grown in aggressively addressing moral issues such as birth control, sexual impurity, and the death penalty. Orthodoxy leaves these issues to the individual and his conscience (or lack thereof).

We needed to move from our Cape Cod home, which by now had become too expensive for us to take care of. With the help of a Catholics priest, who has been my spiritual director for three years now, and the director of St. Luke's Mission of Mercy, we moved into a home in Buffalo, New York, which they helped us acquire. It is an old home in a poor area of the city, but it is acceptable for all of us. It is a joy to be near my spiritual mentor, and to be able to help at St. Luke's Mission of Mercy (a kitchen and shelter for the homeless) whenever I can.

I eventually met with the bishop of Buffalo who was so pastoral and loving that he brought tears to my eyes. He agreed to do whatever he could to help me in my endeavors to have any canonical impediments removed in the proper way, and to make sure that I get all the proper education and needed spiritual formation that was lacking in my Antiochian Orthodox diaconal formation. I also worked with a canon lawyer as a mentor in these proceedings. My prayer was that one day, by God's mercy and grace, I could serve the Holy Catholic Church as a deacon in the Diocese of Buffalo.

I took courses at Christ the King Seminary in East Aurora, New York, and continued studying under my local priest to learn the practical aspects of serving in the Catholic Church. I assist him in his nursing home ministries, help teach RCIA at St. Luke's Mission of Mercy, and have taught an altar servers' class there. I also help with the First Friday devotions at the Holy Infant Jesus Shrine. I am at the disposal of the Diocese of Buffalo. I am freely obedient in whatever is asked of me by my bishop, as well as those whom the bishop has assigned to help me.

Then in the summer of 2005, by God's merciful grace, I was graciously accepted by the Holy See and the bishop of

Buffalo, New York, to fully serve as a deacon in the Holy Catholic Church.

Thanks, glory, and praise be to God, for bringing me into the fullness of the Christian faith and His Church. I also thank my father, who himself had converted to the Catholic faith not long before he died and who had me baptized in the Church.

Rev. Deacon Joseph Pasquella was formerly a Pentecostal pastor. He was ordained to the Holy Order of deacon in the Antiochian Orthodox Church in 1996 and was incardinated into the Diocese of Buffalo, New York, in 2005. He is assigned to St. Lawrence Catholic Church in Buffalo, New York.

FROM CONFUSION TO THE ORDER OF TRUTH

CLYDE PEARCE

former Mormon missionary and bishop

My pathway home to the Catholic Church required an all-terrain vehicle to negotiate the steep, rocky, tortuous roads, including dead ends, cul-de-sacs, and detours. Unlike many of the *Journey Home* stories, I was not trained in theology or doctrine. I attended no seminary, Bible college, or religious institute. But a great deal of informal education in those areas plus years of lay ministry led me to the Catholic Church. And it all started early.

When I was seven years old, my father was killed in an auto accident. I was the eldest, with a brother and two sisters. My mom was six months pregnant with her fifth child. My brother suffered brain damage at birth. He was mentally handicapped and suffered from grand mal epilepsy. For most of my growing up years, we barely survived on Social Security and county welfare.

That's when I began to talk to God. I asked Him to forgive me my sins and to please keep our family safe. Except for several summers of Bible camps (Baptist and Nazarene) I had little religious activity, but prayer was not completely foreign to me. So I grew up mostly without any specific religious discipline. We were, however, taught Christian morality and principles.

All the while, I remained desperately alone and afraid, without any assurances from God.

But a saving grace was about to emerge into my life: competitive sports, beginning with Little League baseball. My mom scrounged up the enrollment money, and when they gave me a real uniform, I was in embarrassed disbelief. I couldn't afford baseball shoes, but my old tennis shoes were all right. I had a uniform. Baseball would play a big role in my life. I went on to play four years of varsity baseball in high school, as well as football and basketball. I also played football and baseball in college.

My coaches, God bless them, became surrogate fathers not only for me, but also for a number of other guys. Several of us never had our dads see us play. We tried not to let it show when the other guys walked off the field with their dads, while we walked off alone. My high school football coach, a good Christian man, is one of the finest men I've ever known. From him, I learned discipline, honor, sacrifice, teamwork, and to always get up again. His quiet modeling of honesty and generosity remain with me today.

When I began my junior year in high school, I hadn't an inkling of what lay ahead for me. We had a new history teacher that year. He was bright, young, and even made history interesting for a bunch of teenagers. One day he called me into his classroom on a lunch hour. He had gone over my transcript and told me that my performance was way below my abilities. For the first time in my education, I began to study and experience what getting an A felt like. Up until then, I felt that academic mediocrity was my lot.

After a few months, he began to engage me in religious discussions. I soon learned that he was a Mormon, which piqued my curiosity. He spent a few hours setting out the basic principles of Mormonism, which I found unusual, to say the least, but interesting.

I need to state clearly that I know and love many devout Mormons, many of my own family. They are, as a people, generally upstanding, kind, and generous folk, devoted to family and church. What I write here is not intended to denigrate these wonderful people in any way. My problems with Mormon doctrine, however, cannot be lightly treated, for, I went from a faithful, one-hundred-percent immersed, true-believing member to a distraught, betrayed, and angry one.

Eventually, my teacher invited me to attend church with him on Sundays, and I went. The congregation (called a "ward") was small, but in it were a couple of attractive girls my age and three guys who were also juniors. They were a warm welcoming committee. Being on the debate team — and just being argumentative by genes and environment — I challenged some of what I was hearing. The whole Joseph Smith story seemed like, well, a story. But my teacher friend and my new Mormon friends solemnly testified that it was all true. I read the Book of Mormon.

I'll never forget the strange feeling I got when I opened the Book of Mormon for the first time. Dismissing that eerie feeling, I plowed through the book over the next few months. The language rang familiar since it was after the King James style. Then I was "challenged" to pray about its truthfulness and that, if I did so "with real intent" and an open heart, its truthfulness would be "manifest unto me."

I prayed about it a lot. But no angel visited, no overwhelming divine confirmation warmed me. Since all these other people *knew* it was true, I assumed that I was the problem, not the Book of Mormon. I read several books written by church leaders all pounding the same theme: Jesus set up His Church on earth; soon after the death of the Apostles, a great apostasy set in, and all keys and authority were withdrawn until 1820, when fourteen-year-old Joseph Smith was visited by God, the Father, and Jesus Christ, His Son; they told him that none of the churches on earth was the true one, that they were all "an abomination" to God, and that Smith would be God's instrument for restoring the full, pristine, and true Church; and that through divine guidance, Joseph was led to some "Golden Plates" written in "reformed Egyptian," which Smith translated as the Book of Mormon. Eventually, in the spring of my senior year of high school, I agreed to be baptized into the Church of Jesus Christ of Latter-day Saints, LDS, or the Mormons. Of course, I lent no credence to my mother's concerns and objections.

I had all-star seasons in football and baseball that year, and got several good scholarship offers. At the last minute, however, some of the people in the ward got together and decided that I should go to Brigham Young University (whose athletic scholarships were gone by then) and advanced money for my freshman year. So, off I went to Provo, Utah, leaving behind an unhappy and upset mother.

Coming from a high school of fewer than five hundred students, I found walking onto the BYU campus of more than sixteen thousand students somewhat overwhelming. I had never seen so many Mormons. That it was not a completely homogenous campus quickly became obvious to me. We California kids were different from those Utah and Idaho students. They looked down on us as being liberal and not very faithful; we, in turn, looked at them as parochial bumpkins. We wore shorts and flip-flops to class. They reported us to the honor committee for dress code violations. This was the distant, early warning signal to me that compliance was going to be required in more than just belief in Joseph Smith, the Book of Mormon, and the succeeding prophets of the church.

Overall, I was happy. My girlfriend from home was also at BYU; I walked on and won the starting quarterback position on the freshman football team (this was before all the great QBs to follow), was the third baseman on the baseball team, and was awarded a full baseball scholarship. Culturally, I was completely seduced.

A year and a half later, my local bishop called me to go on a two-year mission for the church. I willingly accepted and was soon in the North British Mission that included northern England, Scotland, and Ireland. My first assignment was to Dublin, Ireland. My companion (Mormon missionaries always come in pairs) and I were the only two elders (as the missionaries are called) in all of free Ireland.

The Irish loved Americans. They loathed Mormons. Knocking on doors for twelve hours a day taught me a lot. The people considered themselves "Irish Catholics" not Roman Catholics, a distinction not lost on me. We almost never got invited into a home. When we did, the first time the conversation turned to religion and to questions about Catholicism, we were shown the door.

Two particular experiences deeply impressed me. One day we knocked on the door of a Jesuit priest. He, unfortunately, did invite us in. Arrogant in my competitive debating skills, I was ready to teach this priest a thing or two. But nobody had warned me about Jesuits. Although I started on the attack — Mary-worship, the Trinity, apostasy, infant Baptism, etc. — I soon was backing and filling, in hasty retreat and defense. He was polite but pointed. He skillfully took apart Mormonism, and rebuilt it as Catholicism. To my great relief, my companion — who had not entered into the discussion at any point to help me — excused us for another "appointment." Furious, I yelled at my companion for not stepping in to help me. "We're not here to argue," he said, "but to bear our testimonies and teach our lessons." I would later learn the real meaning of his answer: the last resort of a true believing Mormon is his or her "testimony." For many who are born in the church, it is both the first and last defense, even — especially — when faced with lucid, powerful facts contradictory to their basic beliefs. Faith trumps facts. Yet, the author of Hebrews tells us in the New

King James version that faith has *substance* and *evidence* at its roots (cf. (11:1).

The second experience, more memorable than the first, happened on a sunny morning. It was my turn to knock. A lovely young woman holding a newly born infant in her arms answered. She gave us a warm smile, and she appeared to be glowing. After I went through my spiel and she nicely declined, I whipped out my testimony that what I brought her I knew to be the truth. With her countenance becoming more radiant, she said that she knew her Catholic Church was true, that Jesus was the center of her life, that He loved her, and came to give Himself to her in the Mass. I was stupefied. We were told that other people couldn't bear testimony because they didn't have the truth. But this beautiful young mother and baby gave a warm and divine witness.

During my time in Ireland, we received a book from our mission president (*A New Witness for Christ in America*) that we were directed to place in a public library. I thought I'd better read it first, so I could deal with someone who may have also read it. The first half of the book dealt with arguments and claims against the validity of the Book of Mormon. I found these critical positions to be quite convincing, but hoped that the second half of the book would easily and clearly refute them. Even reading the latter half of the book from the bias of accepting its apologetics, I found them weak, requiring more "testimony" than analysis and deduction. But the busyness of missionary work let me put my doubts away.

While in Ireland, I concluded that the Catholic Church and the Mormons were much alike in many ways, especially as to authority, but exact opposites in many others. It was easy for me to see why the Book of Mormon, and many writings and sermons by Mormon leaders — even within the past fifteen years or so — refer to the Catholic Church as "the church of the devil," that "great and abominable church," the "whore of the earth" who leads men to hell. At the same time, Protestants were given short shrift. After all, they all splintered off from Catholicism, and you can't take good fruit from a bad tree. And the fact that Protestants worshipped in over thirty thousand denominations proved to me that just reading the Bible did not lead to unity.

Over time, I had a temple marriage ("for time and all eternity"), was ordained a high priest at age twenty-two, served in many positions, including five years as a bishop. Being "active" in the Mormon Church means having a "temple recommend" (which admits one to any Mormon temple), tithing, and fulfilling callings in the church, leaving little time for study and thought. As a bishop, I served between fifteen to forty hours a week while still working full-time and attempting to be a husband and father.

God has gifted me, however, with an unrelenting intellectual curiosity. I kept digging into Mormon history and came upon facts that to my mind are indisputable.

My serious inquiry began when I entered law school, where I met other questioning LDS students. They challenged my apologetics. And, like many who have shared their stories on *The Journey Home* program who set out to prove the Catholic Church false, only to discover its truth, I began to search and read, looking for evidence to buttress the Mormon claims. What I found, instead, was clear and convincing evidence that Joseph Smith was a pretender, steeped in magic, who used a seer stone to look for buried treasure, concocted the Book of Mormon (which he translated by placing his seer stone in a hat and then putting his face into the hat and translating the words that appeared on the stone), a book that has had thousands of changes made to it. He proclaimed polytheism: that God, the Father, and Jesus Christ, the Son, were separate and distinct, with bodies of flesh and bones, and that the Holy Spirit is a separate and distinct body of spirit.

The heinous practice of polygamy as introduced by Smith repelled me, when I found that he had an affair with a seventeen-year-old (Fannie Alger) some three years before he had a "revelation" that he was to take plural wives, and that he did not "commit adultery" because he was merely obeying the revelation. Moreover, he and Brigham Young and succeeding prophets taught that polygamy (really polygyny) is the obligatory order of the highest heaven.

Brigham Young taught that Adam was our God, who had come to earth to get his body and then progressed to where he is today. Most blasphemous, Young also taught that we can do the same thing. In Mormon's Celestial Kingdom, men will have all these wives with whom they will procreate innumerable spirit children. They will then create worlds where they will send these spirit children, replicating our mortal experience. "As man is God once was; as God is man may become," expresses in couplet form the Mormon belief.

Young also taught in quite clear language the doctrine of "Blood Atonement." If a man's sins are of a serious nature, that man should shed his own blood in atonement for those sins. Until 2004, the lingering evidence of Young's doctrine was found in Utah's permitting criminals about to be executed to choose as their form of death a firing squad, whereby their blood would be spilt.

Recently, studies of DNA of Indian tribes have shown that about 98% of them (as traced through their mitochondrial DNA) are of Asian descent. The rest are from Europe, mainly Spain. There are no traces of Jewish ancestry, which confutes the Book of Mormon claims that the people written of therein came from Israel. No archeological evidence validates the history as suggested in the Book of Mormon.

The behavior of more recent Mormon leaders failed me. "When the prophet speaks, the thinking is over" has become a motto. When the leaders speak, you follow, for "obedience to the Lord's anointed" requires such response. The problem with that fiat — besides the theocratic approach to stifle free thought and speech — is that the leaders have dissembled.

Time and space restrict me from going more deeply into such examples, but they are plentiful, beginning with Smith and continuing.

I learned firsthand that leaving the Mormon Church exposes one to agony deeper than could have been imagined. Such extrication is like having one's heart removed without the benefit of anesthesia. In my case, it resulted in four years of separation, ending in divorce; alienation from friends and family members; and shunning by most of my children. My wife had come from generations of Mormons. My children were born in the church and received its teachings from age two onward; three of them went on missions; they have married Mormons in the temple (where I was not allowed) and now have their own children.

My anger and bitterness targeted not only Mormonism, but also God. How could He have let this happen to me? Why? I spiraled into agnosticism and depression. I didn't know any longer if there was a God, and what's more, I didn't care.

Only an opportunity at a new job gave me any enthusiasm. The job was only for a year, but it was so intensive, with a lot of traveling, that it helped crust over my woundedness, giving me little time to think about it.

During this time, I renewed my acquaintance with a friend I had known some fifteen years earlier through work. She had just ended her marriage and was in the process of annulment by the Catholic Church. Our friendship grew into courtship, and we were married four years later.

Mary Patricia (Trish) is a cradle Catholic, fully educated in Catholic schools from Sacred Heart kindergarten through Dominican University. During our courtship, I had fully vented my Mormon experience and told her unequivocally that I would never be part of organized religion again.

My wife is as bright as she is lovely. She didn't push me. But before too long, I was going to Mass with her and my three stepchildren. I often sat defiantly, with my arms folded, refusing to stand or kneel at any time. During the Mass, I parsed every word of the homily, the mispronunciations of the lectors, and the perfunctory prayers. I limited the sign of peace to my family. If Trish asked me about the homily or the Scriptures, I answered with caustic assessments.

After serving as the general counsel to a large U.S. government agency, and then accepting a partnership in a national law firm, I moved my family from Washington, D.C., back to California, where I practiced in our Century City office. Blending families challenges the best of marriages. Blending faiths — or, in our case, one faith with no faith — exacerbates the struggle.

Through the next several years, a number of difficult things happened. God crashed through my arrogance and my hubris, trying to get my attention. Like Jacob wrestling with an angel, the outcome was not in doubt, except for me.

One day, when the cruel, whirling riptide sucked me under for what felt like the final time, I found myself inside Sacred Heart Catholic Church. But for one other Person, I was alone. I sunk to my knees and buried my face in my hands. The only words I could whisper were, "Please, love me." Soft, warm, assuring, loving arms engulfed me. I wept. The boy who had always been afraid and alone heard: "Be not afraid; I am with you always."

While I could no longer deny God, I wasn't ready for any church, let alone the Catholic Church. Church hurt; it betrayed; it lied. God did not get my attention, however, for purposes of leaving me there.

Within a couple of months, the Rite of Christian Initiation of Adults (RCIA) began. Trish suggested that since I once said I might be interested in learning more about the Catholic Church, this might be a good time. I cautiously agreed.

When I arrived for my first meeting — the group had already met three or four times — I wore my shield of aloofness. The director of the group made a couple of announcements and then said, "We have a new face among us. Would you please tell us your name and tell us why you are here?"

With a smug reply about my face certainly not being new, although they might be seeing it for the first time, I said, "And I don't know why I'm here." An awkward silence followed before the director collected herself and moved on. I folded my arms across my chest.

Just about ten minutes later, the parish priest stepped in to greet the RCIA group. I will never forget what he said. After a few words of greeting he declared: "Some of you may not even know why you're here. But that's okay, because God does."

I sat up, unfolded my arms, and listened. I listened for seven months, and I read. The evidence stood firmly on a rock foundation. The chain links of authority from Peter to John Paul II for two thousand years put to rest all remnants of the notion of a "great apostasy." I discovered the truth about Jesus Christ, His incarnation, His life, death, and resurrection, for my sins and the sins of the whole world. I fell in love with Mary, His mother, the Mother of God, the Queen of Heaven, my Mother. The sacraments compelled me. The Holy Trinity made sense. Beginning to understand the Eucharist, I longed to partake. The early Church Fathers (Sts. Ignatius, Irenaeus, Polycarp) clinched the evidence. The essential role of Tradition made sense. (I had often wondered about the closing verse in the Gospel of St. John 21:25: "But there are also many other things which Jesus did; were every one of them to be written, I suppose that the world itself could not contain the books that would be written."

Amen.) The Scriptures themselves came from oral history and Tradition, not all of which was canonized. Thank God for the Magisterium of the Church. I began to embrace the Church of smells and bells, of icons, stained glass, and holy water.

I was won over by the unique recognition and respect the Church gives to the individual conscience. An informed, prayerful, and studiously prepared one it must be, for, in the end, I decided to follow it. Can you understand how vivifying that is for one who was taught to be "immediately obedient" when the leaders speak, no thinking required or allowed?

But most of all, I experienced the living Jesus Christ. (See Pope John Paul II's *Ecclesia in America*.) I have read dozens of conversion stories published by the Coming Home Network International, many about the treks of Protestant ministers steeped in their beliefs. For them, a long intellectual undertaking seems to be the *sine qua non* for their conversion. But even for each of them — as for me — the final step across the threshold is experiential. That part was primary for me.

As I prepared for the Easter Vigil that Saturday in 1994, I spent the day praying, meditating, listening. I had decided to fast from Friday night to the Vigil, so that I would break my fast with the Body and Blood of Jesus. The cleansing Baptism, the gifting of Confirmation made my soul exultant. And then when I looked at my priest's eyes, and he said to me, "The Body of Christ, for you, Clyde," tears flowed of their own will and continued as I received the Blood of Christ. My fast was broken; I had now the Bread of Life to feed me and the Cup of Salvation to slake my thirst. I was home.

And just when I thought I was finally out of tears, we sang:

> Do not be afraid, I am with you.
> I have called you each by name.
> Come, and follow me, and I will bring you home.
> I love you, and you are mine.

The little boy and the man were now no longer afraid and alone.

Clyde Pearce, a former Mormon missionary and bishop, is a member of Sacred Heart parish in Salinas, California. Active in lay ministries, he was a founding member and director of the parish's stewardship committee; founding member and convener of the Small Faith Sharing Groups Committee; director of the RCIA; founding member of the Evangelization Task Force, and has worked on the finance committee. His wife, Mary Patricia, has joined him in all these activities. He is a California attorney and has practiced in Arizona, Utah, Washington, D.C., and Virginia. In a notable career achievement, he filed and won the very first North American Free Trade Agreement case against the United Mexican States.

A Glorious Journey

Father Paul Schenck

former Evangelical Anglican pastor

When it became apparent to me that I no longer could confess the Creed — in which I made the claim to believe in the one, holy, Catholic, and apostolic Church — and not be in communion with the bishop of Rome, the successor of St. Peter, and pastor of the universal Church, I chose to enter into full communion with the Catholic Church.

Unity is the foremost characteristic of the Body of Christ. The two most splendid descriptions of the Church, the *Body* and the *Bride of Christ*, can only be conceived of as one, and never, as many. Our Lord has only *one Body* and only *one Bride*. St. Paul emphatically declares this in Ephesians 4:4–5: "There is one body and one Spirit, just as you were called to the one hope that belongs to your call, one Lord, one faith, one baptism, one God and Father of us all, who is above all and through all and in all."

There was no such unity outside the Catholic Church. My brother and I researched hundreds of denominations in a book we called *The Constitutions of American Denominations*. They conflicted with each other in the most important and the most trivial matters. Those divisions have wounded and weakened the Body of Christ, and have sapped her strength and vitality. The visible Church in true unity with Christ and His members is the true Church.

Pope John Paul II lamented our current situation in *Ut Unum Sint*, where he quotes the Decree on Ecumenism of the Second Vatican Council. "Division," he says, "openly contradicts the will of Christ, provides a stumbling block to the world, and inflicts damage on the most holy cause of proclaiming the Good News to every creature" (no. 6).

When I refer to the Catholic Church as the true Church, I do not mean that all others are false. I use it in the way a carpenter might use a level: as the standard against which all others are measured. *Mysterium Ecclesiae,* the statement of the Congregation for the Doctrine of the Faith, quoting *Lumen Gentium,* unambiguously states, "'Outside her visible structure,' namely, in Churches and ecclesial communities which are joined to the Catholic Church by an imperfect communion, there are to be found 'many elements of sanctification and truth [which], as gifts properly belonging to the Church of Christ, possess an inner dynamism towards Catholic unity'" (no. 1).

Indeed, in numbers 818 and 819, the *Catechism,* quoting the Vatican II documents *Unitatis Redintegratio* and *Lumen Gentium,* is quite clear:

> "All who have been justified by faith in Baptism are incorporated into Christ; they therefore have a right to be called Christians, and with good reason are accepted as brothers in the Lord by the children of the Catholic Church" (*UR* 3, sec. 1).
> "Furthermore, "many elements of sanctification and truth" (*LG* 8, sec. 2) are found outside the visible confines of the Catholic Church: "the written Word of God; the life of grace; faith, hope and charity, with other interior gifts of the Holy Spirit, as well as visible elements" (*UR* 3, sec. 2). Christ's Spirit uses these Churches ... as means of salvation, whose power derives from the fullness of grace and truth that Christ has entrusted to the Catholic Church. All these blessings come from Christ and

> lead to him (cf. *UR* 3), and are in themselves calls
> to "Catholic unity" (cf. *LG* 8).

For these and many other good reasons, I have not repudiated my conversion to Christ, my baptism, discipleship, or my training in God's Word outside the Catholic Church. I have in fact brought them with me into the Catholic Church, where they belong.

I was raised Jewish. My father and his siblings were the first American generation, born to descendants of Polish and Austrian Jewish immigrants. My mother was not born Jewish. Her mother was Catholic and her father Episcopalian. My mother's mother, only sixteen years of age when she gave birth to my mother, saw to it that she was baptized in the Roman Catholic rite. On the way to St. Mark's parish, where my mother was baptized, is a small mission called "St. Margaret's," while my mother's given name is Marjorie, her Christian name is Margaret.

My maternal grandmother died while my mother was still young, and her father raised her in the Episcopal Church. After a tragic first marriage that ended in her husband's suicide, my mother was left a young widow struggling to raise two daughters. My father met her and came to her aid. She converted to Judaism and married him in the Jewish ceremony. Their agreement was to raise their children Jewish. That is why when my twin brother and I were born, we received ritual circumcision, were inducted into the Covenant of Abraham, given Hebrew names (Hillel and Chaim), and enrolled in Hebrew school for six years.

When I entered high school, I was introduced to a group of Christian young people who took their faith seriously. They met for prayer in the mornings, gathered for late-night Bible studies in homes, and were conscientious about church attendance. They were Protestants and Catholics. I began attending a small Methodist chapel in our neighborhood. The minister was a Salvation Army officer, as the congregation could not afford a pastor. I attended the Sunday school, the youth group, and Sunday church services. It was there my brother and I requested Baptism, after responding to the call to accept Christ in a parish mission. I was baptized "in the Name of the Father, and of the Son, and of the Holy Spirit" on October 11, 1974, by immersion in the river.

My brother and I both became involved in Christian fellowship in school. We attended the prayer meetings, the Bible studies, joined the youth group on evangelistic efforts such as sharing witness in church services, in public places like malls, and door-to-door visitation. I became a volunteer youth counselor with the Billy Graham Association and the Christian Broadcasting Network. I discerned a call to Christian service and thought at first that I would attend a Methodist college and seminary. Then I learned about a missionary Bible college nearby. I arranged to graduate from my high school a year early, and I applied. It was necessary to obtain two referrals from ordained ministers. The pastor of a large Evangelical church and my own minister provided the requisite letters, and I was accepted.

I had begun a special friendship with Rebecca Wald, whom I had met at the prayer meetings. It became an exclusive relationship, which did not include "dating," but a friendship based on our mutual church activities. Before leaving for college, I asked her parents for permission and their blessing in asking her to marry me. We intended to marry when I completed my program. However, after the first year, we were married, and I returned to school. I had to suspend my program, and then resumed my studies part time. Our first born child came two years later, after our first child miscarried. My wife and I became house parents for Baker Hall, a publicly funded, Catholic program for delinquent boys. During the day, I was also the director of an Evangelical Christian drug and alcohol intervention program called Teen Challenge. I attended school at night.

After five years, I received a Pastoral Ministries certificate, and after two more years, a bachelor of arts degree in biblical studies. I was examined and called as pastor of a nondenominational community church in western New York.

In the course of my studies, I read the Church Fathers in addition to the Scriptures. As I followed Church history, I became aware of the distinct differences between the beliefs and practices of the Evangelical churches and the apostolic Church. These differences were explained in reference to the Reformation. For a time, that was sufficient for me, but after a while, it was no longer an effective explanation. I was becoming aware that the Fathers were Catholic.

While I was still a minister in the community church, it quietly troubled me that we were not in communion with the Catholic Church. As I matured in the ministry of Christ, I recognized that the Church was the guardian of the great truths of revelation: the Scriptures, the Trinity, the councils and creeds, the episcopacy. The more I learned from Church history, and especially the Fathers, the more I yearned for rootedness and continuity with the early Church. In 1983, I was invited to conduct a preaching mission in the U.K. I was stationed at St. John's (Anglican) Church in Poole, Dorset. In long discussions late into the night, the vicar and I explored the liturgy, the Church Fathers, and the first ecumenical councils. I returned from the U.K. with the Book of Common Prayer and an appreciation for the history of the Church of England. In a very basic way, I saw the Anglican Church as a connection between the Evangelical churches and the apostolic Church. I introduced the Creed, certain parts of the liturgy, vestments, and a higher view of the Lord's Supper into our community church, and it was generally received. I had begun my journey to the Catholic Church.

I began to look for attachment to a church that embraced the ancient liturgical forms of worship and had a high view of the sacraments and a visible hierarchy. My grandparents (my mother's father and her first father-in-law) were Church of England men, and my interest in the Anglican Church developed. At that same time, I had begun a collaboration with a professor of systematic theology at Wycliffe College, University of Toronto. He was a third-generation Jewish Christian and an Anglican priest. He had been rector of St. John's Church, East End London, and was in residence at the Church of the Messiah in Toronto. Through him, I was introduced to Anglican men in Canada and at the same time met an Episcopal priest from the Diocese of Birmingham who urged me to consider the Episcopal priesthood.

I contacted the Reformed Episcopal Seminary in Philadelphia and eventually petitioned the bishop for entry. I resigned from the pastorate, and my family and I moved from Buffalo to Chesapeake, Virginia, where I joined the American Center for Law and Justice, a public interest law firm advocating for pro-life, family, and religious liberty issues. I read theology, Church history, and liturgical studies for the Reformed Episcopal bishop.

After completing the program of guided independent studies, I stood my examinations for ordination at the Reformed Episcopal Seminary in 1995. I was received as a deacon in St. John's Episcopal Church (ECUSA), Portsmouth, Virginia. The following year I was ordained a presbyter by the Most Rev. Leonard W. Riches (Yale Divinity School), by then the presiding bishop of the Reformed Episcopal Church in the United States.

The year previous, my brother and I had challenged a federal district court injunction that restricted pro-life "sidewalk counselors" from approaching abortion clinic clients and others, with Bibles, tracts, and a peaceful, pro-life message. I was sentenced to two years in federal prison for violating the federal judge's order for counseling a couple leaving the clinic, passing a Bible to a woman who thanked me, and speaking with a man who refused a Bible. The case, called *Rev. Schenck v. Pro-Choice Network*, reached the U.S. Supreme Court, which ruled 8–1 in my favor, striking down the judge's order as a fundamental violation of the First Amendment right of freedom of speech.

When I began my prison sentence, I was told that the Protestant chaplain was "pro-choice" and wanted nothing to do with me. My conscience would not allow me to worship in her chapel or receive communion from her. When the Catholic sacristan heard about it, he came to me and said, "Father says that you're welcome at Mass!" Because I was a good prisoner, my family was allowed to worship with me. So every Sunday my wife packed up our seven children and drove nearly two hours to attend Mass with me in the prison chapel. That was when the Church opened wide her arms to us. Each week I eagerly awaited Mass, where I could commune spiritually with our Lord and pray with my family.

After my release on appeal, I was appointed vicar in the Reformed Episcopal mission in Virginia Beach and chaplain to the law faculty at Regent University. There a Catholic deacon began tutoring me in Catholic doctrine, especially ecclesiology. I attended the campus Mass and discussed theology with priests and deacons who visited the campus. The deacon also had faculties in the Melkite (Greek Catholic) Church, and he invited me to join him at the eparch's residence in Methuen, Massachusetts. When I explained my earnest interest in entering the Catholic Church, the eparch invited me to a diaconal formation week at St. Basil's Seminary, and I attended (he later explained that Anglican men go to the Roman archbishop).

About the same time, I was elected a trustee of Thomas More College in Merrimack, New Hampshire, a Catholic school, which also granted me the honorary doctor of humanities. I found myself being drawn ever closer to the Catholic Church.

I started praying for the reunion of the whole Church Catholic, but began to realize it would have to start with my heart. When I became the rector of an old Evangelical Anglican parish in Baltimore, I was welcomed by the Catholic priest in the next parish, (now the bishop emeritus of St. Augustine), who began joining me for the stations of the cross at the abortion mill. We became friends and then co-counseled a couple that was about to divorce. The husband was a member of my parish; the wife was a member of his. So the priest and I co-counseled them, and they were wonderfully reconciled. At the same time, another couple in my parish was separating. The husband said, "I know its God's will that Julie be my wife, but I don't want to live with her. We'll have separate houses, and we can share the children."

"No," I insisted, "there must be an organic unity to marriage. It is not enough to be 'legally' married; you must share the same bed and board, live together under one roof, in mutual submission, with Christ as your head. These are the visible signs of your union."

When they left, I said to myself, "You hypocrite! You told them there has to be an organic unity to marriage, but you're content to be separated from Christ's true Body." I began praying more fervently for reunion with the Church.

Then, in 2000, our oldest child, at twenty-one, told me that she intended to become Catholic. She would be confirmed at the Easter Vigil the following year. I told her she had my support, and I would be present with her.

In Baltimore, I shared our church campus with an Ethiopian Orthodox parish. When the Ethiopian bishop learned that I was traveling to Egypt to teach at a Protestant minister's conference in Alexandria, he asked if I would visit the Ethiopian bishops in Jerusalem. They were in a crisis of faith as some of the faithful had begun converting to Judaism. He thought I might have some helpful advice, which I did not, but in charity I offered to go. There was also a priest who had immigrated to Washington, but his wife and children were still in Jerusalem, and the Intifada had broken out — and he needed someone to intercede for them at the Embassy in Israel. I promised to help and was successful, and the family was reunited.

After my visit to Jerusalem, I went on to Egypt. When a former student of mine, who was an Egyptian national, from a Coptic family, and living in Cairo, picked me up at the airport, he announced, "You have an appointment to go to the Basilica tomorrow where Pope John Paul II is conducting an ecumenical encounter!" We went early the next morning and waited for nearly two hours as our host, the president of the Evangelical college, argued with police. We were denied entrance, and I returned to my hotel dejected. I felt so strongly that an encounter with the Holy Father would somehow seal my reunion with the Catholic Church. It did not happen, and I went on to teach in Alexandria and returned to the U.S. crestfallen.

I was teaching at the Reformed seminary in Philadelphia when I was informed that the Melkite Eparch of Methuen, Massachusetts had arranged for an invitation from the Greek Catholic archbishop of Jerusalem, Lufti Laham (now Patriarch Gregorious III), to accompany him on the Papal Pilgrimage from Bethlehem to Jerusalem.

When I returned to the Old City, the archbishop received me and said, "Now, Father Chayam (He called me by my Aramaic name), you did bring your Eastern vestments, and you will concelebrate with the Holy Father in Bethlehem?" I realized he did not know I was not yet Catholic. I said, "Your Grace, I'm not Catholic; I'm an Evangelical Anglican."

"Oh!" he exclaimed. "Nevertheless, you will have an honored seat among the priests in Bethlehem. You will see, the Holy Father will be there, I will be there, and you will be there. You will see; you will be absorbed!"

The next day indeed, I was seated to the right of the Holy Altar in Manger Square. John Paul the Great was offering the Sacrifice of the Holy Mass, the Body and the Blood all around me — "a sacrament of love, a sign of unity, a bond of charity." A sea of humanity flowed forward to receive the Communion of the precious Body and Blood of Christ. There, where Christ was born, was every "tribe and tongue and people and nation." There was every hue of skin and nap of hair, every kind of dress. Everything that wasn't stone was a human head. It was an oasis of love and peace in the midst of the storm of hatred and conflict. It was the grandest display of unity I had ever seen in my life. It was truly "a Paschal banquet."

We went to the grotto of the Nativity with the Holy Father and prayed there. As we walked abreast with the Holy Father and the Latin Patriarch Michael Sabah, the archbishop turned and said, "Here is the Holy Father, here am I, and here you are — and you see, you're absorbed; you've been absorbed!" We went on throughout Palestine and Israel, and finally, at the end of the week to Jerusalem. There, in the Church of the Holy Sepulcher, the Holy Father declared with a jubilant countenance, "He is not here; He is risen!" Before the sanctuary was a truly ecumenical assemblage: the Anglican bishop, the Lutheran bishop, the Coptic, Armenians, and Ethiopians. When it was time for the Peace, the bishops embraced one another, as did all the faithful — born Jews and Palestinians, black, white, and Asian. And they were all praying and participating in the Holy Mass in one tongue: Latin.

After the Mass, the Pope lingered for some time like a Great Father amidst his affectionate children. Then, as he left, the congregation swelled and rose behind him like a torrent sweeping through the cavernous manmade mountain that is the Sepulcher Church. As he passed through the ancient doors, the Israeli officials pushed the doors closed — something they were not expected or permitted to do, as there is an ancient protocol conducted by the Muslim sergeants-at-arms. A hue and a cry went up, followed by a muted sigh and then a hush as the daylight was shut out and the Church became gloomy. It was as if the Holy Father had been stolen away. Then, panicked security personnel reopened the doors, and the Holy Father was there again, above the crowd on top of his vehicle, and he imparted his blessing to all of us below. There — in the midst of the Anglican and Lutheran bishops, the Ethiopians and Copts, Jewish Holocaust survivors and Palestinians, every language and nationality, I believe I became Catholic in my heart.

I had already become Catholic in my head, but in Jerusalem, I became Catholic in my heart. It was a biblical journey — from the footsteps of Christ in Jerusalem, down into Egypt, out of the Holy Land, only to be swept back again to the sacred sites. I had walked from Bethlehem to Jerusalem, speaking French badly with a Franciscan Friar from Cote d'Ivoire. I followed the papal train to the place of Christ's saving death and glorious resurrection. I had prayed in Hebrew, Greek, Ethiopic, Arabic, and Latin. When the Holy Father entered the convent in Bethlehem to meet barely more than a handful of us, I fell to my knees and clutched a rosary so tight that it left its imprint on my palm. I knew there was no place else for me to go, but to the one, holy, Catholic, and apostolic Church, and to its one true Pastor.

When I returned to Baltimore, I began praying for a doorway through which I could bring my family and myself into the Catholic Church. Full-time Christian service was all I had ever known, my entire adult life and throughout our whole marriage. We lived in the church rectory, drove a church car, and my children attended the church school.

I had been reading the biography of the Holocaust martyr Edith Stein, St. Teresa Benedicta of the Cross. There was so much I could identify with, being the descendant of European Jewish ancestors. I asked St. Teresa Benedicta to join her prayers to those of the Blessed Mother, to intercede with the Lord to find a way into the Catholic Church for my family and me.

I left it in the Lord's hands, and I was at peace. I began making arrangements to leave our home, our community, our children's school, and step out into the deep.

The next year, I was told that Father Frank Pavone wanted to talk to me. He invited me to his office in Staten Island, and I told him about my desire to enter into full communion with the Catholic Church. He invited me to join *Priests for Life*, and six months later, I was received into the Church with the proper permissions in the archdiocese of New York. I received the Sacraments of Penance and Reconciliation, Confirmation, Marriage, first Holy Communion, and I was inducted into the Confraternity of Our Lady of Mount Carmel, and invested with the brown scapular. I was in the ark!

My wife and children were some steps behind me, and they remained members in my former church for another year. We began looking for a good Catholic school for the children and found it at York Catholic High School in the Diocese of Harrisburg. We sold the rectory, which we had purchased from the former church, and relocated to York, Pennsylvania, so that the children could begin their Catholic formation and education. We joined Holy Infant Church in York Haven, and began our formation as a Catholic family. My wife and our children at home were confirmed on January 8, 2005, and our youngest is now in formation for first Holy Communion.

Our journey has been an adventure that has presented its trials and triumphs. In many ways, the journey reflected the experiences of the first believers and those who have persevered within the one, holy, Catholic, and apostolic Church. I am a latecomer, but have inherited the great legacy of this glorious Catholic Church!

Father Paul Chaim Benedicta Schenck is a priest of the Diocese of Harrisburg, where he is director of Respect Life Activities, bishop's liaison to the Catholic Medical Association guild, and a parish administrator.

Raised Jewish, Father Schenck was baptized at the age of sixteen. He attended a Missionary Bible college, an Evangelical seminary, and a Catholic university. He was ordained in the Evangelical Anglican tradition, where he was a pastor, college and seminary instructor. He was united with the Catholic Church in 2004. Today he is the chairman of the National Pro-Life Center near the Supreme Court in Washington, D.C.

I Wonder What Sort of a Tale We've Fallen Into?

Peggy Gibson, M.D.

former Anglican priest's wife

This question concludes one of my favorite passages from J. R. R. Tolkien's *The Lord of the Rings* (book IV, chapter VIII, "The Stairs of Cirith Ungol"). In the "tales that really mattered, or the ones that stay in the mind. Folk seem to have been just landed in them, usually — their paths were laid that way ... but I expect they had lots of chances, like us, of turning back, only they didn't.... We hear about those as just went on." Is my own life being crafted by my Creator with the same care that Tolkien took with his tale? My hope is kindled in the best Book; there I find one of my favorite titles of God: Jesus is "the author and finisher of faith" (Heb 12:2, Douay-Rheims). Each of our lives is a heart-stirring story that can resound with the glory of our Creator.

My story began as a cradle Anglican, which means I have been surrounded by beautiful words of prayer my whole life. As long as I can remember I have come into God's presence on the Lord's day, praying, "Almighty God, unto whom all hearts be open, all desires known and from whom no secrets are hid: cleanse the thoughts of our hearts by the inspiration of thy Holy Spirit, that we may perfectly love thee, and worthily magnify thy Holy Name." Each week we approached Holy Communion, praying, "Grant us therefore, gracious Lord, so to eat the flesh of thy dear Son Jesus Christ, and to drink his Blood, that our sinful bodies may be made clean by his Body and our souls washed through his most precious Blood, and that we may evermore dwell in him, and he in us" (Book of Common Prayer).

With such a rich patrimony, it seemed my pilgrimage had been well supplied with food for the journey. But as the recent history of Anglicanism has shown, when we as prodigals leave our generous Father's home, no matter how rich the inheritance we take with us, our wealth will be exhausted, and we will one day know our hunger and long to return to His table.

THE MEANING OF SUFFERING

My family of origin rejoiced in the love of our parents and the gifts they both brought to their marriage. However, we struggled with the consequences of my father's illness. For the last several years of his life, until his death at forty-two, he and my mother tried to support his health in the midst of the demands of professional and family life. Losing a parent in childhood set my heart on my invisible Father: I was convinced that what is invisible is even more real than what is visible. Our family is quite close; my mother and three siblings are all thankful for the gift of faith and are active in their church communities, both Anglican and nondenominational.

My husband, Jonathan, and I both renewed our commitment to discipleship as young adults; we met during our undergraduate studies in music and were married in 1984, before undertaking our professional degrees. He was ordained to the Anglican priesthood in 1988, and I graduated from medical school in 1989. My first hunger for deeper Catholic truth came after our first child was born in 1992 with a rare, sporadic genetic disorder that included a lethal, congenital heart malformation and a developmental disability that is an obstacle to independent living. We were loved and prayed through our son's open-heart surgery at the age of six months, and he is now a healthy young man with a love of life.

Despite the blessings of his "happy ending," I was left wrestling with the meaning of suffering, particularly what Paul meant by the words, "Now I rejoice in my sufferings for your sake, and in my flesh I complete what is lacking in Christ's afflictions for the sake of his body, that is, the Church" (Col 1:24). Many well-intentioned friends offered the comfort that one day we would understand God's purposes ... but what about our son? What about the meaning of his day-to-day experience of limitations and isolation? The potential intellectual satisfaction of understanding was a faint glimmer compared to the radiant joy of Paul's incarnated fellowship in Christ's redemptive suffering. Was that joy meant for all believers or just the Apostle? Turning elsewhere in Scripture for comfort, I took solace in knowing that the sword of Jesus' suffering had pierced His Mother's heart (Lk 2:35), and so I was not alone on my journey. Even before we knew our son's diagnosis, we had named him Thomas, the disciple who knew the Lord through the privilege of touching His wounded Body. Reading the meditations of Henri Nouwen and Jean Vanier on disability was like water in a desert. I still love John Paul II's thoughts, as quoted by Vanier: "Disabled people are ... living icons of the crucified Son. They reveal the mysterious beauty of the One who emptied himself for our sake and made himself obedient unto death" (*Message of John Paul II on the Occasion of the International Symposium on the Dignity and Rights of the Mentally Disabled Person*).

How could we truly complete Christ's afflictions as members of His Body and manifest His beauty? Around this time, a dear Catholic friend from medical school gave us a beautiful, hand-carved crucifix. The mystery of participating in God's ongoing work of creation through sharing Christ's sufferings became precious to me.

And so, God was still graciously giving me food for my journey: the joys and busyness of family and professional life were still deeply satisfying. We welcomed a healthy daughter, Elspeth, in 1996 and delighted in the unique way in which she too reflects the beauty of her Creator. A Catholic friend and I invited each other to be godmothers to our second children.

DESIRE FOR UNITY

My husband and I dearly loved our parish, and it grew into a life-giving community, where many felt they encountered God in Word and Anglican sacraments just as the disciples had done on the road to Emmaus (see Lk 24:13–35). It was as though we lived in the joy and peace of Tolkien's Shire, but there were dark clouds gathering on the Anglican horizon. As we matured as a family and a parish, we began to take seriously the need for faithful leadership on the larger stage of national and international Anglicanism. Theological and moral dissent was threatening the ability of local congregations to proclaim the Word and faithfully administer the sacraments by undermining the trust between pastors and their bishops.

As the Anglican Communion approached the once-a-decade meeting of all the world's Anglican bishops at Lambeth in 2008, it became clear that Anglicanism as we had known it was in crisis. Rather than honoring Christ's prayer for unity in John 17, bishops in North America were reinterpreting Scripture in order to bless relationships that could not reflect the "great mystery" of Christ the Bridegroom's union with His Bride the Church (see Ephesians 5). Consequently, many bishops would no longer share Holy Communion with the revisionist bishops or support a meeting that did not take the need for unity seriously.

As a family, we planned pilgrimages to Great Britain to affirm God's faithfulness in bringing us the Gospel through our Anglican roots despite all the storms of history that have battered that family tree. In 2008, we explored how the Christian faith had come to Britain through unknown Roman citizens and began to put down roots and bear fruit. Beginning in 385, the withdrawal of the Roman legions from Britain led to the breakdown of cohesive governance. We were particularly drawn to the witness of the Celtic church, which through strong monastic communities had effectively evangelized many in the midst of the social upheaval. We stood on the holy Island of Lindisfarne, where St. Cuthbert lived and prayed, and knew that nothing could separate us from the love of God. St. Cuthbert had presided over the Celtic monastic community on Lindisfarne in 664, when they accepted the authority of Rome at the Synod of Whitby, requiring reform of their traditions. Their faith inspired the "Father of English History," St. Bede, and survived the Viking raids of the ninth century and the Norman Conquest of the eleventh century. We stood in St. Mary the Virgin in Oxford and read the plaque marking both Catholic and Protestant martyrs of the sixteenth century as members of one community. In Westminster Abbey, at the tombs housing the remains of Elizabeth I and Mary I, we prayed for the unity hoped for in the inscription on Elizabeth's tomb: "Partners both in throne and grave, here rest we two sisters, Elizabeth and Mary, in the hope of one resurrection."

We thought we had fallen into a story like that of the Celtic church: we were entering a storm of dissolution, and with our little community we needed to work for the reestablishment of the larger Anglican Church's stability. Were we called to live through a period of ecclesiological chaos by faithfully witnessing to the Gospel with our local community? We did not yet discern that the true storm was the English Reformation itself, which had separated the English church from its true roots. As in the Celtic church, only by welcoming reunion with Rome would we know the full joy of God's faithfulness. It would not be a revitalized Anglican *via media* (Latin: "middle way") between Protestantism and Catholicism, but Roman Catholicism that would again offer the unshakeable foundation on which Jesus intended His Church to be built.

In 2010, we traced the roots of our favorite stories: *The Lord of the Rings* and *The Chronicles of Narnia*. We had the privilege of visiting Oxford, in the ancient kingdom of Mercia, which is depicted by Tolkien as the Shire, and Northern Ireland, the landscape that shaped Narnia. We hoped that our lives would resemble these great stories: that despite the temptation to turn back in the face of darkness, we might grasp the chance to persevere and take our place in a "tale that really mattered" and to travel "farther up and farther in" to our true home beyond this world.

Without realizing the significance of July 12, we were in Belfast on Orangemen's Day, when Northern Ireland Protestants celebrate the defeat of the Catholic pretender to the throne of England. We realized the truth of Tolkien's observation on C. S. Lewis' conversion to Christianity: "Lewis would regress. He would not re-enter Christianity by a new door, but by the old one: at least in the sense that in taking it up again he would also take up again, or reawaken, the prejudices so sedulously planted in childhood and boyhood. He would become again a Northern Ireland Protestant." The unimaginable depth of hostility between the communities shocked us and made us realize how far Lewis had come by embracing sacramental reality to the extent that he did.

"The Weight of Glory," a sermon delivered by C. S. Lewis from the pulpit of St. Mary's Oxford, is a breathtakingly beautiful exposition of the things that "God has prepared for those who love him" (1 Cor 2:9). His wisdom seemed to witness to the integrity of the Anglican Church, and yet now we wondered whether "mere Christianity" was enough.

The next summer we were visiting with my faithful Catholic friend and updating her on our ecclesiological struggles. With a mixture of sympathy and exasperation, she pointed out (not for the first time) that I was her "most Catholic friend," and why weren't we Catholic? In 2009, Pope Benedict XVI had announced *Anglicanorum Coetibus*, an Apostolic Constitution that invited Anglicans to come into full communion with the Catholic Church. By 2011, the structures were starting to be put in place for Anglican groups to come into full communion and retain elements of their worship tradition, such as those well-loved prayers that really were *lex orandi, lex credendi* (Latin: "the law of prayer, [is] the law of belief"). Our friends had heard a radio interview with a former Anglican priest who had been ordained within the Catholic Church under Pope John Paul II's Pastoral Provision; it seemed obvious to them where our future lay. But at the time, we explained our hopes for Anglican renewal and confidence in conciliar government rather than the Petrine ministry. Their persistent welcome to us lived out paragraph 819 of the *Catechism of the Catholic Church*. That passage acknowledges the "many elements of sanctification and of truth" that are to be found beyond the "visible confines of the Catholic Church" and that the Lord uses other Christian denominations as a means of salvation, drawing on the power of "the fullness of grace and truth … entrusted to the Catholic Church."

"Reformed Catholicity"

One of the most respected international Anglican leaders declined the "gracious offer" of *Anglicanorum Coetibus*, but as an alternative expressed his vision for Anglicans to live out "reformed catholicity." I decided that if we were to grasp "reformed catholicity," I needed to have a firmer grasp of how Anglicanism grew from its Catholic roots. Week by week, Anglicans affirm their faith in the words of the Nicene Creed, but what did it really mean to say "I believe in one, holy, Catholic, and apostolic Church"?

During that same visit in 2011, my friend recommended Scott Hahn's *Signs of Life: 40 Catholic Customs and Their Biblical Roots.* Perfect! I thought; when we got home, I found that, while the title my friend had recommended had been checked out from our public library, they did have the same author's *Reasons to Believe: How to Understand, Explain, and Defend the Catholic Faith.* Being an avid reader, I thought I'd get a better sense of Hahn's point of view if I read more than one of his works. And so I unsuspectingly brought home a book that would change the direction of our quest.

Hahn's book of apologetics not only covered the familiar grounds for conversion to Christ, but also boldly made the case for conversion to the Catholic Church, including exegesis of Matthew 16 that pointed to Isaiah 22. I had never before encountered the scriptural underpinnings of the keys given to Peter: that they represent not just his confession of faith, but also the office of the Davidic steward. Disconcerted, I checked the many study Bibles in our home and could find no cross-references to Isaiah 22.

The absence of references to this compelling exposition of Jesus' solution to the problem of authority within the Church was unsettling — why was this not being taught in our Anglican tradition with its high view of the sufficiency of Scripture? Our consciences were formed by the sixth of the foundational Thirty-Nine Articles of Religion found in the Book of Common Prayer (1662): "Holy Scriptures containeth all things necessary to salvation: so that whatsoever is not read therein, nor may be proved thereby, is not to be required of any man, that it should be believed as an article of the faith, or be thought requisite or necessary to salvation." The Articles go on to recognize the need for the Church to exercise "authority in controversies of faith" (Article XX) and for the Church to give her authority publically to those sent to minister in the Lord's Vineyard (Article XXII). But who was giving the Church *her* authority?

We had a pressing need for a rock on which to build our house! In John 17, Jesus promised that it was unity amongst His disciples that would witness His love to the world. And yet it was becoming painfully obvious that, even with the formation of a new North American Anglican province in 2009, Anglican ecclesiology was no closer to the creedal marks of being "one, holy, Catholic, and apostolic," as differences remained in sacramental theology. Could it be that we were living in the time when Lewis' hope that the "tragic farce which we call this history of the Reformation" was being healed by "mature and saintly disputants"?

BLESSED MARY

Throughout the fall of 2011 and the spring of 2012, I read voraciously, participated in online forums, and regularly prayed in the Catholic perpetual adoration chapel near our home. Being in the presence of the Blessed Sacrament was enough to convince me that transubstantiation was true; the Real Presence I had been taught by the Anglican catechism was only *part* of the truth. I was trying to work out whether I could truly accept that Jesus had gifted the Petrine office with the authority that would allow me to say, "I believe and profess all that the holy Catholic Church believes, teaches, and proclaims to be revealed by God."

I needed to work at reforming my conscience to recognize that the Church, which had grown from a mustard seed to a great tree (Lk 13:18–19), had been led into truth (Jn 16:13) when she promulgated the dogma of the Immaculate Conception in 1854. Anglicans regularly pray the Magnificat in Evening Prayer, and I truly wanted to "call [Mary] blessed" (Lk 1:48). Marian dogma at the time of the English Reformation had not been captured in the Book of Common Prayer, and so there is a wide range of belief and practice within the Anglican Communion. Some Anglican churches continue to bless

"Mary, ever Virgin", but increasingly, this devotion has fallen away from common worship. As for the Immaculate Conception, our estrangement from the See of Peter meant we were missing the centuries of discussion and exegesis that had led to its promulgation. Hadn't Thomas Aquinas himself contested the doctrine? Why was it now taught as dogma?

I rejoiced in the generosity of God that could have granted the Virgin Mary freedom from our first parents' fall. But could Mary's seemingly effortless holiness, as depicted in popular piety, really make her the model disciple (Lk 8:21) or help her be a mother to God's fallen, struggling children? Could God not have rendered the Holy Child immaculate in the Blessed Virgin's womb and given her the grace she needed minute by minute: to mother Him and to battle the impulses of a fallen heart? It was when I began to contemplate the meaning of Mary's Immaculate Heart that light began to dawn, and with St. Augustine, my belief in the Church grew into understanding of her dogma: "Therefore do not seek to understand in order to believe, but believe that thou mayest understand." Mary's Immaculate Conception gave her the freedom and strength to truly guard the door of her heart against the whisperings of Satan who stalks all the decisions of our lives (1 Pet 5:8) with these haunting words: "Did God truly say …?" (Gen 3:1). Her holiness was not effortless. She clung to God's grace, so that she was truly full of grace; we see in her question, "How can this be …?" (Lk 1:34), the habits of a strong and practiced holy heart. Her lifelong experience of *cooperating* with grace prepared her to say, "Let it be to me according to your word" (Lk 1:38) and to become a spiritual mother to us all (Jn 19:27, Rev 12:17). The beauty and power of her self-giving became like the burning bush: a radiant, unconsumed witness to God's longing to see holiness brought to birth once for all in Jesus and in the ongoing incarnation of His Body, the Church.

BLESSED WITH HOPE

By 2012, on the Feast of the Annunciation, March 25 (the day Tolkien had chosen for the destruction of the Ring), both my husband and I had become convinced that the Catholic Church is who she says she is. We were incredibly thankful that, through all the reading and heartache of discovering the inherent tension between the founding tenets of Anglicanism and biblical ecclesiology, we were given the grace to walk together on this new journey. We were received into the Catholic Church on July 18, 2012, through the Anglican ordinariate in North America (Ordinariate of the Chair of St. Peter), the community sharing the liturgy shaped by Anglican tradition that has been constructed at Pope Benedict's invitation.

The heartbreaking work of sharing our conversion with our friends and family is only recently behind us. In John Henry Newman's autobiography, *Apologia pro Vita Sua*, he described the years of conversion as "the '*infandum dolorem*' [Latin: "unutterable grief"] of years, in which the stars of this lower heaven were one by one going out." I am certain that there were prayers of many in the communion of saints, some of whom I will never know, who lightened that journey and sped our steps. The metaphor of stars again brings Tolkien's Sam Gamgee to mind, as he labored through doubt and exhaustion on his quest:

> There, peeping among the cloud-wrack above a dark tor high up in the mountains, Sam saw a white star twinkle for a while. The beauty of it smote his heart, as he looked up out of the forsaken land, and hope returned to him. For like a shaft, clear and cold, the thought pierced him that in the end the Shadow was only a small and passing thing: there was light and high beauty for ever beyond its reach.

(*The Lord of the Rings*, book VI, chapter II, "The Land of Shadow")

While our lower heaven darkened, we were taught how to offer up our sufferings and were blessed with hope.

There is a dreamlike quality to becoming Catholic as an Anglican. As the darkness of loss fades and the light of faith dawns, it is like waking up in the house I've lived in all my days and finding that there is so much more life in it than I have been shown. A bit like going through the wardrobe to Narnia. The "stately home" of creed and liturgy is familiar, but is becoming so much more vivid; it's as though long-loved statues and paintings can now come to life and speak and move to reveal so much more of their Creator's heart. All the prayers I have treasured are found in the ordinariate's Liturgy of the Eucharist, enriched with the full Catholic truth of the eucharistic sacrifice and Real Presence. What seemed to be "private interpretations," such as my cherishing of Colossians 1:24 as a key to suffering, is no longer a simple tune I hum to myself, but the theme of great symphonic variations such as Pope St. John Paul II's *Salvifici Doloris*. We are so thankful for the faithfulness of Pope Emeritus Benedict XVI and Pope Francis to Jesus' commission to "strengthen your brethren" (Lk 22:32). The new depths of sacramental grace and the full communion of saints will sustain us as our story continues to unfold. We are only beginning to explore ...

And therefore we also having so great a cloud of witnesses over our head, laying aside every weight and sin which surrounds us, let us run by patience to the fight proposed to us: Looking on Jesus, the author and finisher of faith, who having joy set before him, endured the cross, despising the shame, and now sitteth on the right hand of the throne of

God. (Heb 12:1–2, Douay-Rheims 1899 American Edition)

My husband, Jonathan, was ordained first to the transitional diaconate, then to the Catholic priesthood in May of 2013, on the memorial of St. Bede. He is actively fostering the New Evangelization. Our children were young adults at the time of our reception, and they continued to attend our former parish at first. Our daughter began attending both the ordinariate and Anglican parishes for several months then chose to be received into full communion at Easter Vigil 2013. Our son is beginning to attend the ordinariate parish more regularly; I wonder what sort of tale he has fallen into?

LEAD KINDLY LIGHT

FATHER DOUG GRANDON

former Free Church missionary and pastor

Just yesterday, an Evangelical Free Church pastor inquired over lunch about my journey from the Free Church to the Episcopal Church and on to the Catholic Church. As John Henry Newman, once noted, one's conversion story is a bit too complicated to be quickly recounted between the salad and main course of a dinner.

I became a Christian after first hearing the Gospel from a young man named Dan in a Christian coffee shop in downtown Sterling, Illinois. It was there that I was first confronted with the question, "Are you a Christian?" When I replied that I wasn't sure, Dan arranged to meet with me every other week for Bible study and conversation. In November 1972, I prayed that Christ would forgive my sins. In February 1973, at the age of fourteen, I was baptized.

During the next five years, I attended Dan's church, a small Pentecostal church, on the "wrong side of the tracks." The pastor was a self-taught, but serious, Bible teacher, who emphasized that God had called us to holiness and service. However, his leadership style was overly dictatorial, and he was much too confident in his ability to hear the voice of the Holy Spirit. It was in that church that I first met my future wife, Lynn, when I was fourteen, and there, at sixteen years of age, that I felt a definite call to ordained ministry.

After five years in that Pentecostal church, and having completed two years of college, I was invited by a faithful missionary to spend a summer with a Protestant pastor in Belgrade,

Yugoslavia, where I was tutored in Serbo-Croatian. That missionary offered to support me if I would remain in Belgrade and enroll in the Institute for Foreign Languages, which I was happy to do. For the next five years, I assisted his mission as a translator/interpreter in Communist Yugoslavia.

Upon returning to the U.S., I married Lynn, completed my final two years at Bradley University in Peoria, Illinois, and then proceeded to seminary. I first earned an M.A. in Religion from Liberty University, then an M.Div. from Trinity Evangelical Divinity School, the Evangelical Free Church seminary. I was ordained in the Free Church, and started Glen Hill Evangelical Free Church in Peoria, which still exists today.

During that time, I met Edward MacBurney, bishop of the Episcopal Diocese of Quincy, a committed Evangelical and Anglo-Catholic, and a godly man. We enjoyed each other's company and met regularly for lunch. During the course of our numerous conversations, he recommended that I read Tom Howard's *Evangelical Is Not Enough*. (Dr. Howard was kind enough to meet me one day for breakfast in Wheaton.) Bishop MacBurney convinced me that my Evangelical experience was deficient.

Several points of Catholic theology became clear to me at that time: apostolic succession, the Real Presence of Christ in the Eucharist, the role of saints as mediators, the value of liturgy, the sacrifice of the Mass, etc. My early Pentecostal experience had infected me with a strong prejudice against the Catholic Church. To overcome this, God led me into the Church in short steps, from Pentecostalism to mainstream Evangelicalism, and across the bridge of Anglicanism. To this day, I am grateful for each of those churches.

When the timing was appropriate for me to leave my Evangelical Free Church, I became Episcopalian. Bishop MacBurney made it very clear to me that the Episcopal Church was rapidly abandoning its Catholic and biblical roots. I was aware, however, that the worldwide Anglican Communion included a strong Evangelical wing, which was profoundly committed to evangelization, good preaching, holy living, and serious academic work — and that Anglo-Catholics still defended those Catholic convictions championed by John Henry Newman, prior to his conversion to Catholicism. I felt comfortable exploring the Catholic tradition in a church populated by such Evangelical leaders as Alister McGrath, Jim Packer, and John Stott.

During my Anglican years, I completed my doctoral course work at St. Louis University. With my doctoral advisor (a convert himself), I engaged in a serious reading of Newman. With his help, I began to understand the profound importance of Newman's *Essay on the Development of Christian Doctrine.* (*Development* was the answer to *sola scriptura*, which seemed more and more untenable.) My dissertation research on Flacius Illyricus, an immediate successor to Luther and the first Protestant historian, reinforced my doubts about Protestant separation from Rome.

In preparation for ordination to the Anglican priesthood, I was sent to Oxford for a year of postdoctoral theological study. Oxford was fantastic. However, at St. Stephen's House, I witnessed firsthand the serious degeneration of the Anglo-Catholic movement. I was shocked that the principal allowed a practicing homosexual to remain in residence and was admitting women, who would eventually be ordained to the priesthood.

My Episcopal bishop, Keith Ackerman, allowed me to transfer to Wycliffe Hall, the Evangelical Anglican college, on the other side of Oxford. Scholarship was much more serious there, as was an Evangelical commitment to the faith. Wycliffe Hall was marvelous in many ways, although sacraments, episcopacy, and other Catholic hallmarks were given minimal attention.

I flew back to the U.S. to be ordained to the transitional diaconate in May 1999, but backed out. I almost became Catholic at that point. My wife and I discussed the matter after I returned to England. We concluded that I should proceed with ordination, in order to support my bishop, who had himself indicated that he might one day become Catholic. Later that summer, I was ordained to the diaconate. Bishop Ackerman assured me that he had authority to ordain me, not simply an Episcopal priest, but a priest in the "one, holy, Catholic, and apostolic Church." After all, he told me, Anglicans do represent the third branch of the Catholic faith. (The first and second branches are, according to this theory, Roman Catholicism and Orthodoxy.)

As Bishop Ackerman later observed, I was a faithful and obedient Episcopal priest. Nevertheless, I began to question the validity of Anglican orders, which, of course, directly led to doubts about the validity of Anglican sacraments. For me, the fundamental problem was neither the ordination of women nor the toleration of homosexual practice. Most fundamentally, I could no longer confidently assert that Anglican orders were valid. As a result, I contacted Bishop Daniel Jenky, who had been recently ordained as Ordinary for the Catholic Diocese of Peoria, to whom I expressed my desire to take concrete steps toward entering into full communion with the Catholic Church.

For a number of years, I had been reading Catholic authors and the Church Fathers. In Oxford, I had met an elderly French Jesuit at a Newman Conference who kept in touch, encouraging my conversion and my application for Catholic priesthood. Also in Oxford, I had heard lectures that offered a revisionist (and true!) explanation of the nature of the English Reformation. Others were also quite helpful, including a Catholic, former undergraduate professor, several Catholic priests in the Dioceses of Peoria and Davenport, and numerous Catholic laymen active in the pro-life movement.

When I first met with Bishop Jenky, I made it clear that I was coming with no expectations whatsoever. I needed the Church; the Church did not need me. The Church did not owe me employment nor, even more certainly, Catholic priesthood. Bishop Jenky was kind enough to respond that he was certainly open to having a married, former Anglican minister/priest among his diocesan clergy. (He subsequently made sure this was the case with his Presbyteral Council.) We also spoke about my interest in Russia, where I had lectured each winter for the previous four years. Bishop Jenky spoke most encouragingly about this as a possibility for future ministry. Bishop Ackerman attended my second meeting with Bishop Jenky. He graciously and semi-officially transferred me from his jurisdiction to that of Bishop Jenky. (A bronze bust of John Henry Newman hovered over the table where we spoke.)

It was a bittersweet day when I left Christ Episcopal Church. I loved celebrating the Eucharist on Saturday, Sunday, and during the week. I spent hours preparing my homilies. I joyfully taught adult education, First Communion, and Confirmation classes. I enjoyed visiting my flock, especially the sick and elderly, and most especially when I could bring them communion. We had just completed a large addition to our church building, without incurring debt. I had a good reputation in the community, and I was quite well paid. When I departed, I wondered, like Newman (who also converted in his mid-forties), whether the best chapters of my life had already been written. My wife and I weren't sure how we would support our family of six.

My wife, our four children, and I entered the Church at a vigil Mass at Sacred Heart Church in Moline, Illinois, on the Feast of the Sacred Heart in 2003. My first year in the Church, I was blessed to serve as spiritual director and chairman of the theology department at Assumption High School in Davenport, Iowa. At the end of that year, Bishop Jenky appointed me the director of the office of catechetics for the Diocese of Peoria, where I served with great delight.

In September 2006, I traveled to Immaculate Conception Seminary in the Archdiocese of Newark, for the seven initial examinations required by the Pastoral Provision for former Anglican clergy. In November 2007, the Congregation for the Doctrine of the Faith officially notified Bishop Jenky that they were "positively disposed" toward my candidacy for priesthood. In February 2008, I successfully completed the final written and oral examinations on the seven subjects. On April 18, the Congregation authorized Bishop Jenky to proceed with my ordination. On May 24, 2008, Bishop Jenky ordained me, along with five seminarians, to the Catholic priesthood. (Three of the six are former Episcopalians, although I am the only former Episcopal priest/minister.) I then served as parochial vicar (associate pastor) at Sacred Heart Church in Moline, where I was received into the Church.

It appears as I write this testimonial [2008], that there may be a sizeable exodus of bishops, priests, and lay people from the Church of England into the Catholic Church. Please pray for all those who find themselves in the Valley of Decision. My message to those pondering full communion with the Catholic Church: "Be not afraid. Obey your informed conscience. If you depart your present church, make sure you leave honorably. Be not afraid."

Father Doug Grandon became Catholic in 2003, after serving as a Protestant missionary and pastor for twenty-five years. In 2007, Pope Benedict XVI granted Father Doug permission to be ordained a married Catholic priest for the Diocese of Peoria, Illinois. He presently serves as parochial vicar at St. Thomas More Church in Centennial, Colorado, and teaches Homiletics at St. John Vianney Seminary in Denver. Father Doug's wife, Lynn, serves as the director of the Respect Life Office of the Archdiocese of Denver and as founding director of the Lighthouse Women's Center in Denver.

Father Doug holds three certificates from the Institute for Foreign Languages in Belgrade, Serbia, and degrees from Bradley University, Liberty University, and Trinity Evangelical Divinity School. He earned a Ph.D. in Historical Theology from St. Louis University and completed a year of postdoctoral study at Oxford University. Father Doug also serves on the board of the Mary Mother of God (Russian) Mission, whose priests are restoring the Catholic presence to the Russian Far East, where the Church suffered the martyrdom of thirty thousand Catholics in the 1920s and '30s.

LONGING FOR TRUTH

BY LEAH DESGEORGES

former Evangelical

> *"My longing for truth was a single prayer."*
> *- St. Edith Stein*

As a thirteen-year-old Evangelical Protestant, I spent a day in a sporting good store asking people, "If you died tonight, do you know for sure that you would go to heaven? Would it be worth two minutes of your time to know for sure?" Today, at twenty-seven, I am a devout Catholic, in formation to become a Catholic sister with the Carmelite Sisters of the Most Sacred Heart of Los Angeles. Surely, God has a sense of humor, but when I reflect on how He brought me here, I know that it was His providential hand guiding each step.

A FERVENT FOUNDATION

I grew up in a nondenominational Evangelical church in Boulder, Colorado. I "accepted Jesus as my personal Lord and Savior" for the first time when I was three, again when I was seven, and several other times after that for good measure. My parents, both fervent believers who met each other at church, made it a point to raise my two younger sisters and me to know Jesus. We went to church together every Sunday, and I don't remember a time in my life when I didn't believe in God.

My parents taught us that the first and most important thing in life is to love Jesus Christ, and I am incredibly in-debted to them for that. In the charismatic, evangelical church we attended, I saw firsthand the beauty of fellowship among Christian believers. My parents hosted a weekly home Bible study, where they and their friends would sit in our living room and discuss God and the faith for hours. When we were little, we would play in another room while they conversed, but as I grew older, I began to sit and listen to them talk. It seemed to me that there, in our living room, true Christianity was being lived out, permeating the lives of everyone there.

At our church, we understood communion to be entirely symbolic, so there was usually no formal communion service. Instead, we had baskets of small crackers and cups of grape juice on tables at the front of the church, and during the time of worship, as you felt led, you could go up and help yourself. Sometimes I would partake of the bread and juice very reverently, imagining that it really was the Body of Christ broken for me, and the Blood of Christ shed for me. I remember wanting to be connected to Jesus through this communion. For a time, I helped to prepare the wafers and juice cups in the kitchen before service. I remember asking the woman in charge about this communion, why we do it and what it means. She told me that Jesus told us to eat His Body and drink His Blood, so we do what He tells us to. She said it helps us to remember how He died for us on the cross. I remember her answer was unsatisfying: I wanted it to mean something more.

FAITH NOURISHED BY TRUTH

Growing up in Boulder, one of the least religious cities in the country, I found vibrant and open opposition to my Christian faith from my teachers and friends at the public schools I attended. This opposition didn't deter me from my faith; instead, it drove me to seek a deeper understanding of what I believed and why. I learned what made Christianity different from other religions and how it differed from the build-your-own-spirituality mentality around me. I began looking for apologetic arguments for the faith. Surrounded by a secular, relativistic culture, Christian authors like C.S. Lewis and G.K. Chesterton bore witness to something much more solid. I became convinced, first of all, that truth exists outside of myself and my own experience. I became even more convinced that the truth is always found in Christ. This deep conviction originated in my own personal experience of Christianity in my church, and especially in our charismatic worship services. I became active in my church's youth group, as well as in the *Young Life* and Student Venture ministries at my high school. A Christian friend and I met at the flagpole of our school every Friday morning at 6:30 for two years, snow or sun, praying for our friends and teachers. My own experience of God's love in my life deepened, and during high school my identity as a Christian became deeply rooted in my heart.

When choosing a college, I decided that I wanted to find a Christian school where my faith would be nourished. It was also important to me to find a school that took questions of faith seriously, without any fear of asking hard questions. I was convinced that honest questioning would always lead to the truth, to Christ. I wanted to be around other Christians where I could delve more deeply into the faith. I found what I was looking for at Wheaton College in Illinois, a beautiful community where I found many students and professors genuinely committed to Christ and seeking truth. My new friends were from many different Christian denominations: Presbyterian, Anglican, Baptist, Lutheran, and others.

I found through these friendships that, although we were united in our search for truth and our deep love of Christ, there were also vast theological differences that existed between our faith traditions. As each of us looked to Holy Scripture as the infallible and only source of truth, we came to different conclusions about almost every aspect of the faith. We all believed in Baptism, but we disagreed on when to baptize (infants, adults, or somewhere in between), and whether Baptism was regenerative or merely symbolic. We disagreed about whether the Holy Spirit is active in the Church today and, if He is, *how* the Holy Spirit is active. We disagreed about whether Christ died for all or only for the elect. We disagreed about whether the human person has free will to accept or reject Christ's atoning sacrifice. We disagreed about issues of morality and how to discern when something was acceptable or unacceptable for Christians. For each item of faith there was a broad spectrum of thought.

I heard over and over that this disagreement was normal and even desirable; that among Christians there should be "in essentials unity, in non-essentials liberty, in all things charity." However, no one agreed on what was essential and what was left up to personal discernment, so subsequently almost every issue was considered non-essential, a matter of personal liberty. One day, in a theology class, our professor instructed us to define the central gospel of Christ — to make a list of what we believed were the essentials of the faith, the non-negotiable items of that must be believed in order to fall within orthodox Christianity. Each of us in the class wrote down a different list with a different number of items. It was striking to see how much we disagreed even on what was essential to agree upon. And ultimately, no one had the authority to say with any true confidence what was essential or what was non-essential, so we left the class, each with our own list in hand, unified only by the lowest common denominator. Each of us was left to discern the truth for ourselves. I found it hard to believe that this fractured church was what Christ had in mind when He prayed for Christian unity in the High Priestly prayer "that they may all be one, as you, Father, are in me and I in you, that they also may be in us, that the world may believe that you sent me" (Jn 17:21). I began to wonder if any one church had preserved the truth revealed by Christ, beyond any personal opinion.

350

MATTER MATTERS

After my first year at Wheaton, I began to attend an evangelical Anglican church. For the first time, I experienced liturgy and formal prayers. It was also the first time I experienced a church service where the central event was not the sermon, but rather the Eucharist. At first, I worried that the liturgy would become monotonous, but I discovered that the opposite was true: the more deeply I learned the prayers and the liturgical dance (stand, sit, kneel, stand ...), the more fully I could enter into it. Knowing that Christians had been praying these same prayers for years, I felt connected for the first time to the universal Church beyond my own time and place. Pronouncing the Nicene Creed each week, I felt more connected to the common belief of Christians, in all times and places. I began to work with the middle and high school students in the youth group. The youth pastor assured me that I didn't need to be an Anglican to work with their students, but he asked that I be "open to a sacramental worldview." I wasn't sure what that meant. He explained that as Anglicans, they believe that Baptism and the Eucharist are sacraments; that is, that God uses matter (water, bread and wine) to convey His grace to us. In other words, "matter matters."

As I began to consider the idea of the sacraments, it occurred to me how fitting it would be that the God of the Incarnation, who chose to send His Son to bring salvation to the world by His life and death in a physical Body, would also choose to use matter to minister His grace to us. When we received the Eucharist as Anglicans, we believed that Christ was really present, spiritually at least, in the bread and wine. We also believed that while the elements of bread and wine remain in their own substance, Christ becomes spiritually present alongside that, consubstantially, during the consecration. Because Christ is really present, we receive actual grace when we receive Him in communion; thus, the sacrament affects a change in us.

THEOLOGY OF THE BODY

Through my Anglican church, I was also introduced to the Theology of the Body of Pope (now Saint) John Paul II. For the first time, I met Protestants who thoughtfully and lovingly chose to follow God's natural plan for their families by using Natural Family Planning. ("NFP" refers to methods of achieving or avoiding pregnancy by cooperating with a woman's natural fertile and infertile periods.) At first, I thought it was a strange choice, but I also saw the beautiful fruit which it bore in their marriages: along with their precious children, their marriages were open, loving, and radiated an astonishing depth of love and trust in God.

I learned first of all about the intrinsic and uncompromising value of each human person — persons of soul and body, not a Gnostic dualism, but embodied spirits. I also learned that marriage is intended by God to be to the world an image of the Trinitarian nature of love: as God the Father loves the Son, eternally pouring Himself out in love, and the Son loves the Father, eternally returning that love to the Father, the love between them is so real that it is the Person of the Holy Spirit. Thus, as the husband loves his wife in the marital union, and the woman loves her husband in return, the love between them is so real that it brings forth a new life in their child. The marital act is intended to be an act of total self-surrender, affirming the personhood and value of both husband and wife.

For the first time, I understood why Catholics believe that this sacramental image of marital love is distorted by contraception; it turns the definitive marriage act into a self-gratifying experience, rather than an act of total self-gift. Although challenging, I found this Catholic teaching morally consistent and beautiful. I was surprised to find something that rang with truth coming from the direction of Rome. I was also surprised to learn that Christians of every denomination had always rejected the use of contraceptives throughout the entirety of Church history, until the Anglican Church decided at the Lambeth Conference in 1930 that contraception was morally permissible in certain circumstances within marriage. This decision less than a century ago opened the door to the current state of the church, wherein the vast majority of Christians — even many Catholics — use contraceptives without even considering their moral permissibility.

A DRAW AND A DREAD

As a Protestant, I never gave much thought to Christians of the past. My vague impression of Church history was based on an assumption that the early Church was evangelical and charismatic. I believed early Christians instinctively trusted in faith alone for salvation and looked to Holy Scripture as the sole authority for that faith: in other words, I believed that the early Church was full of Protestants. I believed that at some point in history, the Catholic Church had infiltrated the unadulterated gospel belief of these early Christians, usurping the pure teaching of Christ and introducing heresies like purgatory, indulgences, and the worship of Mary and the saints. This assumption was the only way to explain what changed between Jesus' death on the cross and the heretical practices that necessitated Martin Luther's 95 Theses. I believed that the Reformation had restored the church to its original purity.

During my junior year, I took a class on St. Augustine. I was interested to see what the Church Fathers actually believed. I was hoping to find in St. Augustine teachings similar to Martin Luther and the Reformers, to reinforce my own view of the early Church as essentially Protestant in theology. As I read St. Augustine's writings first hand, however, I found him to be disturbingly Catholic; much more Catholic to me than

I expected. His comments about the Church, the Eucharist, Mary, and the saints were strikingly Catholic. Most shocking to me was how strongly St. Augustine viewed the sacraments; he said that "the importance of these sacraments cannot be overstated, and only scoffers will treat them lightly." If anyone had a "sacramental worldview," it was St. Augustine. And if anyone was a Catholic, it was St. Augustine. This terrified me, because it meant that my own narrative of the early Church was wrong: if the early Church was Catholic in its teachings, then the Reformers weren't actually restoring the Church to its early purity as I had believed.

I felt both a draw toward the Catholic Church and a dread of what I would find once I began exploring. I signed up for a class on Roman Catholic theology to put an end to my Catholic questions. I wanted to prove to myself that the Reformers were right in leaving the Catholic Church. But, as I learned about each doctrine from the Church herself, reading books like Karl Adams' *The Spirit of Catholicism*, and *Mary: The Church at the Source* by Joseph Cardinal Ratzinger (now Pope Emeritus Benedict XVI) and Hans Urs Von Balthazar, I was surprised to find that the Catholic teachings were far from what I thought they were, and that they were more convincing than any Protestant rebuttals. The actual teachings of the Church, when I heard them directly from a Catholic source, weren't at all what my perceptions of them had been. The Catholic view of the world, of human nature, and of God intrigued me. I tried to ignore it, to shake off the growing suspicion that I had been wrong about the Catholic Church, but the Church's teachings made too much sense for comfort, and were (most surprising of all) too in line with Scripture, to dismiss offhand.

I had assumed that the Reformation had restored the Church to its Protestant roots, but I saw now that the Church was Catholic from its very beginning. And while the Church has developed over the years, as a tree grows out of an acorn, it is still the same organism. Or, as an old man looks very different than he did as a baby, he is still the same person. I had a sinking feeling that I had been wrong about the Catholic Church: she looks different today than she did on the day Christ handed the keys of the Kingdom to St. Peter, but I realized it was, indeed, the same Church. And I, a Protestant, suddenly saw myself standing outside of full communion with that Church founded by Christ. It is a historical fact that the evangelical church I grew up in would have been unrecognizable to early Christians, to the Church Fathers, and even to the Reformers themselves.

Though, at that point, I was interested in Catholic theology, I still held firm to *sola fide*, the belief that we are saved by faith in Christ's all-sufficient work on the cross, and that we are saved only by faith and not by any works that we do. I had always been told that while Protestants believe salvation is by faith alone, Catholics believe that salvation is by works alone. But when I learned the actual teaching of the Catholic Church on justification, I found that this is far from a fair distinction. The Catholic Church teaches that we are saved by faith in the atoning work of Christ, that justification is a work of the Holy Spirit, merited for us by the Passion of Christ, and which requires our cooperation. This justification comes from the grace of God, which is the free and undeserved help given to us by God. It is the grace of God, which justifies and sanctifies us, and it will necessarily result in the fruit of good works (see: *Catechism of the Catholic Church* 1987-2016). I had to admit that this view of justification was more consistent with several passages of Scripture that had always made me nervous and clashed with my "once saved—always saved" views (see Mt 25:31-46; Lk 12:41-48; Lk 13:23-28; Lk 18:18-30; Jn 14:21-24; Jas 2:14-22; 1 Jn 3:4-10).

In good conscience

After graduating from college, as I continued learning more and more about Catholic teachings, I began to struggle more with whether I could remain a Protestant in good conscience. I realized that I actually believed that the Catholic Church was who she claimed to be — the very Body of Christ on earth — and I believed that she had been given authority by Christ to minister His sacraments to the faithful. I also believed that Christ was present in the Eucharist — Body, Blood, Soul, and Divinity. But still not wanting to convert, I consulted a friend of mine who had converted to Catholicism that year. I told him of all that I had come to believe, but asked whether he thought I could remain a Protestant. He told me that if God had revealed to me the truth of His Church, that it would be wrong for me to walk away from that knowledge. I knew he was right.

I began RCIA in the fall of 2009, a little over a year after finishing college. There were still things with which I struggled: Mary and the saints were especially problematic for me, as were some other Catholic practices, which seemed superstitious upon first glance. Mary proved to be the most difficult hurtle to overcome. To me, the doctrines of Mary's Immaculate Conception and Assumption seemed unnecessary, and many of the devotions to Mary seemed overly sentimental and even superstitious. In fact, it was less the Marian dogmas that bothered me, and more the Catholic practices of Marian devotion. But once I began to see for myself that Catholics don't worship her as they worship God, but revere her because of her singular role in salvation, I began to open myself more to understand the Marian teachings and they began to make more sense. It was also helpful for me to see Mary as the fulfillment of the Old Testament type of the Ark of the Covenant, which contained the stone tablets of the law. Mary, who contained within herself the Word made flesh, was singularly set apart for that task: it is because of this that she has a special place within the life of the Church.

But because I had come to believe in the Real Presence of Christ in the Eucharist, I wanted more than anything else to be admitted to the sacraments. I wanted to be able to finally receive Christ's Body, broken for me, and His precious Blood, shed for me. I wanted to be able to receive Him physically, not just symbolically. I wanted to be able to commune with my Lord in the most Holy Eucharist. This overcame any other doubts or scruples I may have had.

THE BEGINNING OF A JOURNEY

When I received the Sacraments of Confirmation and First Communion on Easter of 2010, I felt as if I had finally found what I was searching for: the fullness of truth. I discovered in the Catholic Church a depth and breadth I can never plumb — centuries of theology, philosophy, prayer, mysticism, and sanctity. In the lives of the saints, I find the gospel mirrored in unique ways in the lives of real people, in real times, in real places — mystics, virgins, martyrs, and doctors. Living alongside the witness of the saints has made me strive for holiness in my own life. The saints are not statues to adorn church buildings. They are people, our older brothers and sisters who have triumphantly gone before us, who are helping those of us who are still on our way to heaven.

The grace of the sacraments has transformed me. I thank God every day for bringing me to the Eucharist; I want to receive the Eucharist every day for the rest of my life. It is truly the "source and summit of Christian life" (*Lumen Gentium*, no. 11) It was during eucharistic adoration that I began to discern whether God is calling me to follow Him in Religious Life, and I am currently in formation with the Carmelite Sisters of the Most Sacred Heart of Los Angeles. That has been another unexpected journey.

It was difficult to explain my decision to become Catholic to many of my friends and family, most of whom were Protestant. Some of my friends who knew me during college weren't surprised, since they had seen the progression of my journey and could see that I was heading in the direction of Rome. Other friends and family were surprised by my decision, and couldn't understand my reasons for it. Many people assumed that it was a matter of taste or preference — as if I chose to become Catholic for the music, the liturgy, the incense, or the hats. But it was only because I was convinced of the truth of her teachings, and for no other reason, that I decided to come fully into communion with the Catholic Church.

I am entirely convinced that Catholicism is the fullness of the Christian faith. I didn't lose anything when I was received into the Church — I *gained* more than I can express. My faith was real before I came into the Church, I truly loved Christ before I knew that He was present in the Eucharist, and I experienced the healing of God in my life before I had the Sacrament of Reconciliation. But, by the help of the sacraments, through His Church, I know Him more deeply than ever. Through the Church, my faith has been incarnated in my life and in every aspect of who I am, body and soul.

Leah DesGeorges is in formation with the Carmelite Sisters of the Most Sacred Heart of Los Angeles. After growing up as a nondenominational charismatic evangelical, she spent five years as an evangelical Anglican before coming home to the Catholic Church in 2010.

Resources for
the Journey Home

The following list of books is provided to help those on the journey understand more clearly the various teachings, practices, and history of the Catholic Church. The sad reality is that too few Protestants have actually read books written by Catholics about the Catholic Church. They have relied too often on books written by people who have only seen the Church from the outside or who have left the Church sometimes with great bitterness and anger.

This is in no way a comprehensive list. Rather it represents our personal choices of books that we and others in the Coming Home Network International have found particularly helpful. The two main criteria for these choices were: (1) faithfulness to the historic magisterial teachings of the Catholic Church, and (2) ease of understanding.

Published by CHResources

Adam, Karl. *The Roots of the Reformation*. Trans. Cecily Hastings. Zanesville, OH: CHResources, 2012. An unbelievably powerful, succinct, and candid summary of the issues that led to the Reformation and their implications for today.

Choy, Leona. *My Journey to the Land of MORE*. Zanesville, OH: CHResources, 2010. After a lifetime of missionary work in China and on university campuses, and writing, publishing, and broadcasting — all within the Evangelical Protestant context — Leona Choy never dreamed she would write a book chronicling her surprise journey into the Catholic Church, which she calls "The Land of MORE." At the age of eighty and after four years of biblical and historical research, she faced the prospect of abandoning her lifelong reputation in Evangelical leadership; the potential misunderstanding of family, friends and coworkers; and loss of the readership of her books. Nevertheless, she took the risks rather than reject the truth she knew that God had shown her.

Grodi, Marcus C. *How Firm a Foundation.* Zanesville, OH: CHResources, 2011. Stephen LaPointe believed in Jesus. For him, the Bible was the only sufficient, firm foundation for his life. He wanted to obey God in all things, and he had given up a secular career to become an ordained minister. He loved to preach the Word and knew that one day he would stand before God, accountable for everything he preached. But there was only one problem: How could he be certain that what he was preaching was true?

———, ed. *Journeys Home.* Zanesville, OH: CHResources, 2011. This book contains the stories of men and women who, having surrendered their lives to Jesus Christ, heard a call to follow Him more completely. Many of them were pastors or missionaries. Others were lay men and women who, though working in secular jobs, took their calling to serve Christ in the world very seriously. In each case, their desire to follow Christ faithfully to remain faithful to the truth He taught and to the Church He established through His Apostles led them to embrace the Catholic Church. These conversion stories provide insight, encouragement, and inspiration for those who are thinking about making the same journey and for Catholics born in the faith as well.

———. *Pillar and Bulwark.* Zanesville, OH: CHResources, 2011. The sequel to *How Firm a Foundation.* After nearly losing his life to an assassin, Stephen LaPointe resigned from his pastorate as a Congregational minister. He made this radical decision as the result of a crisis of truth. This decision had many immediate ramifications for his vocation, his career, and most significantly for his marriage and family. Now a year later, no one knows where he is. He has disappeared. Out of love, as well as remorse, several people and old friend, his estranged wife, and a potential enemy set out separately to find him. This is a story of conversion — of heart, of mind, and of love.

———. *Thoughts for the Journey Home*. Zanesville, OH: CHResources, 2010. This book is a collection of essays by Marcus Grodi. His thoughts provide wisdom and strength for those who are exploring the claims of the Catholic Church, those who are on the path to the Church, and those who have already entered the Church yet need encouragement. Lifelong Catholics will also find the book useful in helping friends and family members they hope will someday come home.

———. *What Must I Do to be Saved?* Zanesville, OH: CHResources, 2012. A growing majority of Christians today believes that all that is necessary for salvation is an individual's faith in Jesus. Mega-churches everywhere proclaim this Jesus and Me theology, built around a simple application of John 3:16, belittling the need for membership in any religious community, the practice of any rituals, the reception of any sacraments, the submission to any leaders, or the adherence to any set of doctrines. Salvation is merely by faith *alone* in Jesus *alone* by grace *alone*. But is this biblically, theologically, and historically sound? This book argues, from the perspective of a biblical hermeneutic or interpretation of continuity, that salvation has always involved more than this simplistic expression of modern individualism.

Howell, Kenneth. *Clement of Rome and the Didache: A New Translation and Theological Commentary*. Zanesville, OH:

CHResources, 2012. The *Letter to the Corinthians* by Clement of Rome and the *Didache* are two of the most important documents from the earliest days of Christianity. Here we stand at the very fount of Christian teaching outside the New Testament. Clement's letter and the *Didache* reveal how Christians were implementing and living out the faith taught by Jesus and passed on by the twelve Apostles. The constant threat of schism and doctrinal deviation prompted these earliest writers to pen some of the most enduring wisdom known to the Church.

———. *Ignatius of Antioch and Polycarp of Smyrna: A New Translation and Theological Commentary.* Zanesville, OH: CHResources, 2009. Ignatius of Antioch and Polycarp of Smyrna were two of the greatest leaders of the Church in the first half of the second century. Their combined writings provide a unique window on the faith, life, and practice of the early Christians. Careful reading of these writings demonstrates the unique place that the early Fathers of the Church hold in establishing the foundations of historic Christianity. Their relevance for contemporary ecumenical discussions is beyond dispute.

Sullivan, Bruce. *Christ in His Fullness.* Zanesville, OH: CHResources, 2007. Details the journey of the author, who was a Church of Christ minister for seven years before entering the Catholic Church. This book explains the joys, struggles, fears, and peace that come from an individual's realization that the fullness of truth is found within the Catholic Church. Sullivan presents an in-depth study of the issues that prevent many from ever considering the Catholic Church while emphasizing in a positive way the great gift awaiting all who will embrace the Catholic faith, the gift of having Christ in all of His fullness.

Additional resources

Adam, Karl. *The Spirit of Catholicism*. Tacoma: Angelico Press, 2012. A classic study of the essence of Catholic faith.

Akin, Jimmy. *The Fathers Know Best*. El Cajon: Catholic Answers, 2010. This unique resource introduces you to the teachings of the first Christians in a way no other work can. Features more than nine hundred quotations from the writings of the Church Fathers, as well as from rare and important documents dating back to the dawn of Christian history. The volume also contains mini-biographies of nearly a hundred Fathers, as well as descriptions of dozens of key early councils and writings and a concise history of the dramatic spread of Christianity after Jesus told His disciples to evangelize all nations.

Bennett, Rod. *Four Witnesses: The Early Church in Her Own Words*. San Francisco: Ignatius, 2002. What was the early Church like? Rod Bennett shows that, contrary to popular belief, there is a reliable way to know. Four ancient Christian writers — four witnesses to early Christianity — left us an extensive body of documentation for this vital subject, and this book brings their fascinating testimony to life for modern believers. With all the power and drama of a gripping novel, this book is a journey of discovery of ancient and beautiful truths through the lives of four great saints of the early Church: Clement of Rome, Ignatius of Antioch, Justin Martyr, and Irenaeus of Lyons.

Butler, Scott, Norman Dahlgren, and David Hess. *Jesus, Peter and the Keys: A Scriptural Handbook on the Papacy*. Santa Barbara, CA: Queenship, 1996. An extensive collection of exegetical and historical sources that bear on the Petrine doctrine. This book contains most of the important data that any view of the papacy must explain.

Catechism of the Catholic Church. Rome: Libreria Editrice Vaticana, 1994. The first universal catechism of the Church to be published since the sixteenth century, this volume is the standard reference for learning Catholic teaching today. Every Catholic should have one.

Chesterton, G. K. *The Everlasting Man*. San Francisco: Ignatius, 1993. Considered by many to be Chesterton's greatest masterpiece, this is his whole view of world history as informed by the Incarnation. Beginning with the origin of man and the various religious attitudes throughout history, Chesterton shows how the fulfillment of all human desires takes place in the Person of Christ and in Christ's Church.

Connor, Charles P. *Classic Catholic Converts*. San Francisco: Ignatius, 2001. The compelling stories of well-known converts to the Catholic faith from the nineteenth and twentieth centuries. These are powerful testimonials to God's grace in the lives of men and women from all walks of life in Europe and America whose search for the fullness of truth led them to the Catholic Church.

Currie, David. *Born Fundamentalist, Born Again Catholic*. San Francisco: Ignatius, 1996. The author wrote this book to explain to family and friends why he became Catholic. He presents a lucid, systematic, and intelligible account of the reasons for his conversion to the ancient Church that Christ founded. He also provides a detailed discussion of the important theological and doctrinal beliefs that Catholics and Evangelical Protestants hold in common, as well as key doctrines that separate us, particularly the Eucharist, the papacy, and Mary.

Drake, Timothy. *There We Stood, Here We Stand: Eleven Lutherans Rediscover Their Catholic Roots*. Bloomington, IN: AuthorHouse, 2002. These thought-provoking testimonies by eleven former Lutherans reveal how far the Lutheran Church has strayed from Luther. They include moving stories from four former female pastors, three former male pastors, and others. Their intensely personal stories address the differences between Lutheran and Catholic faith, differences so profound that they have led many into the Catholic Church.

Hahn, Scott and Kimberly Hahn. *Rome Sweet Home*. San Francisco: Ignatius, 1993. A moving testimony of the grace and the trials that led Scott Hahn in 1986, and his wife, Kimberly, in 1990, from the Presbyterian tradition into the Catholic Church. One of the best publicized conversion stories in the late twentieth century.

Hahn, Scott. *A Father Who Keeps His Promises*. Cincinnati: St. Anthony Messenger, 1998. This book focuses on the "big picture" of Scripture: God's fatherly plan in making and keeping covenants with us throughout salvation history, so that we might live as the family of God.

———. *Reasons to Believe: How to Understand, Explain, and Defend the Catholic Faith*. Colorado Springs: Image, 2007. This book unravels mysteries, corrects misunderstandings, and offers thoughtful, straightforward responses to common objections about the Catholic faith.

———. *Signs of Life: 40 Catholic Customs and Their Biblical Roots*. Colorado Springs: Image, 2009. *Signs of Life* is a clear and comprehensive guide to the Biblical doctrines and historical traditions that underlie Catholic beliefs and practices. Devoting single chapters to each topic, the author takes the reader on a journey that illuminates the roots and significance of all things Catholic, including: the Sign of the Cross, the Mass, the sacraments, praying with the saints, guardian angels, sacred images and relics, the celebration of Easter, Christmas, and other holidays, daily prayers, and much more.

Howard, Thomas. *Evangelical Is Not Enough*. San Francisco: Ignatius, 1984. Convert Thomas Howard describes his pilgrimage from Evangelical Protestant faith to a more liturgical Christian tradition. He soon afterwards became a Catholic. He describes Evangelical faith with great sympathy and then examines more formal, liturgical worship with the freshness of someone discovering for the first time what his soul had always hungered for. This is a book of apologetics without polemics. A persuasive account by a former Evangelical of the liturgical riches of ancient Catholic worship.

Keating, Karl. *Catholicism and Fundamentalism*. San Francisco: Ignatius, 1988. This book, which effectively refutes the common fundamentalist misconceptions of and attacks on the Catholic Church, has served as the initial stepping stone for many modern converts.

Kreeft, Peter. *Fundamentals of the Faith*. San Francisco: Ignatius, 1988. In this helpful book, the author — a prolific writer and convert to the Catholic faith — considers all the fundamental elements of the Christian tradition and the Catholic faith, explaining, defending, and showing their relevance to our life and the world's yearnings.

Longenecker, Dwight, ed. *Path to Rome*. Leominster, England: Gracewing, 2010. This is a collection of stories of English converts, related with typically English reserve.

Madrid, Patrick, ed. *Surprised by Truth*. San Diego: Basilica, 1994. This collection of modern conversion accounts is the first of a series of three volumes (see below). They are packed with biblical, theological, and historical evidence

for the Catholic faith, presented in a winsome and enter-
taining way.

————. *Surprised By Truth 2*. Manchester, NH: Sophia Institute, 2000.

————. *Surprised by Truth 3*. Manchester, NH: Sophia Institute, 2002.

Merton, Thomas. *The Seven Storey Mountain*. 1948. Reprint,
Orlando, FL: Harcourt Trade Publishers, 1998. This spiritual autobiography of a secular man turned Trappist monk
has often been compared to the *Confessions* of St. Augustine and is one of the most influential religious works of
the twentieth century.

Michuta, Gary. *Why Catholic Bibles Are Bigger: The Untold
Story of the Lost Books of the Protestant Bible*. Port Huron,
MI: Grotto Press, 2007. Why do Catholic Bibles have more
books in their Old Testaments than Protestant and Jewish
Bibles? Did the Catholic Church add books to Scripture,
or did Protestants remove them? What was the Bible of the
earliest Christians? In this fascinating book, Gary Michuta
traces the path of the Deuterocanon (called by Protestants
the "Apocrypha") from its pre-Christian roots through the
Protestant Reformation to the nineteenth century. Many
commonly held myths are exposed while uncovering little-
known and surprising facts about these "lost books" of the
Protestant Bible.

Newman, John Henry. *An Essay on the Development of Christian Doctrine*. 1878. South Bend, IN: Reprint, University of
Notre Dame Press, 1986. Newman's classic study, in which
he originally set out to prove that the Anglican Church
was the "via media" or middle way between the Catholic
Church and the Protestant movement, but in the process
became convinced that only in the Catholic Church is

found the fullness of the deposit of faith as delivered by Jesus to His Apostles. This book has proved a great source of inspiration and conviction for many converts.

———. *Apologia pro Vita Sua*. 1880. Reprint, London: Penguin, 1994. This classic narrates the conversion of one of the greatest English cardinals of the nineteenth century. Newman tells how his doubts about the Anglican tradition began and how he gradually converted to the Catholic faith. The book was intended as an answer to charges that he was a Catholic all his life and had been trying to "subvert" the Church of England from within.

Nordhagen, Lynn. *When Only One Converts*. Huntington, IN: Our Sunday Visitor, 2001. A candid collection of conversion accounts from married couples in situations in which only one spouse wanted to become Catholic. The stories reveal the stresses this problem caused in their marriages and how they coped or even grew spiritually through the ensuing difficulties.

Pearce, Joseph. *Literary Converts*. San Francisco: Ignatius, 1999. A biographical journey into the faith of some of the greatest modern writers in the English language, all Christian converts: Oscar Wilde, Evelyn Waugh, C. S. Lewis, Malcolm Muggeridge, Graham Greene, G. K. Chesterton, Dorothy Sayers, T. S. Eliot, and J. R. R. Tolkien.

Ratzinger, Joseph (Pope Emeritus Benedict XVI) and Hans Urs Von Balthazar. *Mary: The Church at the Source*. San Francisco: Ignatius Press, 2005. Two great theologians offer a spiritually rich approach to Mariology that brings into new relief the Marian contours of ecclesial faith. Ratzinger and Balthasar show that Mary embodies the Church and co-operates in giving birth to the Church in the souls of believers. At once profound and accessible, this book offers a theologically balanced and biblically grounded presentation of traditional and contemporary thought on Marian doctrine and spirituality.

Ratzinger, Joseph (Pope Emeritus Benedict XVI). *Anglicanorum Coetibus*. 2009. Apostolic Constitution that authorized the creation of "ordinariates," geographic regions similar to dioceses but typically national in scope for Anglicans coming into full communion with the Catholic Church. Parishes in these ordinariates are to be Catholic yet retain elements of the Anglican heritage and liturgical practices.

Ray, Stephen K. *Crossing the Tiber*. San Francisco: Ignatius, 1997. A moving account of the conversion of an Evangelical Protestant, thoroughly documented with more than four hundred biblical and patristic quotations and commentary.

Shea, Mark P. *By What Authority? An Evangelical Discovers Catholic Tradition*. San Francisco: Ignatius, 2013. Interspersed with an account of his own journey from Evangelical Protestant faith to the Catholic Church, Mark Shea skillfully explains how and why Sacred Tradition occupies a central role in Divine Revelation.

Wojtyła, Karol Józef (St. Pope John Paul II). *Christifideles Laici* (The Lay Members of Christ's Faithful People). 1988.

———. *Salvifici Doloris* (On the Christian Meaning of Human Suffering). 1984.

———. *Ut Unum Sint* (On commitment to ecumenism). 1995.

How to become a member of
THE COMING HOME
NETWORK INTERNATIONAL
and support its work

The Coming Home Network International was established in 1993 to help inquiring clergy as well as laity of non-Catholic Christian traditions to discern whether God is calling them to come home and then be at home to the Catholic Church, by providing:

Contacts, assistance, and fellowship for those who are exploring the teaching and history of the Catholic Church, and are considering coming into full communion with the Church;

Continued fellowship and encouragement for those who have entered the Church and want to live fully Catholic lives;

Resources that give clear expressions of the Catholic faith.

The goal of the CHNetwork is to assist the Catholic Church in fulfilling her mission of evangelization and her call for Christian unity, as proclaimed by Pope John Paul II in his 1995 encyclical *Ut Unum Sint.*

One of the strongest desires of all members of the CHNetwork is to help all Catholics appreciate the wonderful faith they have always had and sometimes have taken for granted.

How Can I Help?

You can support the work of the Coming Home Network International in several ways:

Become a member of the CHNetwork. As a member you'll receive a free year of the CHNewsletter and other special Coming Home Network International mailings.

Pray for the CHNetwork, its staff and members. All members are encouraged to pray regularly for the needs of the CHNetwork and to present these needs at least one hour each month before the Blessed Sacrament.

Tell others about our work and encourage them to support it. Let your priest and bishop know about our apostolate. Often when non-Catholic Christians become interested in finding out about the Catholic faith, they do not know where to turn. We want to help them.

Be an evangelist by distributing our brochures, literature, CDs, and DVDs to clergy and laity of other traditions. Most non-Catholic Christians have been misinformed about the teachings of the Catholic faith. By sharing our published media and online resources, you are being an active part of the New Evangelization.

Schedule one of our staff members to speak at your parish or at a conference. Marcus Grodi, Dr. Kenneth Howell, and other staff members are experienced speakers and enjoy sharing their conversion stories as well as other topics to strengthen the faith of Catholic laity.

Make a contribution to the CHNetwork. The Coming Home Network International is a non-profit 501(3)c Catholic lay apostolate, solely funded through the generous contributions of its members and friends. All donations are tax-deductible and are greatly appreciated.

How Can I Become a Member?

If you are interested in becoming a member of the CHNetwork, contact us at info@chnetwork.org, go to chnetwork.org, or write or call us:

The Coming Home Network International
P. O. Box 8290
Zanesville, OH 43702-8290
Phone: 800-664-5110 or 740-450-1175